Orientalism, postmodernism and globalism

It is often thought that the development of capitalism and the modernization of culture have brought about a profound decline in religious belief and commitment. The history of Christianity in the last two centuries appears to be a good illustration of this general process of secularization with the undermining of belief and commitment as Western cultures became increasingly industrial and urban. However, in the twentieth century we have seen that Islam continues to be a dominant force in politics and culture, not only in the Orient but in Western society. The strength of Islam raises fundamental questions about the nature of modern culture. At the same time, there has been much discussion about the so-called postmodernization of cultures, suggesting a decline in high culture, a pluralization of lifestyles, celebration of cultural differences and a new emphasis on consumerism and simulation, parody and irony. What is the relationship between these forces? Within the intellectual sphere, there has been a profound criticism over the last twenty years of orientalism, that is, an academic framework which negates and denies the significance of non-Western cultures, seeing them as lacking some essential feature of rational modernization. Can Christianity and Islam survive these changes in popular and high culture?

In this challenging study of contemporary social theory, Bryan Turner examines the recent debate about orientalism in relation to postmodernism and the process of globalization. He provides a profound critique of many of the leading figures in classical orientalism. His book also considers the impact of globalization on Islam, the nature of oriental studies and decolonization, and the notion of 'the world' in sociological theory. These cultural changes and social debates also reflect important changes in the status and position of intellectuals in modern culture who are threatened, not only by the levelling of mass culture, but also by the new opportunities posed by postmodernism. He takes a critical view of the role of sociology in these developments and raises important questions about the global role of English intellectuals as a social stratum. Bryan Turner's ability to combine these discussions about religion, politics, culture and intellectuals represents a remarkable integration of cultural analysis in cultural studies.

Bryan S. Turner is Dean of the Faculty of Arts and Professor of Sociology at Deakin University, Australia.

Orientalism, postmodernism and globalism

Bryan S. Turner

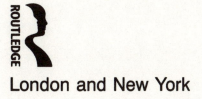

London and New York

First published 1994
by Routledge
11 New Fetter Lane, London EC4P 4EE

Simultaneously published in the USA and Canada
by Routledge
29 West 35th Street, New York, NY 10001

© Bryan S. Turner

Phototypeset in Times by Intype, London

Printed and bound in Great Britain by
Mackays of Chatham PLC, Chatham, Kent

British Library Cataloguing in Publication Data
A catalogue record for this book is available from the British Library

Library of Congress Cataloging in Publication Data
A catalogue record for this book has been requested

ISBN 0–415–10861–6
ISBN 0–415–10862–4 (pbk)

To Adelaide, Mathilde and Karen

Contents

Part V Modernity

Tables

Acknowledgements

Chapter 1 was first given as a lecture at the Australian Middle East Society meeting at Stonnington House, Deakin University in 1993. I am grateful to members of the society for their critical but sympathetic response to the lecture. Chapter 2 appeared in A. Hussain, R. Olsen and J. Qureshi (eds) *Orientalism, Islam and Islamists*, London, Amana Books, pp. 23–43. Chapter 3 was originally published in D. MacEion and A. Al-Shahi (eds) *Islam in the Modern World*, London and Canberra, Croom Helm, 1983, pp. 9–26. Chapter 4 was a lecture delivered to the Hull Group on Middle East Studies and subsequently appeared in *Review of Middle East Studies*. Chapter 5 was also a seminar paper given at Hull University to the Middle East Studies Group and later appeared in A. Hussain, R. Olsen and J. Qureshi (eds) *Orientalism, Islam and Islamists*, pp. 193–201. Chapter 6 was a conference paper given at the Saint Martin Conference on Religion and Globalization. This lecture appeared in R. Robertson and W. R. Garrett (eds) *Religion and Global Order: Religion and the Political Order*, vol. 4, New York, Paragon House, 1991, pp. 161–81. Roland Robertson has for many years been both friend and academic mentor, and obviously whatever views I may have about globalization have been profoundly influenced by his work. Chapter 7 was initially a seminar paper given in the Middle East Studies Department at the University of Montreal which then appeared in *Sociology*, vol. 23, no. 4, 1989, pp. 629–38. Chapter 8 was a lecture given to the Society for the Scientific Study of Religion at Pittsburgh University as part of a symposium on the sociology of Roland Robertson which then appeared in the *Journal for the Scientific Study of Religion*, vol. 31, no. 3, 1992, pp. 296–323. I am grateful for the critical comments on this chapter from Frank Lechner, William Garrett, Edward Tiryakian and Roland Robertson. Chapter 9 started as a lecture at the New Delhi International Sociological Association meeting and was then developed with Georg Stauth as an article in *Theory, Culture and Society*, vol. 5, nos 2–3, 1988, pp. 509–26. Chapter 10 first appeared in *Theory, Culture and Society*, vol. 7, nos 2–3, pp. 343–58. I am grateful to Mike Featherstone for comments on this paper. Chapter 11 was a seminar paper on contemporary intellectuals given at the University of Utrecht. I am grateful to Jan Rupp for his comments on the original paper, which was published in *Theory, Culture and Society*, vol. 9, no. 1, 1992, pp. 183–210. Chapter 12 was a seminar given to the Department of Sociology at the Australian National University in 1993. Once more I am grateful to the participants for their comments. Chapter 13 was a lecture to the conference on detraditionalization held at Lancaster University in 1993. This paper represents part of the more general project on the sociology of the body. I am grateful for permission to reprint these articles from these various sources. However, each chapter has been slightly modified in order to introduce new references, change emphasis and eliminate unnecessary repetition or overlap.

My original interest in Islam and orientalism owes a great deal to Professor Trevor Ling, previously of the University of Manchester and to Georg Stauth, University of Bielefeld. My involvement in the debate about globalization is a product of intellectual exchanges with Roland Robertson over a number of years but particularly as a result of our mutual interest in the sociology of religion. As Zygmunt Bauman has observed, all intellectuals are naturally interested in intellectuals. My specific and current interest in the intelligentsia is a consequence of observing British intellectual migrants in a variety of university settings around the world, a topic about which I have intended to write for some years. It is difficult not to be interested in current problems of the academic intellectual, given the managerial and professional revolution going on inside state-owned universities. However, my current focus on the problem of the intellectual is probably a consequence of various seminars which took place in the Department of General Social Sciences at the University of Utrecht, with Hans Adriaansen, John Shotter, David Ingleby, Jan Rupp and Lieteke van Vucht Tijssen. My recent interest in risk and somatization has been stimulated by the work of Ulrich Beck, Anthony Giddens and Scott Lash. Chris Rojek has been both as friend and editor critical and supportive. Finally I should thank Mike Featherstone the editor of *Theory, Culture and Society* for his unselfish commitment to social theory.

Monika Loving kindly retyped the entire manuscript with her usual cheerful efficiency. I am also grateful to Stephanie Louise for correcting the bibliography.

Bryan S. Turner
Ocean Grove
1994

Part I

Orientalism

Chapter 1

Orientalism, postmodernism and religion

The problem of social and cultural diversity has been a classic issue in the humanities and the social sciences throughout the period we refer to as the modern age. With the rise of the world economy and cultural globalization, this question of cultural difference has become even more acute in contemporary politics. In the 1970s academics were interested in a specific feature of this inter-cultural problem, namely how Western societies have understood and interpreted oriental societies through the period of imperial expansion. The debate about orientalism (Said 1978a) gave rise to a new approach to decolonization and the writing of history, especially the writing of Indian history. These 'subaltern studies' (Guha 1981) marked the arrival of a new confidence and radicalism among third-world academics in the struggle for decolonization at both the cultural and political levels. This critical tradition came to be known eventually as 'cultural discourse studies' (Bhabha 1983). It became clear in the 1980s that there were strong intellectual connections between the orientalist debate, subaltern studies and feminism which were all struggles for an authentic voice. Orientalism and colonial discourse studies are concerned to explore the problems of subjectivity and authenticity among social groups or cultures which are excluded from power. I explore some aspects of this debate in Chapter 13. In the 1990s there is equally strong evidence to suggest a connection between anti-orientalism and postmodernism as alternatives to modernist rationalism. This collection of essays examines these interconnections and attempts to understand the role of intellectuals in the modern world.

I have an ambiguous relationship to orientalism in the sense that in the year that Edward Said published *Orientalism* (1978), I also brought out a modest volume called *Marx and the End of Orientalism* (Turner 1978a); Edward Said's book has deservedly become famous while my study remains marginal. My contribution to these new directions was to consider a limited range of problems in the social sciences. Said has been working on a larger canvas. My ambiguity about orientalism is also that I have never done fundamental research in the area of Islamic and Arabic cultures. My own writings were originally about Max Weber and, because very few sociologists were writing about Islam, my work was of some interest to sociologists in the late 1970s. It is only with the recent development of postmodern theory that sociologists in general have become interested in Islam and orientalism. Otherness has become the issue.

Although Said's writings have received much specific attention, I want to talk about the long-term implications of his work. While the book is now obviously outdated, many of the problems raised by Said continue to exercise the minds, not only of Arabic researchers and Islamists, but of feminists and scholars working on alternative philosophies and methodologies. In the 1970s Said was enormously intellectually challenging; within the Anglo-Saxon world, he introduced many of us to the wonderful scholarship of Michel Foucault, whose work on historical discourses continues to influence research in the humanities and social sciences. At the time, Said presented us with a very profound critique of liberalism by showing how power and knowledge are inevitably combined and how power relations produced through discourse a range of analytical objects which continue to impact on scholarship in a way which is largely unanticipated and unobserved. In his argument with liberalism Said also provided us with a critique of what was a conventional view in American social science and epistemology, namely the alleged separation of facts and values and the neutrality of science. Said's work was significant in showing how discourses, values and patterns of knowledge actually constructed the 'facts' which scholars were attempting to study, apparently independently. Over the years this classical approach to orientalism has largely shaped what people understand by the notion of 'Otherness', and the problem of the 'Other' in human cultures has been taken up first of all by feminism, by black studies and more recently by postmodernism. An exciting and important challenge of Said's work was what one may call 'the methodology of the text', that is, Said was able to apply the more advanced aspects of American literary studies to the analysis of history and social sciences; and through what is popularly called deconstructionism, Said was able to provide new directions for the analysis of historical and social phenomena. Certainly Said's approach was very attractive at the time because he provided a model of what we might call the intellectual hero. Said was not simply someone who sat on the margins of literary studies and analytical research, he was actually seen to be at the forefront of Palestinian politics and Middle Eastern politics.

My own work in the 1970s was much more influenced by the work of Marxists like Louis Althusser and, in the United Kingdom, radical groups in Middle Eastern studies turned to theory, being influenced specifically by Marxist sociologists such as Nicos Poulantzas. The attraction of Marxism was to provide a critique of many of the taken-for-granted assumptions of a liberal, individualistic, social science. At the time there was much debate about the so-called 'Asiatic conditions' of despotism and more specifically about the Asiatic mode of production which exercised much of our time in the late 1970s and early 1980s. Both Said and Althusser offered an alternative challenge to the legacy of positivistic sociology which in North America was associated with a value-free individualistic approach. In so far as my own work had any critical merit, it was really to show that Marx also shared much of this Western legacy of perceiving the Orient as a unified system, one characterized by stationariness, lack of social change, the absence of modernization, the absence of a middle-class bourgeois culture, and the absence of a civil society. From this critical stance, one could see how both Marx and Weber fitted into the legacy of Western analysis of the East. The Marxist notion of the Asiatic mode of production and Weber's concept of patrimonialism shared common assumptions. This feature of the orientalist legacy in the social sciences is investigated in Chapters 3 and 7.

I want to turn now to some problems with this critical anti-orientalism that came from writers like Said. There are some standard criticisms of Said's work which are well known. While Said's Orientalist critique dawned upon younger scholars as a new approach, much of his work had already been done in a more mundane way by writers like V. G. Kiernan (1972) in *Lords of Human Kind*. For example, Said was a significant critic of French orientalism, but he was particularly weak in terms of German and British orientalism. These questions are examined in Chapters 4 and 5. In retrospect, there were in fact many forms of orientalism and it was inadequate to lump so many diverse traditions into a single orientalist tradition. Many of these questions are raised in a recent book by Lisa Lowe on *Critical Terrains* (1991) in which she examines French and British orientalism and illustrates many aspects of this argument. I would say, however, that the problem of 'other cultures' has always been a central problem of anthropology from Herodotus onwards. Modern anthropology had its origins in seventeenth-century debates about people from newly acquired colonies. Otherness raised a deep theological problem about the 'Great Chain of Being', namely how did these strange cultures fit into God's plan? The idea of outsiders and insiders is actually a standard form of all anthropological problematics, particularly the anthropological tradition that embraces hermeneutics and textuality. This has become increasingly clear in the work of postmodernists like G. Vattimo who have been analysing the end of modernity and the end of history with reference to a radical hermeneutic anthropology. With Vattimo, I think that textual or hermeneutic radicalism is close to an anti-orientalist critique because it is primarily concerned to grasp the nuances and ambiguities of local practices and beliefs. Much of the central work of classical anthropology was concerned with this problem of, to put it rather naively, understanding other cultures.

The other political condition that has changed very profoundly since the 1970s of course is that Said's *Orientalism* appeared when communism was still a viable political option and for radical social scientists Marxism was still available as a vibrant and possible tradition in the universities. The secular collapse of organised communism actually makes the intellectual credibility of Marxism as a general theory of society very doubtful; many Marxist writers in the West would of course like to argue that nothing significant has changed, but such a position is ultimately untenable. The early critique of orientalism was associated with a process of decolonization which assumed that Marxism provided an alternative to capitalism in terms of theory and politics. Perhaps Islam, in the argument of Ernest Gellner, is the only global, credible political system. We are writing in a post-communist world and that fact ought to have profound implications for how we see the role of Islam or feminism or humanism or any other social movement as a plausible mode of thinking or living. Post-communism as an intellectual and political condition explains much of the current interest in Islam and postmodernism.

Another criticism of the legacy of Said relates to the problem of Michel Foucault and politics. Here again, this is rather a large issue and I am only going to touch on the edges of this question. It is a controversial issue, but it is very difficult to derive a coherent political position from the work of Foucault. One is aware of the fact that Foucault's work does lend itself, for example, to critical criminology. His writing on Soviet psychiatry and his analysis of French penal traditions provide a way of moving from his analytical working to a political position, but generally it has been rather difficult to derive systematic radical politics from Foucault's critical analysis. Foucault's critique of dominant paradigms of knowledge in conventional systems suggests at best a form of romantic anarchism. The same issue arises for Said because his own politics relating to Palestine cannot be derived easily from the epistemological position of his book *Orientalism*. That is, there is an hiatus between the philosophy and the practice which has proved very difficult to fill. If you read Said's book *Covering Islam* (1978b) you will see that there he adopts what you might call a realist epistemology; that is, that he believes that the problem of covering Islam journalistically is simply that journalists are badly trained. They pop in and out of countries for a few days, talk to a few taxi drivers and then write a lead article about Arabic politics. Said's criticisms here are perfectly reasonable and valid, but they are not related analytically or philosophically to his own work or to orientalism – one could write *Covering Islam* without having read a single word of Foucault or Derrida. Deconstruction as a technique merely identified the problems of representation without offering many solutions. This difficulty is very evident in attempts to develop alternative histories (O'Hanlon and Washbrook 1992).

Another criticism of Said's approach to history, which again, is problematic, is the concentration on textuality and textualism. An exclusive focus on 'textual practices' has negated the social dimension of language and meaning, and confused the materiality of social relations with an alleged materiality of the context. Textualism has resulted in a vicious solipsism in which there can be no distinction between fictional writing and social reality. Jean Baudrillard's claim that the Gulf War was merely a television event is a particularly notorious example of this focus.

A further problem in this area has been the rather difficult issue of fascism and deconstructionism. Said's intellectual foundations come from Foucault but behind Foucault's social philosophy is the work of Martin Heidegger, in particular the philosophical critique of metaphysics. It has been very difficult to disassociate Heidegger and deconstructionism from the legacy of fascism. Heidegger's work is essentially anti-modernist in my view, and his writings on technology show all the signs of a massive conservative reaction to democracy and modernization. However brilliant Heidegger's philosophy may be, there are some genuine political problems in this legacy, which has been further illustrated by the case of Paul de Man. There is guilt by association which is not easy to throw off.

I have outlined these criticisms of Said simply as a collection of notes, primarily because they are well known. My main concern lies elsewhere. Another consequence of the debate about orientalism was an equally pernicious occidentalism, that is, a rejection of everything to do with the West and an implicit rejection of the legacy of modernization. This anti-modernist dimension of critical theory may explain some of the attraction of Heidegger's cultural elitism; some aspects of this issue are examined in Chapter 9. Now some aspects of this rejection of the West obviously are justifiable in connection with the indigenization of knowledge which has occupied much anthropological debate about the growth and fostering of the social sciences in third-world society. More pertinent to this discussion is the so-called problem of the Islamization of knowledge. One peculiar consequence of the legacy of Foucault and Said has been a defence of a fundamentalist reading of Islamic knowledge and tradition which involve an opposition to secularism and the disenchantment of modernization as conceptualized in Max Weber's *Sociology of Religion*. This involves a claim about the authenticity of tradition over inherited, imported or alien knowledge. In sociology you see this argument in particular in the endless attempts to demonstrate that Ibn Khaldun was in fact the founding father of all social sciences against the claims of Marx, Weber and Durkheim. However interesting Ibn Khaldun may be, his work does not offer a very useful analysis of late, industrial urban civilizations. There is a debate about the epistemological imperialism of the West, and Said's recent (Said 1993) work on culture and imperialism lends support to this idea that a post-colonial period still involves cultural domination. One of the problems of the Islamization of knowledge is that there is difficulty in deciding whether the fundamentalist claims about this Islamization of knowledge are modernist or anti-modernist. This leads to a problem about whether one can embrace Western technology without Western values. Sociology suggests that you cannot have modernization, technology, urbanization and bureaucratization without the cultural baggage that goes with it and this baggage is essentially a post-Enlightenment system of thought. Now academic indigenization is obviously attractive, but can you have an indigenous methodology or an indigenous epistemology? One might agree with the idea that there are some facts which are peculiar to certain societies; for example, because there was not a history of feudalism in societies like Australia and New Zealand one cannot generalize from the works of Western sociologists working on European cases to the societies of the southern hemisphere where typically there was not a transition from feudal society to capitalism. These problems are further analysed in Chapters 2 and 3. Much of the work of Marx and Durkheim presupposed a feudal society and therefore much of the legacy of Western sociology is not applicable to Asian societies. If we adopted this argument in an analysis of Nepal or Saudi Arabia or Central Africa, the weight of the indigenization argument is quite profound. However, I am not convinced that you can have an indigenization of rationality or indigenization of methodology. This debate is primarily a debate about the authority of local versus global knowledge, and hence about the cultural authority of intellectuals as a universal category.

A similar argument applies to claims about so-called feminist methodology. Feminist methodology is just good sociology. The argument in feminist sociology is that you have to interact with your audience, you have to understand their knowledge and to utilize knowledge to bring about change and so forth. Feminist methodology is sensitive to the social and political needs of audiences and clients. Much of the argument about feminist methodology is really a repeat of symbolic interactionism and ethnomethodology from the 1960s. One would have the same problem with the fundamentalist paradigm. It would not be possible to develop something called Islamic social science, for the same reason that you cannot have Christian social science or Jewish social science or any other type of ethnic social science. There is a basic logic and theory to the social sciences which cannot be subsumed under a particular ethnic or cultural or historical label. Furthermore, while the claim for Islamization of knowledge is influential, all cultures are undergoing a profound process of globalization. It is odd that in a period of strong localistic and regional tendencies, we live in a world in which the globalization of civilization is one of the profound facts of modern life. I return to this argument in Chapter 7.

Globalization is an extension of the emergence of world economic systems, but sociologists are more concerned with cultural globalization. There is a profound sense of globalism brought about by tourism, by world sport, world news, McDonaldization, AIDS, human rights and so on. Globalization and localization go together. Wherever you have the emergence of global consciousness, there will be a reaction which promotes an anti-global movement. Globalization is an important idea, but we have to be aware of the fact that the world religions have always claimed to be global and that part of the problem of trying to understand Islam and the Christian legacy is how to understand the concept of 'the world' in traditional cultures and how that relates to the concept of globalization in modern society. Here again the processes of globalization raise very interesting and important questions about the role of intellectuals as carriers of globalism. This question of the world religions is examined in Chapter 8. One criticism of globalization is that it is simply Westernization. However, there are profound cultural movements coming out of Japan and other strong economies in the Asian region which are shaping the globe to such an extent that one could equally talk about the orientalization of modern cultures. What has globalization got to do with the Islamization of knowledge and the legacy of Said? It is simply the case that globalization makes it very difficult to carry on talking about oriental and occidental cultures as separate, autonomous or independent cultural regimes. The possibility of moving from an out-of-date orientalism to global sociology is explored in Chapter 7.

It is equally important to connect globalization with the debate about postmodernity. We do not need to enter into an endless discussion of what postmodernity means. Some of these debates about definitions are considered in Chapter 9. Briefly, postmodernity refers to the extension of the processes of commodification to everyday life and the impact of mass consumer cultures on cultural systems, blurring the distinction, for example, between high and low culture. Postmodernism means the use of simulation in cultural production, and in stylistic terms it involves self-parody and irony. Now much of the postmodern debate has been concerned to assert the importance of difference and otherness, so there is a connection between a postmodern critique of universalistic categories and the process of indigenization. That is, both indigenization and post-modernism have a fascination for the textuality of knowledge; its local, embedded, contextual quality and the problems of universalizing or generalizing about 'religion' or 'human nature'. Postmodern methodologies are sensitive to the richness and complexity of local meanings of folk practices and beliefs, and particularly sensitive to ironic meaning and intention. The main threat to the Islamization of knowledge is not, however, cognitive. The main threat to religious faith is in fact the commodification of everyday life. People do not adopt or reject beliefs systems simply on the rationalistic grounds that they are not intellectually coherent. Beliefs are adopted or rejected because they are relevant or not relevant to everyday needs and concerns. What makes religious faith or religious commitment problematic in a globalized postmodern society is that everyday life has become part of a global system of exchange of commodities which are not easily influenced by political leaders, intellectuals or religious leaders. The corruption of pristine faith is going to be brought about by Tina Turner and Coca-Cola and not by rational arguments and rational inspection of presuppositions and the understanding of Western secularism. This is what is wrong fundamentally with Gellner's book *Postmodernism, Reason and Religion* (1992) and Ahmed's book on *Postmodernism and Islam* (1992). They are both talking about intellectual cognitive problems of religious leaders and intellectuals, not the problems of everyday life. What they both fail to emphasise is that the Ford motor car did more damage to Christianity than any type of argumentation.

Let us dwell initially on *Postmodernism and Islam*. Ahmed's important and wide-ranging discussion of the place of Islam within the debate over postmodernism has to be understood against the background of the complex analysis of the cultural roots of modernity. In speculating about the origins of the modern (Western) world, social philosophers from David Hume onwards have been impressed by the impact of world religions in shaping modern cultural reality. However, the sociological problem has been to decide which of these world religions has been most significant in determining the contours of modernity. Within the sociology of religion, the ascetic Protestant sects were regarded as fundamental in the push towards rational modernity. The inner-worldly asceticism of Calvinistic Protestantism transformed Western culture towards an anti-magical, disciplined life-world. The alternatives to this Weberian thesis suggested that it was Jewish culture, according to Sombart (1962), which had provided the roots of modernist rationality, but this debate has remained fundamentally unresolved.

There were two major issues within the argument concerning the Protestant ethic thesis. First, it tied the idea of instrumental rationality to modernity: to become modern, a society had to undergo and embrace the disciplines of goal-directed rational conduct. Second, the thesis gave a privileged position to north-western Europe as the cutting edge of this global process, and by casting the West in this role 'the Orient' became the Other. The rationalism of the West was fundamental to the teleological processes of world history. The consequence has been to place Islam in a problematic relationship to rationalist modernity and to the Christian West.

Throughout much of the twentieth century, modernist apologists for Islam have argued that Islam as a religion was not in any essential manner anti-rational or incompatible with capitalism, nor was it culturally traditionalist. Orthodox Islam was in fact an anti-magical, radical, ascetic and disciplined culture; it could provide the same inner-worldly asceticism that one finds in Calvinism. In fact, Islamic monotheism was seen to be more rational than Christianity, within which there are polytheistic strains in the doctrines of the Trinity. The problem was to explain how this rationalist dynamic in Islam had been repressed. Several answers were available to explain this alleged historical retardation of the Islamic world, which included reference to the negative consequences of mystical Sufism, folk religiosity, the rigidity of Islamic law, or the closing of the gate of *ijtihad*, the effects of *Zakat* in relation to more profitable investments, and the absence of an autonomous urban culture within civil society. These various solutions were produced by what we might call the problematic of 'Islamic decline' which exercised Western academics. The issue produced a considerable body of scholarship which was broadly sympathetic towards Islam such as the work of Maxime Rodinson in *Mahomet* (1961) and *Islam et capitalisme* (1966). I examine this feature of the orientalist debate in Chapters 2 and 3.

In the 1970s and 1980s Western critics of orientalism and colonialism lived in a world where there appeared to be a viable alternative to Western capitalism, namely communism. In addition, there was a well-established tradition of scholarship which sought to explain, not only the origins of capitalist exploitation and colonialism, but also the historical stages by which the hegemony of Western capitalism would be brought to a final, brutal end. Two major changes have rendered this world obsolete: the fall of communism and the rise of postmodernity. These two changes are without doubt closely interconnected in cultural and social terms. The consequence has been that there is no significant political or economic alternative to organized socialism as the antagonist of Western capitalism, but it may be that this gap in the world system will be filled by either Islam or postmodernism. The role of the radical intellectuals has been profoundly changed by these events, an issue to which I return in Chapters 10 and 11.

For many Western intellectuals, the enthusiasm for postmodern philosophies may be, at least covertly, a function of the demise of socialism as a credible anti-capitalist system. Following J.-F. Lyotard in *La Condition postmoderne* (1979) we can define postmodernism simply as 'incredulity towards metanarratives'. Postmodern philosophy offers a simultaneous condemnation of exploitative capitalism and bureaucratic socialism as 'grand narratives' which have imposed a barren sameness on the modern social world. Postmodernism, which has found important allies in feminism and anti-colonialism, condemns the uniform, patriarchal, rationalist and hierarchical structures of Western modernism. While many critics of postmodernism have mistakenly assumed that it has no political message, postmodernism suggests a new vision of justice which gives primacy to difference, to heterogeneity, to paradox and contradiction, and to local knowledge (Turner 1990). To understand such profound changes, we need to question many of the traditional assumptions of sociology. This topic, the need for new paradigms, is considered in Chapter 12.

These political and intellectual developments in postmodernism challenge orientalism. The collapse of Soviet communism (the consequent challenge to the intellectual authority of Marxism and the growing influence of postmodernism) make the global position of Islam crucial but problematic. At one level it may be possible to argue that, given the history of the Islamic world since the French revolution, Islam can now function as the major alternative, perhaps even the only alternative to Western capitalist hegemony. For many writers, such as Ali Shari'ati in his *Marxism and Other Western Fallacies* (1980), Islam has been simultaneously opposed to the secularism of the communist world and to the consumerism of the Western world; hence, it can operate globally as an oppositional force. Furthermore, since postmodernism is also opposed to the instrumental rationalism of both capitalism and communism, there could be an alliance between Islam and postmodernism. At another level of analysis, however, Islam may be regarded as itself a 'grand narrative' of religious orthodoxy and uniformity, which has been fundamentally committed to ideas of universal rationalism, discipline and asceticism.

These possibilities represent the 'predicament and promise' of Islam, and hence Ahmed's *Postmodernism and Islam* (1992) will assume a centrality to the contemporary analysis of the place of Islam in postmodernity. The book implies that there can be a convergence between postmodernist criticism and the hegemony of the West and an Islamic critique of Western materialism, media hegemony, military power and global dominance. His thesis fails ultimately, because he wants, somewhat indirectly, to employ postmodernism to attack the traditional assumptions about Western supremacy and modernist rationality, but he does not fully face up to the critical implications of postmodernism for traditional Islam.

Setting his discussion within the contemporary context of the Rushdie affair, the Gulf War and the collapse of BCCI, Ahmed provides an extensive historical review of the struggles and conflicts between the Christian West and Islam. Among radical Muslim scholars, Ahmed recognizes the development of a negative discourse of the West which is as blinkered as the old orientalism: over the last decade the passionate reaction among African and Asian scholars against orientalism has created a kind of 'occidentalism' among them. 'This is as much a rejection of colonialism, with which orientalism is associated, as it is an expression of revolt against the global civilization dominated by the West' (Ahmed 1992: 177). Ahmed is equally judicious in his criticisms of the legacy of Said, because

However powerfully Said argues his case, the work of the older orientalists was marked by many positive features. These included a lifetime's scholarship, a majestic command of languages, a wide vision and breadth of learning and an association with the established universities.

(Ahmed 1992: 180)

These 'older orientalists' included Hamilton Gibb, Bernard Lewis, Arthur Arberry, Montgomery Watt and Louis Massignon. In general, Ahmed is optimistic that the younger generation of scholars are post-orientalist and that their work will be better appreciated by Muslim academics for its balance and neutrality. The post-orientalists include people like Lois Beck, John Esposito, Barbara Metcalf, William Chittick and Michael Gilsenan. The new scholarship may create the conditions whereby the old confrontations of orientalism and occidentalism will disappear.

One consequence of these post-orientalist intellectual encounters is that the traditional view of Islam as a monolithic religion has been replaced by a full appreciation of the diversity and complexity of Islamic cultures around the globe. Ahmed asserts that

In our discussion of culture and change I wish, once again, to dispel the notion that there ever was – or is – one unified and monolithic Muslim Society. Consider Muslim South Asia and its main language, Urdu: both display synthesis and eclecticism.

(Ahmed 1992: 200)

In adopting this line of argument, Ahmed is associating himself with a common intellectual strategy which claims there are many Islams.

What is more problematic for the reader of *Postmodernism and Islam* is quite where the author himself stands in relation to postmodernism. At first sight his obvious understanding of and fascination with Madonna, Queen, 'Twin Peaks' and Batman suggest a sympathy with postmodern culture. How many Cambridge dons are able to chat with Ken Livingstone and Gillian Shephard on 'Any Questions' about Madonna's costumes? Thus, Ahmed is clearly very familiar with postmodern theory, he obviously enjoys many of the phenomena of popular culture and he appears regularly on such programs as 'Newsnight', 'The World This Week', 'Outlook', 'Any Questions?', 'The World Today' and 'Analysis', but his views on Islam and the West turn out to be quite traditional.

Let us take some examples of these ambiguities. Ahmed produces a conventional criticism of Western materialism. Western culture is characterized by the 'obsession to out-buy, out-eat and out-sex the Joneses next door' (Ahmed 1992: 109). He adopts a conventional attack on vulgar consumerism, but surely postmodernism wants to question 'serious' criticism of consumerism, presenting instead a celebration of the consumption of signs? Against the rampant consumerism of the West, he suggests that

Islam is by contrast a green movement which is deeply concerned with the politics of the environment. He notes that 'Islam's very colour is green and its concept of the good life, Paradise, is replete with gardens, orchards and rivers' (Ahmed 1992: 120).

Ahmed rather inflates the idea of postmodern in order to suggest that the Kashmiri expression of independence is an example of Muslim postmodernism. He fears, however, that the combination of feminism and postmodernism will prove to be a lethal attack on manhood; for example, 'To be a male in authority is to be suspect. The media – led by feminist writers – reverse Freud: the penis is the source of all evil, to be publicly and ritually denounced' (Ahmed 1992: 244). The conclusion is that the West is morally bankrupt, because the 'lies, the hypocrisy and moral bankruptcy' (Ahmed 1992: 245) of the 1980s have taken their toll.

These arguments present a straightforwardly conservative critique of the vulgarities and corruption of the West, and of course the function of the book is to warn a rather complacent Muslim leadership that Islam is itself now challenged by postmodernism: 'The postmodernist age in the 1990s hammers at the doors of Muslim *itjihad*; Muslims ignore the din at their peril' (Ahmed 1992: 260). The function of *Postmodernism and Islam* is to explain the nature of the threat and the corrupting power of the (Western) media. Madonna is, as it were, not just a pretty face; she is the sign of postmodernism, which is a threat simultaneously to manhood and to truth. However, if Ahmed wants to defend Islam against the threat of a castrating Madonna, then the implication is that Islam is yet another grand narrative which requires protection from the sexual and cultural diversity represented by Madonna, Freddie Mercury and Michael Jackson.

Apart from the ambiguities of Ahmed's own stand towards postmodern consumerism, there is a more general problem about the precise nature of postmodernism. Ahmed wants to warn Muslim leaders about postmodernism, but it is not really clear what the nature of that threat is. Although he provides a reasonably full account of postmodernism, he fails to resolve an important question: is postmodernity after modernity or against modernity? Alternatively, is postmodernity in fact a form of high modernity? The academic community is sharply divided over the issue of whether postmodernity is a radically different alternative to modernity, of which Islam might be a part, or indeed of whether postmodernity exists. At least one step towards solving the first issue would be to make a distinction between postmodernism and postmodernity. By the former, we should mean the philosophical critique of grand narratives, and by the latter we should mean the postmodern social condition which is an effect of informational technologies, globalization, fragmentation of lifestyles, hyper-consumerism, deregulation of financial markets and public utilities, the obsolescence of the nation-state, and social experimentation with the traditional life-course. Clearly both postmodernism and postmodernity are a significant challenge to the values and institutions which grew out of the Abrahamic faiths. Perhaps Christianity is already in a state of post-religion, but Islam has yet to experience the full impact of postmoderniz-ation. Secularization is certainly assumed to have brought about a con-dition of post-history, because there is no shared understanding of the meaning of history. The subterranean erosion of grand narratives by commercial TV, MTV, videos, head-sets and the global catwalk is a serious possibility. In this sense, Ahmed is probably right: the threat to Islam is not the legacy of Jesus, but that of Madonna.

I have rather similar difficulties with Gellner's contribution in *Postmod-ernism, Reason and Religion* (1992) to the debate on postmodernism. Gellner is well known for his extensive and influential contribution to the defence of rationalism in the social sciences. For many years, Gellner has been concerned to defend rational argument against any attempt to reduce logical and analytical thought merely to a function of language, grammar or textuality. He has been hostile, for example, to ethnometho-dology which he believes is an attack on the possibility of inter-societal agreements about meaning and value. He is also equally well known for his contributions to the sociology of Islam and to the political analysis of Islamic social systems. It is hardly surprising that Gellner would take such strong objection to postmodernism. Gellner, again for reasons which are perfectly obvious and acceptable, is primarily concerned with the impact of postmodern thought on anthropology. In fact he discusses no other forms of postmodernism. Anthropology as a classical social science has been concerned with the problem of meaning, the interpretation of sym-bolism and the inquiry into the fundamental features of human societies via the analysis of culture. To some extent, therefore, anthropology can be seen as a hermeneutic inquiry into belief systems, rituals and cultural practices. It is equally unsurprising that postmodern forms of analysis should have a certain sympathetic reception within academic anthro-pology since postmodernism, like hermeneutics, is concerned with the detailed analysis of irony, parody, satire and other literary devices in belief systems and cultural practices. The impact of postmodernism on anthropology therefore has been to suggest to anthropologists that they are primarily concerned with the interpretation or reading of the textual-ity of rituals and other cultural practices. Gellner objects to this impact of postmodernism on anthropological methodology since, from his per-spective, such a tendency represents a turn away from any universalistic assumptions about the significance of religion, rituals and belief. Gellner is therefore deeply suspicious of the postmodern turn in the modern history of anthropology. Gellner treats the debate between modernists and postmodernists as merely a replay of an earlier intellectual conflict between classicism and romanticism in which the classical tradition was associated with European domination and romanticism expressed the beliefs and practices of folk (or at best national) cultures (Gellner 1992: 26). As it turns out, he is quite scornful of postmodern anthropology's concern for local cultures: 'So the postmodernist will try to communicate the anguish of his field experience, in which he and his subjects tried to break out of their respective islands and reach out to each other. Of course, they must fail!' (Gellner, 1992: 36). The incommensurability of cultural differences logically rules out communication, and hence translation must fail.

Although I am sympathetic to some aspects of Gellner's attack on this current trend, his approach to the problem runs into a number of difficulties. In concentrating on the debate in anthropology, he does of course take a rather narrow view of postmodernism, which in fact is a highly diverse set of trends and movements within intellectual discussion and debate. This narrow approach to postmodernism is illustrated by the fact that Gellner treats postmodern analysis as merely a contemporary form of ancient relativism. For Gellner, postmodernism is a type of hyper-relativism which reduces all practices and beliefs to subjective orientation within which there is no possibility of universalism. The role of the anthropologist is to provide a reading of local cultures; conventional Western anthropological accounts become yet another grand narrative which is to be relativised by postmodernism. Gellner is able to dismiss postmodernism as nothing new simply because he reduces it to conventional relativism, a position against which he can mobilize many of his own conventional arguments. Although the postmodern critique of grand narratives as universal discourses might appear as a conventional form of relativism, postmodernism is perhaps better understood as a more wide-ranging approach to parody, irony, simulation and other forms of reflexivity in literary devices.

Second, Gellner, like many commentators on the current postmodern intellectual scene, makes no significant distinction between postmodernism as a form of thought or trend within the humanities and the social sciences and postmodernity as a social condition of late capitalism. If we regard postmodernism as a response, initially within the arts, to the rationalism of modernism, as sociologists we should also be concerned with the social, cultural and economic risks of postmodernity as a condition or state of modern social systems. Postmodernity in this sense can be seen as a feature of advanced consumerism, the reorganization of cities in the late twentieth century, the impact of new forms of technology and information on social life, the consequences of global tourism and the increasingly risky nature of the social environment. Postmodernity as a social movement or condition within late capitalism is only indirectly related to relativism, irony and parody in that greater cultural diversity, differentiation and heterogeneity might force social actors and social groups into a greater self-reflexive awareness and scrutiny of the diversity and problems of their own systems of belief. Tourism, cultural variation, multiculturalism and the erosion of the sovereignty of the nation-state bring all social groups within the globalizing process into a self-awareness of the relativity of their own belief systems. It is at this point within risk society that postmodernism as a cultural movement and postmodernity as an empirical condition of social systems meet each other.

This relates to a third weakness in Gellner's approach, namely that he is primarily concerned with the intellectual or theological problems of relativizing postmodernism within the academic system or at the level of priests and other intellectual leaders of religious systems. Gellner does not find relativism intellectually convincing on rational grounds and therefore he ultimately dismisses it as a reasonable position which an honest intellectual could occupy. However, this is not the real issue; the real issue is how, at the level of everyday life, the relativization of belief via commodities, travel, tourism and the impact of global TV shakes the bases of faith in the general population. In putting the problem in these terms, I am appealing to an argument in Karl Marx which asserts that it is social being that determines consciousness and not consciousness that determines social being. In order to understand how a dominant ideology functions, one needs to examine how ideological beliefs and perspectives operate at the everyday level of consumption, production and distribution of beliefs. Furthermore, social beliefs of a religious or political kind are sustained when the everyday world has a convergence with abstract systems of speculation. I am therefore returning to the underlying argument of this chapter which is that the erosion of faith through the postmodernization of culture has to be understood in terms of how the diversity of commodities and their global character transform in covert and indirect fashion the everyday beliefs of the mass of the population. It is for this reason that I am arguing via the sociology of knowledge, that the presence of Western forms of consumerism and hedonism have a far more significant impact on the nature of traditional religious belief, at the level of the village for example, than the intellectual beliefs of religious leaders and other intellectual elites within the church or the Academy. Postmodernism does not bring about a change in belief merely by re-organizing the intellectual world of an elite group of intellectuals, but rather, through the medium of cultural change, it brings about social change in everyday life through the hedonistic consumption of commodities in which even in the everyday world there is a profound sense of the simulation and inauthentication of cultures via the endless production of global commodities. As Peter Berger and Thomas Luckmann have argued in their sociology of knowledge, major changes in belief are effects of transformations of the facticity of the everyday world.

These changes in the global nature of consumerism should bring intellectuals to rethink the nature of the social, and in particular to rethink the more traditional ways in which the orientalist debate has been formulated. Here again we might note a certain weakness in Edward Said's *Culture and Imperialism* (1993) since he also fails to give expression to the nature of materialism and its impact on the textual representation of the relationship between cultures. Said is perhaps too prone to see the problem at the level of literary production in the work of famous writers and artists rather than focusing on the everyday nature of imperial penetration of cultures via the materiality of commodity exchanges. The value of articulating the relationship between the material world of commodities and the life-world of intellectuals is that the postmodernization of culture is of course a profound challenge to the monopolistic hold over high culture and elite values which has traditionally been enjoyed by the intellectual within the Academy. The erosion of the distinction between high and low culture, which is part of the process of globalization, the emergence of mass cultures and the postmodernization of lifestyles, has produced a form of nostalgia amongst Western intellectuals who, faced with the indifference or hostility of popular culture, seek in the past, in cultural heritage or primitive forms of culture an escape from the simulation and parody of modern cultural forms.

Critical reactions to popular culture on the part of intellectuals, while overtly about a neutral and objective analysis of capitalist forms, is often covertly a function of their privileged status position within the circulation of signs and symbols as members of elite institutions such as universities. This problem is explored extensively with Georg Stauth in Chapter 9, where we are sceptical of the critical rejection of popular forms of culture via the Frankfurt School and its contemporary followers. In this argument I am also suggesting of course that Muslim intellectuals would be equally critical of the role of mass culture and its postmodernized forms, since postmodern cultures are equally indifferent to the distinction between high and low culture in religious systems. As a result, while postmodernism within the Academy can often be rejected as merely a form of relativism, the relativizing effect of postmodernity in social systems is a much more systematic and profound challenge to the traditional forms of religious practice in the world religions. If postmodernism is a critical scepticism with respect to grand narratives, then the grand narratives of the mainstream religions are equally a target of irony and parody. It is for these reasons that one might anticipate an alliance between the feminist critique of the patriarchal forms of grand narrative in Christianity and Islam and the postmodernization of cultural consumption via a global system of differentiated commodity, production and consumption. This alliance is likely to assume a covert form given the obvious inclination of leaders within feminism to regard postmodernism as an attack on traditional feminist scholarship as a serious activity. Postmodernism is probably only a criticism of unidimensional feminism which weaves its own grand narratives about women and history, but not a critique of a differentiated feminist response to the complexity of modern religion, culture and society.

Chapter 2

Orientalism and the problem of civil society in Islam

While the problems of understanding, comparison and translation are critical issues in philosophy, language and ethical debate, they arise in a particularly acute fashion in sociology because it is a science which attempts comparatively to analyse social structure and culture. In addition to the technical difficulties of bias, distortion and misrepresentation in the methodology of the social sciences, there are the more profound questions of relativism, ethnocentrism and ideology which call into question the whole basis of comparative analysis. It is difficult to imagine what would count as valid sociology without the comparative method and yet there are numerous methodological and philosophical difficulties which often appear to invalidate comparative sociology. There is major disagreement over the issue of whether, following the position adopted by Max Weber, a 'value-free sociology' is either possible or desirable.

In more recent years, social scientists have become increasingly sensitive to the fact that, in addition to these technical and philosophical issues, the structure of power politics is profoundly influential in shaping the content and direction of social science research. In short, the existence of exploitative colonial relationships between societies has been of major significance for the theoretical development of anthropology and sociology. The role of imperial politics has been especially decisive in the constitution of Western images of Islam and the analysis of 'oriental societies' (Daniel 1960; Southern 1962).

In the conventional, liberal perspective, there is the assumption not only that power and knowledge are antithetical, but that valid knowledge requires the suppression of power. Within the liberal history of ideas, the emergence of science out of ideology and common-sense beliefs is conjoined with the growth of individual freedom and with the decline of arbitrary political terror. This view of the contradiction of reason and power has been recently challenged by Michel Foucault, who argues that the growth of bureaucratic control over populations after the eighteenth century required more systematic forms of knowledge in the form of criminology, penology, psychiatry and medicine. The exercise of power in society thus presupposes new forms of scientific discourse through which deviant and marginal groups are defined and controlled. Against the liberal tradition, we are, through an analysis of the Western rationalist tradition, forced to admit that 'power and knowledge directly imply one another, that there is no power relation without the correlative constitution of a field of knowledge, nor any knowledge that does not presuppose and constitute at the same time power relations' (Foucault 1977: 27).

The growth of scientific discourse does not, therefore, inaugurate a period of individual freedoms, but rather forms the basis of more extensive systems of institutionalized power through an alliance of the prison and penology, the asylum and psychiatry, the hospital and clinical medicine, the school and pedagogy. Discourse creates difference through classification, tabulation and comparison and individuates persons for bureaucratic purposes. The categories of 'criminal', 'insane', and 'deviant' are the manifestations of a scientific discourse by which the normal and sane exercise power along a systematic dividing of sameness and difference. The exercise of power over subordinates cannot consequently be reduced simply to a question of attitudes and motives on the part of individuals, since power is embedded in the very language and institutions by which we describe, understand and control the world. Valid comparisons between deviants and normal individuals, between the sane and insane, between the sick and healthy, cannot be achieved by simply reforming attitudes and motives, since these distinctions themselves presuppose a discourse in which conceptual differences are expressions of power relations.

The analysis of knowledge/power in the work of Michel Foucault provides the basis for Edward Said's influential study of orientalism (1978) as a discourse of difference in which the apparently neutral Occident/ Orient contrast is an expression of power relationships. Orientalism is a discourse which represents the exotic, erotic, strange Orient as a comprehensible, intelligible phenomenon within a network of categories, tables and concepts by which the Orient is simultaneously defined and controlled. To know is to subordinate. The orientalist discourse was consequently a remarkably persistent framework of analysis which, expressed through theology, literature, philosophy and sociology, not only an imperial relationship but actually constituted a field of political power. Orientalism created a typology of characters, organized around the contrast between the rational Westerner and the lazy Oriental. The task of orientalism was to reduce the endless complexity of the East into a definite order of types, characters and constitutions. The chrestomathy, representing the exotic Orient in a systematic table of accessible information, was thus a typical cultural product of occidental dominance.

In Said's analysis of orientalism, the crucial 'fact' about the orientalist discourse was that we know and talk about Orientals, while they neither comprehend themselves nor talk about us. In this language of difference, there were apparently no equivalent discourses of occidentalism. The society from which comparisons are to be made has a privileged possession of a set of essential features – rationality, progress, democratic institutions, economic development – in terms of which other societies are deficient and backward. These features account for the particular character of Western society and explain the defects of alternative social formations. As an accounting system, orientalism set out to explain the progressive features of the Occident and the social stationariness of the Orient (Turner 1974a). One of the formative questions of classical sociology – why did industrial capitalism first emerge in the West? – is consequently an essential feature of an intellectual accounting system which hinges upon a basic East/West contrast. Within the broad sweep of this occidental/oriental contrast, Islam has always represented a political and cultural problem for Western accounting systems.

Unlike Hinduism or Confucianism, Islam has major religious ties with Judaism and Christianity; categorizing Islam as an 'oriental religion' raises major difficulties for an orientalist discourse. While the issue of prophetic uniqueness is a contentious one, there are strong arguments to suggest that Islam can, along with Judaism and Christianity, be regarded as a variant of the general Abrahamic faith (Hodgson 1974). Furthermore, Islam has been a major cultural force inside Europe and provided the dominant culture of many Mediterranean societies. While Islam is not ambiguously oriental, Christianity is not in any simple fashion an occidental religion. Christianity as a Semitic, Abrahamic faith by origin could be regarded as an 'oriental religion' and Islam, as an essential dimension of the culture of Spain, Sicily and Eastern Europe, could be counted as occidental. The problem of defining Islam has always possessed a certain urgency for the discourse of orientalism; thus in Christian circles it was necessary to categorize Islam as either parasitic upon Christian culture or a sectarian offshoot of the Christian faith.

The point of Foucault's analysis of discourse is to suggest that the same rules governing the distribution of statements within a discourse may be common to a wide variety of apparently separate disciplines (Foucault 1972). The orientalist problematic is not peculiar to Christian theology, but is a discourse which underlines economics, politics and sociology. If the basic issue behind Christian theology was the uniqueness of the Christian revelation with respect to Islam, the central question behind comparative sociology was the uniqueness of the West in relation to the alleged stagnation of the East. In an earlier publication I have suggested that sociology attempted to account for the apparent absence of capitalism in Islamic societies by conceptualizing Islam as a series of social and historical gaps (Turner 1978a). Western sociology characteristically argued that Islamic society lacked those autonomous institutions of bourgeois civil society which ultimately broke the tenacious hold of feudalism over the Occident. According to this view, Muslim society lacked independent cities, an autonomous bourgeois class, rational bureaucracy, legal reliability, personal property and that cluster of rights which embody bourgeois legal culture. Without these institutional and cultural elements, there was nothing in Islamic civilisation to challenge the dead hand of pre-capitalist tradition. The orientalist view of Asiatic society can be encapsulated in the notion that the social structure of the oriental world was characterized by the absence of a civil society, that is, by the absence of a network of institutions mediating between the individual and the state. It was this social absence which created the conditions for oriental despotism in which the individual was permanently exposed to the arbitrary rule of the despot. The absence of civil society simultaneously explained the failure of capitalist economic development outside Europe and the absence of political democracy.

THE CONCEPT OF CIVIL SOCIETY

There is in Western political philosophy a set of basic categories, which can be traced back to Aristotle, for distinguishing between government in terms of monarchy, democracy or despotism. While it is possible to approach these categories numerically, that is, by the one, few or many, one central element to the problem of government is the relationship between the state and the individual. For example, the notion of 'despotism' typically involves a spatial metaphor of the social system in which there is an institutional gap between the private individual and the public state. In despotism, the individual is fully exposed to the gaze of the despotic ruler, because there are no intervening social institutions, especially voluntary associations, lying between the ruler and the ruled. The individual is completely displayed before the passion, caprice and will of the despot and there are, as it were, no social groups or institutions behind which the ruled may hide. The distance between the despot and the subject may be considerable, but the social space is not filled up with a rich growth of social groupings and institutions which could encapsulate the individual and within which separate interests could develop in opposition to the unified will of the despot. By way of a preliminary definition, we may argue that despotism presupposes a society in which civil society is either absent or underdeveloped. A definition of 'civil society' is that a prolific network of institutions – church, family, club, guild, association and community – lies between the state and the individual, and which simultaneously connects the individual to authority and protects the individual from total political control. The notion of 'civil society' is not only fundamental to the definition of political life in European societies, but is also a point of contrast between Occident and Orient.

In the Scottish Enlightenment tradition, the emergence of civil society was regarded as a major indication of social progress from the state of nature to civilization. The theory of civil society was part of the master dichotomy of nature/civilization, since it was within civil society that the individual was eventually clothed in judicial rights of property, possessions and security. In Hegel's social philosophy, civil society mediates between the family and the state; it is constituted by the economic intercourse between individuals. The Hegelian conceptualization of 'civil society' in terms of economic relationships was the source of so much confusion in subsequent Marxist analysis in that it became difficult to locate civil society unambiguously in the metaphor of economic base and superstructures. For Marx,

> Civil Society embraces the whole material intercourse of individuals within a definite stage of the development of productive forces. It embraces the whole commercial and industrial life of a given stage and, in so far, transcends the State and nation, though, on the other hand again, it must assert itself in its foreign relations as nationality and inwardly must organise itself as a state.
>
> (Marx and Engels 1953: 76)

Since Marx was primarily interested in the theoretical analysis of the capitalist mode of production, it has subsequently been difficult for Marxists to determine the precise relationship between civil society/state, on the one hand, and to analyse such sociological concepts as 'family', 'church', 'community', or 'tribe' on the other. One solution, of course, is to treat this area of social life as explicable in purely economic terms; the primary divisions within society are those between classes, which in turn are explained by the mode of production (Poulantzas 1973).

The difficulties of locating civil society in relation to the economy and the state are exemplified by some recent debates over Antonio Gramsci's analysis of the concept (Anderson 1974). In a famous passage, Gramsci commented that, 'Between the economic structure and the state with its legislation and its coercion stands civil society' (Gramsci 1971). In Gramsci's writing, civil society is the arena within which ideological hegemony and political consent are engineered, and it therefore contrasts with the state, which is the site of political force and coercion. Such a conception complicates the more conventional Marxist dichotomy of base/superstructure, but there is much dissensus over exactly where Gramsci places his theoretical emphasis (Anderson 1977). While there is much disagreement over the extent of hegemonic consent in modern capitalism, it is interesting to note that Gramsci's conceptualization of 'civil society' was important for his view that political strategies were relevant in relation to the extent of coercion and consent in society. Gramsci made a basic distinction between the West, in which there is widespread consensus based on civil society, and the East, where the state dominates society and where coercion is more important than consensus. Speaking specifically of Russia, Gramsci argued that:

> the state was everything, civil society was primordial and gelatinous; in the West, there was a proper relationship between state and civil society, and when the state trembled a sturdy structure of civil society was at once revealed. The state was only an outer ditch, behind which there stood a powerful system of fortresses and earthworks.
>
> (Gramsci 1971: 238)

Where civil society is relatively underdeveloped in relationship to the state, political coercion of individuals is the basis of class rule rather than ideological consent which characterizes the bourgeois institutions of Western capitalism.

Liberal political theory, while clearly fundamentally different in outlook and conclusions, has often approached the East/West, and coercion/consent dichotomies in somewhat similar terms, especially in terms of the notion of constitutional checks and balances. In *The Spirit of the Laws* (Montesquieu 1949) written in 1748, Montesquieu distinguished between republics, monarchies and despotisms in terms of their guiding principles which were respectively virtue, honour and fear (Montesquieu 1949). The main differences between monarchy and despotism were: (1) while monarchy is based on the inequality of social strata, in despotism there is an equality of slavery where the mass of the population is subject to the ruler's arbitrary will; (2) in monarchy, the ruler follows customs and laws, whereas a despot dominates according to his own inclination; (3) in despotism, there are no intermediary social institutions linking the individual to the state. In an earlier work, *Considerations on the Causes of the Greatness of the Romans and Their Decline*, Montesquieu had been particularly concerned with the problems of centralization in the Roman Empire and with the transformation of republics into monarchies (Montesquieu 1965). Montesquieu, who was profoundly influenced by Locke and English constitutional history, came to see the divisions of powers and constitutional checks on centralized authority as the principal guarantee of political rights. His *Persian Letters* (Montesquieu 1923) permitted him to write a critical review of French society through the eyes of oriental observers; it has subsequently not been clear whether Montesquieu's definition of and objections to the despotism of the East were, in fact, directed against the French polity, especially against the absolute monarchy (Althusser 1972).

Emile Durkheim, whose Latin dissertation on Montesquieu and Rousseau was published in 1892, came to see the problem of modern political life not in the effects of the division of labour on common sentiments, but in the absence of regulating institutions between the individual and the state. The decline of the Church, the weakness of the family, the loss of communal ties and the underdevelopment of occupational and professional associations had dissolved those important social relations which shielded the individual from the state. Unlike Herbert Spencer, however, Durkheim did not believe that the extension of state functions in contemporary society necessarily resulted in political absolutism. Durkheim in his 'two laws of penal evolution' defined absolutism in the following terms:

> what makes the central power more or less absolute is the more or less radical absence of any countervailing forces, regularly organised with a view toward moderating it. We can, therefore, foresee that what gives birth to a power of this sort is the more or less complete concentration of all society's controlling functions in one and the same hand.
>
> (Durkheim 1978)

While Durkheim does not specifically employ the term, in the light of his reference to the importance of 'countervailing forces,' it is not illegitimate or inappropriate to suggest that Durkheim's argument is that the weakness of civil society, situated between the individual and the state, is a general condition for political absolutism.

This French tradition in the political sociology of absolutism from Montesquieu to Durkheim cannot be properly understood without some consideration of the debate which arose in France over the nature of enlightened government. What we now refer to as 'enlightened despotism' or 'enlightened absolutism' first arose as an intellectual and political issue in France in the 1760s partly as the result of the doctrines of the Physiocrats (Hartung 1957). The terms favoured by the Physiocrats were '*Despotisme eclaire*' and '*Despotisme legal*'. For example, T. G. Raynal provided a definition of good government as '*Le gouvernement le plus heureaux serait celui d'un despote juste et eclaire*' in his history of trade with the West and East Indies. In their economic doctrines, the Physiocrats adhered to *laissez-faire* policies to free the economy and the individual from the unnatural fetters which constrained efficiency and economic output. However, society was not free from such artificial constraints and it was necessary for radical changes to be brought about by '*Despotisme eclaire*'. The Physiocrats took for granted that such a despotism would be in the hands of an hereditary monarchy which would rationally sweep aside the artificial clutter of the past to restore the natural order of individual freedom. The despot had a duty to force people to be free by a rational policy of education and social reform.

The debate about the virtues of forms of government was generated not only by absolutism in the late eighteenth century but also by the rise of colonialism in the nineteenth. Colonial administrators were forced to decide upon schemes of imperial control for the new dependencies. Raynal's use of the notion of 'legal despotism' is interesting in the context of a discussion of the colonies. Utilitarian commentaries on political organization in Britain were similarly set in the context of criticisms of British government by an hereditary aristocracy and in terms of the colonial administration in India. The utilitarians were concerned both with the problem of the working class and parliamentarian government in Britain and with the question of the government of Indian natives. Thus, James Mill's *The History of British India* was driven in particular by the question of native despotism and government reform. He observed that:

> Among the Hindus, according to the Asiatic model, the government was monarchical, and, with the usual exception of religion and its ministers, absolute. No idea of any system of rule, different from the will of a single person, appears to have entered the minds of them, or their legislators.

> (Mill 1972: 212–3)

For Mill, there was a social hiatus between the traditional, all-embracing life of the Indian village and the outer, public world of kingdoms. The constant break-up of the latter contrasted with the social isolation and stagnation of the former. The principal political solution to this static despotism was a dose of '*Despotisme eclaire*', that is, strong central government, benevolent laws, modernized administration and a redistribution of land rights. In many respects, John Stuart Mill followed his father's line of argument both about political reform in Britain and colonial government. J. S. Mill's basic fear was focused on the effects of majority rule in popular democracies on the life and conscience of the educated and sensitive individual. This fear had been greatly confirmed by the more pessimistic aspects of Alexis de Tocqueville's analysis of American political institutions in *Democracy in America*, which Mill read in 1835 (de Tocqueville 1946). According to de Tocqueville, majority rule on the basis of universal franchise could result in a sterile consensus which was inimicable to individuality and individual rights. The only check to the despotism of the majority would be the existence of strong voluntary associations (that is, civil society) protecting the individual from majority control and protecting diversity of interests and culture. Without safeguards, democracy would produce in Britain the same sterility which tradition had brought about in Asia, namely social stagnation. Mill's fears were consequently, 'not of great liberty, but too ready submission; not of anarchy, but of servility; not of too rapid change, but of Chinese stationariness' (Mill 1859: 56).

In the case of colonial rule, however, the choice was between two types of despotism: native or imperial. Native despotism was always arbitrary and ineffectual, while the enlightened despotism of 'more' civilised people over their dominions was firm, regular and effective in promoting social reform and political advancement.

John Stuart Mill (1806–73) and Karl Marx (1818–83) were contemporaries. In formulating their views on Asiatic society, they were influenced by similar contemporary events and by a similar range of documentary evidence. It is not entirely surprising, therefore, to find that they also shared some common assumptions about Asiatic society, despite very different evaluations and expectations of British rule in India. While Marx's concept of the Asiatic mode of production was primarily formulated in terms of economic structures and processes (or the absence of them), the Asiatic mode was also a version of the conventional political notion of 'oriental despotism'. In Marx's journalistic writing, oriental society was characterized by ceaseless political changes in ruling dynasties and by total economic immobility. Dynastic circulation brought about no structural change because the ownership of the land remained in the hands of the aristocratic overlord. Like James Mill, Marx also emphasized the stationary nature of village life, based on self-sufficiency. No civil society existed between the individual and the despot, between the village and the state, because autonomous cities and social classes were absent from the social system.

While Weber acknowledged a debt to Marx's analysis of Indian village life in his *The Religion of India* (Weber 1958a), Weber's various elaborations of political forms – patriarchalism and patrimonialism – concentrate more on the problem of military organization than on the economic basis of political life. In fact, it is possible to see Weber's sociology as the analysis of the interconnections between the ownership of the means of production and the ownership of the means of violence. He thus established an abstract continuum between a situation where independent knights own their own weapons and provide military services for a lord, and another context in which the means of violence are centralized under the control of a patrimonial lord. Empirically, Weber recognised that these 'pure types' rarely occurred in such simplified forms, but the contrast was important in his analysis of the tensions between centralizing and decentralizing processes in political empires.

In feudalism, where knights have hereditary rights to lands and provide their own weapons, there are strong political pressures towards localism and the emergence of autonomous petty-kingdoms. The crucial political struggles in feudalism are thus *within* the dominant class, not between lords and serfs, because the crucial question is the preservation of the feudal king's political control over other landlords who seek extensive feudal immunities from their lord. In patrimonialism, one method of controlling aristocratic cavalries based on feudal or prebendal rights to land is to recruit slave or mercenary armies. Such armies have little or no attachment to civil society – they were typically foreigners, bachelors or eunuchs who were also detribalized. Hence, slave armies have no local interests in civil society and are, formally at least, totally dependent on the patrimonial lord. As Weber points out, patrimonialism can only survive if the patrimonial lord enjoys a stable fiscal liquidity or access to other resources by which to pay off his armies. Patrimonial empires suffer from two perennial crises: (1) revolts by slave armies and (2) instability of political succession. While Weber did not use the feudal/prebendal distinction as a necessary criterion for distinguishing the West from the East, he did regard patrimonial instability (or 'sultanism') as a major problem of oriental society, especially of Turkey.

The debate about oriental empires in European social thought found its classic expression in the twentieth century in Karl Wittfogel's *Oriental Despotism* (1957). Characteristically subtitled 'a comparative study of total power', Wittfogel presented a technological account of oriental empires. The climatic aridity of oriental regions gave rise to the need for extensive hydraulic systems which, in turn, could be organized only on the basis of centralized political power. The difficulties of hydraulic management could be solved only on the basis of bureaucratization, general slavery and centralized authority. The hydraulic state was forced to obliterate all countervailing social groups within society which could threaten its total power. These 'nongovernmental forces' included kin groups, independent religious organizations, autonomous military groups and owners of alternative forms of property. Oriental despotism thus represented the triumph of the state over society and Wittfogel saw the absence of 'civil society' in hydraulic empires as a necessary basis for total power. In Europe, absolutism was always faced by countervailing forces in civil society:

> the absence of formal constitutional checks does not necessarily imply the absence of societal forces whose interests and intentions the government must respect. In most countries of post-feudal Europe the absolutist regimes were restricted not so much by official constitutions as by the actual strength of the landed nobility, the Church and the towns. In absolutist Europe all these nongovernmental forces were politically organised and articulated. They thus differed profoundly from the representatives of landed property, religion or urban professions in hydraulic society.
>
> (Wittfogel 1957: 103)

To summarize, the political problem of oriental society was the absence of a civil society which functioned to counterbalance the power of the state over the isolated individual.

Although the notion of the absence of civil society in oriental despotism was formulated by reference to Asia as a whole, it has played a particularly prominent role in the analysis of Islamic societies; it is an essential feature of the orientalist discourse. Furthermore, the theme of the missing civil society cut across political and intellectual divisions in the west, providing a common framework for Marxists and sociologists alike. Marx and Engels in their articles for the *New York Daily Tribune* observed that the absence of private property in land and the centralization of state power precluded the emergence of a strong bourgeois class. The dominance of the bureaucracy and the instability of urban society meant that 'the first basic condition of bourgeois acquisition is lacking, the security of the person and the property of the trader' (Marx and Engels 1953: 40).

A similar position was adopted by Max Weber in *The Sociology of Religion* where he suggested that the effect of Islamic expansion had been to convert Islam into a 'national Arabic warrior religion'; the result was that the dominant ethos of Islam 'is inherently contemptuous of bourgeois-commercial utilitarianism and considers it as sordid greediness and as the life force specifically hostile to it' (Weber 1966).

In Western sociological accounts of Islamic societies, it has been argued that, because of the absence of a 'spirit of capitalism' in the middle class, trade in most Islamic societies was dominated historically by minorities (Greeks, Jews, Armenians and Slavs). Recent sociological studies of Islam have continued this tradition by suggesting that in the absence of the entrepreneurial spirit and achievement, motivation was linked to the underdeveloped nature of the middle class in Islam (Bonne 1960; Lerner 1958; McClelland 1961).

The absence of a civil society in Islam and the weakness of bourgeois culture in relation to the state apparatus have been associated, in the orientalist problematic, not only with the backwardness of economic development, but also with political despotism. There is a common viewpoint among political scientists that there is no established tradition of legitimate opposition to arbitrary governments in Islam, because the notions of political rights and social contract had no institutional support in an independent middle class (Vatikiotis 1975). However, the orientalist theme of the absence of a civil society extends well beyond the area of economics and politics. The scientific and artistic culture of Islam is treated as the monopoly of the imperial court which, within the 'city camp', patronized the emergence of a rational culture in opposition to the religion of the masses. The union of science and industry which was characteristic of the English Protestant middle classes in the nineteenth century was noticeably absent in Islamic culture. Ernest Renan, in a forthright commentary on Islam and science, suggested that, 'the Mussulman has the most profound disdain for instruction, for science, for everything that constitutes the European spirit' (Renan 1896: 85).

For Renan, science could only flourish in Islam in association with heresy. While Renan's highly prejudicial attitudes are rarely articulated in an overt fashion in contemporary oriental scholarship, the same arguments concerning elitist patronage of arts and sciences in the absence of a middle class are constantly repeated. This perspective is normally conjoined with the notion that science in Islam was merely parasitic on Greek culture and that Islam was simply a vehicle transmitting Greek philosophy to the Renaissance in Europe (O'Leary 1949). The deficiencies of Islamic society, politics, economics and culture, are, in orientalism, located in the problem of an absent civil society.

ALTERNATIVES TO ORIENTALISM

In the period following the Second World War, orientalism has shown many symptoms of internal crisis and collapse (Laroui 1976), but the alternatives to orientalism have been difficult to secure, since orientalism retains substantial and institutional supports. Orientalism is a self-validating and closed tradition which is highly resistant to internal and external criticism. Various attempts at reconstruction have been presented in, for example, *Review of Middle East Studies* and by the Middle East Research and Information Project (MERIP). One problem in the transformation of existing paradigms is that Marxist alternatives have themselves found it difficult to break with the orientalist perspective which was present in the analyses of Marx and Engels.

Although there have been major changes in Marxist conceptualization of such basic notions as 'the mode of production', much of the theoretical apparatus of contemporary Marxism is irrelevant in the analysis of Islamic societies. Those Marxists who have adopted the epistemological position of writers like Louis Althusser are, in any case, committed to the view that empirical studies of the Orient will not be sufficient to dislodge the orientalist perspective without a radical shift in epistemology and theoretical frameworks. While Edward Said has presented a major critique of the oriental discourse, the conceptual basis on which that critique is founded, namely the work of Michel Foucault, does not lend itself unambiguously to the task of reformulating perspectives. A pessimistic reading of Foucault would suggest that the alternative to an oriental discourse would simply be another discourse which would incorporate yet another expression of power. In Foucault's analysis there is no discourse-free alternative since extensions of knowledge coincide with fields of power. We are thus constrained to 'the patient construction of discourses about discourses, and to the task of hearing what has already been said' (Foucault 1973: xvi). At one level, therefore, Said is forced to offer the hope of 'spiritual detachment and generosity' (Said 1978a: 259), which will be sufficient to generate a new vision of the Middle East which has jettisoned the ideological premises of orientalism.

There may, however, exist one line of development which would be compatible with Said's employment of Foucault's perspective on discourse and which would present a route out of orientalism. By its very nature, language is organized around the basic dichotomy of sameness and difference; the principal feature of the orientalist discourse has been to emphasize difference in order to account for the 'uniqueness of the West'. In the case of Islam and Christianity, however, there is a strong warrant to focus on those features which unite rather than divide them, or at least to examine those ambiguous areas of cultural overlap between them. Historically, both religions emerged, however antagonistically, out of a common Semitic-Abrahamic religious culture. They have been involved in mutual processes of diffusion, exchange and colonization.

In this sense, as I have already suggested, it is permissible to refer to Islam as an occidental religion in Spain, Malta and the Balkans and to Christianity as an oriental religion of North Africa, the Fertile Crescent of Asia. This obvious point has the merit of exposing the fundamental ambiguity of the notion of 'the Orient' within the orientalist discourse. In addition to these mutual contacts in history and geography, Islam and Christianity have, for historically contingent reasons, come to share common frameworks in science, philosophy and culture. Despite these areas of mutual contact, the general drift of orientalism has been to articulate difference, division and separation. One important illustration of these discursive separations can be found in conventional histories of Western philosophy.

Islam and Christianity are both grounded in prophetic revelation and were not initially concerned with the philosophical articulation of orthodox theology. Both religions were confronted by the existence of a highly developed system of secular logic and rhetoric which was the legacy of Greek culture. Aristotle's philosophical system became the intellectual framework into which the theologies of Islam and Christianity were poured. Eventually the formulation of Christian beliefs came to depend heavily on the work of Islamic scholars, especially Averroes (Ibn Rushd), Avicenna (Ibn Sina), Al-Kinda and Al-Razi. Here, consequently, is an area of mutual development in which medieval Christianity was parasitic on the philosophical developments which had been achieved in Islam. However, the orientalist response to this situation has been to claim that Islam simply mediated Hellenism, which subsequently found its 'true home' in the universities of medieval Europe. Thus, we find writers like Bertrand Russell in his *History of Western Philosophy* following the tradition of Renan in simply denying that Islam made any significant contribution to European philosophy. The attraction of connecting Western philosophy with Hellenism is obvious; it provides the link between Western culture and the democratic traditions of Greek society. Greek rhetoric grew out of public debate in the political sphere where systematic forms of argument were at a premium. On this basis, it is possible to contrast the closed world of oriental despotism with the open world of Greek democracy and rhetorical speech. One difficulty with this idealistic equation of Hellenism and political democracy is that it remains largely silent with respect to the slave economy of classical Greece. The majority of the Greek population was excluded from the world of logic and rhetoric by virtue of their slave status.

The philosophical and scientific legacy of Greek civilisation passed to Europe through the prism of Islamic Spain, but here again orientalism treats the impact of Islam on Spanish society as merely regression or, at best, repetition. In Wittfogel's view, the particular combination of population pressure and climatic conditions created the context within which Muslim colonialists in Spain created the despotic polity of hydraulic society. Under Islam, Spain

> became a genuinely hydraulic society, ruled despotically by appointed officials and taxed by agromanagerial methods of acquisition. The Moorish army, which soon changed from a tribal to a 'mercenary' body, was definitely the tool of the state as were its counterparts in the Umayyad and Abbasid caliphates.
>
> (Wittfogel 1957: 215)

Prior to Islamic influence, Spain had, according to Wittfogel, been a decentralized feudal society, but, with the introduction of the hydraulic economy, it was rapidly transformed into a centralized, despotic state. In other words, within an occidental setting, Islam still carried the essential features of an oriental despotic culture. Similarly with the *reconquista*, Spain reverted to a feudal rather than despotic polity. The re-establishment of Christianity 'transformed a great hydraulic civilisation into a late feudal society' (Wittfogel 1957: 216). Contemporary scholarship on Islamic Spain presents a very different picture, emphasizing the continuity of agricultural and irrigation techniques between Christianity and Islam. A complex and regulated irrigation system requires considerable economic investment over a long period. While the Spanish irrigation system was considerably improved under Muslim management, this was on the basis of a system which was already in operation from classical times. It is the continuity of technology and polity in Spain rather than the difference between Islamic and Christian management which is the important issue (Glick 1970; Smith 1970). The conversation of civil society and economy in Spain under Islam and Christianity thus pinpoints the orientalist fascination with difference, a difference constituted by discourse rather than by history.

CONCLUSION: THE INDIVIDUAL AND CIVIL SOCIETY

The concept of 'civil society' forms the basis of Western political economy from the Scottish Enlightenment to the prison notebooks of Gramsci; while the concept has been frequently discussed in contemporary social science, the fact that it has also been a major part of the orientalist contrast of East and West has been seriously neglected. In simple terms, the concept has been used as the basis of the notion that the Orient, is, so to speak, all state and no society. The notion of 'civil society' cannot be divorced from an equally potent theme in Western philosophy, namely the centrality of autonomous individuals within the network of social institutions. Western political philosophy has hinged on the importance of civil society in preserving the freedom of the individual from arbitrary control by the state. The doctrine of individualism has been regarded as constitutive, if not a Western culture as such, then at least of contemporary industrial culture. It is difficult to conceive of the nexus of Western concepts of conscience, liberty, freedom or property without some basic principle of individualism and therefore individualism appears to lie at the foundations of Western society. The additional importance of individualism is that it serves to distinguish occidental from oriental culture, since the latter is treated as devoid of individual rights and of individuality. Individualism is the golden thread which weaves together the economic institutions of property, the religious institution of confession of conscience and the moral notion of personal autonomy; it serves to separate 'us' from 'them'. In orientalism, the absence of civil society in Islam entailed the absence of the autonomous individual exercising conscience and rejecting arbitrary interventions by the state.

Underlying this liberal theory of the individual was, however, a profound anxiety about the problem of social order in the West. The individual conscience represented a threat to political stability, despite attempts to argue that the moral conscience would always conform with the legitimate political authority. In particular, bourgeois individualism – in the theories of Locke and Mill – was challenged by the mob, the mass and the working class which was excluded from citizenship by a franchise based on property. The debate about oriental despotism took place in the context of uncertainty about enlightened despotism and monarchy in Europe. The orientalist discourse on the absence of the civil society in Islam was a reflection of basic political anxieties about the state of political freedom in the West. In this sense, the problem of orientalism was not the Orient but the Occident. These problems and anxieties were consequently transferred onto the Orient which became, not a representation of the East, but a caricature of the West. Oriental despotism was simply Western monarchy writ large. The crises and contradictions of contemporary orientalism are, therefore, to be seen as part of a continuing crisis of Western society transferred to a global context. The end of orientalism requires a radical reformulation of perspectives and paradigms, but this reconstitution of knowledge can only take place in the context of major shifts in political relations between Orient and Occident, because the transformation of discourse also requires a transformation of power.

Chapter 3

Accounting for the Orient

The way we talk about other people is a central problem of all human interaction and one of the constitutive debates within the social sciences. Although as a matter of fact we do talk about other people and other cultures apparently without too much difficulty, there are major philosophical problems which throw doubt on whether we can really understand people who belong to alien groups and foreign cultures. The philosophical issues are ones of translation and relativism. Achieving a reliable, intersubjectively intelligible translation of meaning is the core issue of all hermeneutics. Sociologists and philosophers have come to see the meaning of words as dependent on their usage within a particular language and their function within a particular grammar, which in turn depends upon its setting within the way of life of a particular society. The philosophical task of understanding the meaning of an expression in another culture cannot, according to this view of language, be separated from the sociological problem of providing an exposition of the social structure within which that language is embedded. Taken as a strong doctrine about the dependence of meaning on social structure, such a philosophical position would render translation, if not impossible, at least uncertain and problematic. Unless there is extensive comparability of social structures, one language cannot be intelligibly translated into another. The paradox is that translation is a routine practice and becoming proficient in another language may be difficult but is clearly not impossible.

The question of translation can be treated as a specific instance of the more general problem of cultural relativism. The problem of relativism is as old as Western philosophy itself since it was Herodotus and Aristotle who confronted the fact that 'Fire burns both in Hellas and in Persia; but men's ideas of right and wrong vary from place to place'. If all beliefs and knowledge are culturally specific, then there are no universal criteria of truth, rationality and goodness by which social practices could be neatly compared or evaluated. There are, however, a number of familiar difficulties with relativism, because, taken to its logical conclusion, it demonstrates that our knowledge of the world is merely ethnocentric, subjective preference. It would mean that no objective, valid comparisons between societies could be made and yet it would be difficult to conceive of knowledge which was not comparative or at least contained comparisons. To know something is, in principle, to be able to speak about it, and language necessarily involves contrasts and comparisons between sameness and difference. As with translation, we constantly compare, despite the apparently insoluble philosophical difficulties of doing so.

The questions of translation and relativism inevitably confront the sociologist who attempts a comparative study of two religions, such as Christianity and Islam. In fact, the question of adequate comparisons is so fundamental that it may appear to rule out such an enterprise from inception since the implication of much sociological analysis of Islam is that it is not a 'religion' at all but a 'socio-political system'. The trouble with this implication is that it takes Christianity as a privileged model of what is to count as a 'religion' in the first place; perhaps in this respect it is Christianity, not Islam, which is the deviant case. One way into these conceptual puzzles may be to recognize that our contemporary views of other religions, such as Islam, are part of an established tradition of talking about alien cultures. We understand other cultures by slotting them into a pre-existing code or discourse which renders their oddity intelligible. We are, in practice, able to overcome the philosophical difficulties of translation by drawing upon various forms of accounting which highlight differences in characteristics between 'us' and 'them'. The culture from which comparisons are to be made can be treated as possessing a number of essential characteristics – rationality, democracy, industrial progress – in terms of which other cultures are seen to be deficient. A table of positive and negative attributes is thus established by which alien cultures can be read off and summations arrived at. Any comparative study of religions will, therefore, tend to draw upon pre-existing assumptions and scholarly traditions which provide an interpretational matrix of contrasts and comparisons. The principal balance sheet by which Islam has been understood in Western culture may be referred to as 'orientalism'.

Orientalism as a system of scholarship first emerged in the early fourteenth century with the establishment by the Church Council of Vienna of a number of university chairs to promote an understanding of oriental languages and culture. The main driving force for orientalism came from trade, inter-religious rivalries and military conflict. Knowledge of the Orient cannot, therefore, be separated from the history of European expansion into the Middle East and Asia. The discovery of the Cape route to Asia by Vasco da Gama in 1498 greatly extended the province of orientalism, but it was not until the eighteenth and nineteenth centuries that detailed studies of oriental societies were published in Europe. In Britain, the establishment of the Asiatic Society (of Bengal) in 1784 and the Royal Asiatic Society in 1823 were important landmarks in the development of Western attitudes. Similar developments took place in France with Napoleon's Institut d'Egypte and the Société Asiatique in 1821; while in Germany an Oriental Society was formed in 1845. It was through these and similar institutions that knowledge of oriental societies, studies of philology and competence in oriental languages were developed and institutionalized. While in common sense terms the 'Orient' embraces an ill-defined geographical zone extending from the eastern shores of the Mediterranean to South-east Asia, Islam and the Islamic heartlands played a peculiarly significant part in the formation of Western attitudes to the East.

Within the category of 'other religions', Islam has at least two major distinguishing features. First, Islam as a prophetic, monotheistic religion has very close ties historically and theologically with Christianity. It can be regarded, along with Christianity and Judaism, as a basic variant of the Abrahamic faith. Second, unlike other religions of the Orient, Islam was a major colonizing force inside Europe and from the eighth century onwards provided the dominant culture of southern Mediterranean societies. These two features of Islam raise the question: in what sense is Islam an 'oriental religion'? This deceptively simple question in fact goes to the heart of the orientalist problematic. If orientalism addresses itself to the issue of what constitutes the Orient, then it is also forced ultimately to define the essence of occidentalism. We might, for example, take a number of Christian cultural attributes – scriptural intellectualism, anti-magical rationality or the separation of the religious and the secular – as constitutive of occidentalism in order to mark off the Orient. As we have seen in Chapter 2 this strategy does immediately raise the difficulty that Christianity, as a Semitic, Abrahamic faith by origin, could be counted as 'oriental', while Islam, by expansion part of the culture of Spain, Sicily and eastern Europe, could be regarded as 'occidental'. The problematic religious and geographical status of Islam was recognized by traditional Christian theology which either treated Islam as parasitic upon Judaeo-Christian culture or as a schism within Christianity. In Dante's *Divine Comedy*, the Prophet Muhammad is constantly split in two as an eternal punishment for religious schism.

The problematic nature of Islam is not, however, merely a difficulty within Christian theology. If the motivating issue behind Christian orientalism was the uniqueness of the Christian revelation with respect to Islamic heresy, then the crucial question for comparative sociology has been the dynamism of Western, industrial civilisation versus the alleged stagnation of the Orient. Within Weberian sociology, the fact that Islam is monotheistic, prophetic and ascetic raises important difficulties for the view that Protestant asceticism uniquely performed a critical role in the rise of Western rationality. In *The Sociology of Religion* (1966), Weber provided two answers to remove this difficulty for the Protestant ethic thesis. First, while recognizing that Muhammad's initial message was one of ascetic self-control, Weber argued that the social carriers of Islam were Arab warriors who transformed the original salvation doctrine into a quest for land. Hence, the inner *angst* of Calvinism was never fully present in Islam. Second, the prebendal form of land-ownership in Islam resulted in a centralized state so that Islam became the ideology of a patrimonial structure and precluded the growth of urban asceticism. This argument about social carriers and patrimonial power in Islam permitted Weber to treat Islam as a religion of world acceptance with a formal and legalistic orientation to questions of personal salvation. Since Islam presented no radical challenge to the secular world of power, it failed to develop a rational theodicy which would, in principle, have driven believers to a significant position of world mastery. Islam, by legitimating the status quo, never challenged the political structure in such a way to promote fundamental processes of social change.

Weber's treatment of Islam provides us with the accounting system that constitutes the basis of his comparative sociology of oriental society, of which the central issue is a contrast between dynamic and stationary social systems. The task of Weber's sociology was to provide an historical account of the emergence of what he took to be the characteristic uniqueness of the West, namely the defining ingredients of rational capitalist production. These ingredients included rational (Roman) law, the modern state, the application of science to all areas of social life, especially to the technology of industrial production, the separation of the family from the business enterprise, autonomous urban institutions, an ascetic lifestyle which initially converted entrepreneurship into a 'calling' and finally the bureaucratization of social procedures. These features of capitalist society were the institutional locations of a general process of rationalization in which social relationships were increasingly subject to norms of calculation and prediction. The rationalization of social life involved a continuous alienation of social actors, not only from the means of production, but from the means of mental production and from the military apparatus. The ownership of the means of economic, intellectual and military production are concentrated in bureaucratic, anonymous institutions so that, in Weber's view, capitalism became an 'iron cage' in which the individual is merely a 'cog'. While the individual is subjected to detailed social regulation, rational law, bureaucratic management and applied science provide the social conditions for economic stability by which capitalist accumulation can proceed unhindered by moral conventions or by capricious political intervention.

In Weber's sociology of oriental society, an accounting system is created in which the Orient simply lacks the positive ingredients of Western rationality. Oriental society can be defined as a system of absences –

absent cities, the missing middle class, missing autonomous urban institutions, and missing property (Turner 1978a, 1978b). In Europe, Christianity permitted cities to arise in which urban social relations were based
on a universal faith rather than on particular tribal loyalties; in addition,
European cities enjoyed considerable economic and political independence from the state (Weber 1958b). In the Orient, according to Weber,
cities did not evolve organically as economic centres, but were imposed
on the countryside as military and political sites of state control. The
oriental city did not provide a congenial environment within which an
urban bourgeoisie could emerge free from unpredictable, ad hoc political
control. This analysis of the city in turn depends upon a basic contrast in
Weber's sociology between the feudal structures of Europe and the prebendal organization of land in the Orient. In feudalism where individual
land rights were inherited by a stable system of primogeniture or limited
partibility, land-owning knights enjoy a degree of political freedom from
the feudal monarch in return for military service. In prebendalism, the
prebend was a non-inheritable right which was controlled by a patrimonial
state and as a stratum of cavalry was more directly subject to the royal
household. While some forms of private land-ownership did occur in
prebendalism, legal ownership of private land was restricted in scope and
there was a strong tendency for the wealthy to avoid risk-taking capital
investments. Hence, in Islam, Weber thought that capital was frequently
frozen in the form of investment in religious property. While property
was subject to political interference, it was also difficult to obtain legal
security because religious law was essentially unstable. It is consequently
possible to imagine Weber's comparative sociology as an accounting
system with 'rational law', 'free cities', 'urban bourgeoisie' and the
'modern state' in one column and 'ad hoc law', 'military camps', 'state-
controlled merchants' and 'patrimonial state' in the other. Weber does
the work of translation from one set of social meanings to another context
of meanings by a system of linguistic accounting in which occidental
categories have a privileged location.

It is often claimed that Weberian sociology represents a form of subjective idealism which unwittingly reproduces the contents of common-sense,
bourgeois thought and that, by contrast, the historical materialism of Karl
Marx penetrates the conceptual surface of bourgeois political economy
to reveal the objective structures which ultimately determine social life.
This contrast is difficult to maintain in general terms and particular problems arise with the commentaries of Marx and Engels on oriental society.
In Marx and Engel's early journalistic writing on India, China and the
Middle East, we find the theoretical development of what has subsequently been referred to as 'the Asiatic mode of production' (Avineri
1968). The point of this theoretical device was to contrast the socio-
economic stagnation of the Orient with the revolutionary character of

capitalist society in which capitalists are forced to change constantly the technical basis of production in order to survive economically. The 'Asiatic mode of production' is thus a form of social accounting which bears a close similarity to that employed by Weber. Marx and Engels, forming their theory on the basis of utilitarian analyses of India and Francois Bernier's *Voyages* (1710), focused their concern on the alleged absence of private property in land in Asia where the state controlled the distribution of land-ownership. In some of his journalistic work, such as the article on British rule in India (Marx 1972), Marx emphasized the importance of climate and geography in the desert regions of North Africa and Asia for the rise of the state which had important functions in the control of irrigation works. Because the state controlled the land in order to manage a public irrigation system, social classes based on the ownership of property could not emerge and instead the population was held in a condition of what Engels called 'general (state) slavery'. In the absence of social classes and class struggle, there was no mechanism of social change. Since the history of all societies is the history of struggles between classes, it followed that Asia 'has no history at all, at least no known history' (Marx 1972: 81). In later works, such as the *Grundrisse* and *Capital*, Marx shifted his attention away from the role of the state in irrigation to the nature of economic self-sufficiency of Asiatic villages as the ultimate explanation of oriental immobility. The outcome was still the same: the absence of radical changes in asiatic social structure which, in Marx's terms, would count as historical change.

Weber and Marx adhered to rather similar accounting schemes to explain the presence of history in occidental societies and its absence in the Orient. According to these schemes of translation, the Orient is a collection of gaps or a list of deficiencies – the absence of private property, the absence of social classes, and the absence of historical changes in the mode of production. Since both Weber and Marx also adhered to the notion that state politics in the Orient was arbitrary and uncertain, their view of oriental society may be regarded as yet another version of that more ancient system of accounting, namely 'oriental despotism'. The theoretical impetus for the analysis of despotic politics came from the development of the absolutist state in Europe when philosophical discussions centred on the distinction between legitimate monarchy and arbitrary despotism. Thus, Benigne-Bossuet, instructor to Louis XIV, identified four principal causes of despotic rule which were the absence of private property, arbitrary laws, absolute political power and general slavery (Stelling-Michaud 1960). These causes of despotism were all evident in the imperial structures of Russia and Turkey. A rather similar position was taken by Montesquieu in *The Spirit of the Laws* (1748) where he argued that despotism in the Asiatic empires was brought about by the absence of social institutions intervening between the absolute ruler and the general population who consequently were unprotected objects of the ruler's passions.

Whether or not Marx eventually abandoned the concept of the Asiatic mode of production has subsequently become an important issue in Marxist theory and politics (Wittfogel 1957). In recent years, a number of attempts have been made to jettison the concept by employing Louis Althusser's notion of an 'epistemological break' in the theoretical development of Marx's ideas. According to Althusser (1969), it is possible to divide Marx's work into distinctive periods in which the early idealism and humanism of the Paris manuscripts were eventually replaced by an entirely new scientific interest in the objective laws of the capitalist mode of production. On these grounds it is possible to treat the concept of the Asiatic mode of production as a pre-scientific interest which Marx and Engels abandoned in their maturity. It has also been argued that, in any case, the concept is incompatible with the central element of the Marxist theory of the state as the product of a society divided along class lines. According to this view, class conflict is a 'condition of existence' of the state, and since in the asiatic mode of production there are no classes, it is difficult to explain the existence of the state other than by vague references to 'climate and territory' (Hindess and Hirst 1975). Unfortunately, these attempts to extricate Marx from an orientalist problematic simply bring in their train a series of additional theoretical difficulties. Once the Asiatic mode of production has been abandoned, it is then necessary to conceptualize all pre-capitalist modes of production within the rather narrow framework of either slavery or feudalism, unless Marxist theory is prepared to admit new additions to the existing orthodox list of modes of production.

The question which lies behind the accounting schemes of Marx and Weber concerns the social origins of capitalism in Western society and its absence in oriental society. This question carries with it all the implications of the assumption about the uniqueness of the West, and therefore a dichotomous contrast between the progressive West and the stagnant East. There are two main theoretical strategies by which this basic question can be avoided. In the first, the question of capitalist origins in the Orient is inappropriate because the prior existence of European capitalism and the development of colonialism ruled out the autonomous development of capitalism outside Europe. European capitalism changed the global conditions for independent capitalism elsewhere by creating a world-wide system of economic dependency (Frank 1972). The presence of capitalism in the Occident becomes the explanation for the absence of capitalism in the Orient. In the second strategy, it is possible to deny that capitalism has consistent social characteristics or uniform consequences. Just as England, France and Germany had unique developmental processes which cannot be subsumed under the general label of 'capitalist development', so each oriental society is subject to individual, peculiar features which are contingent and historical. While both strategies are in some respects theoretically attractive, they are not without their own theoretical problems. The first solution is still left with the question: why then did capitalism emerge uniquely in the West? Any list of socio-economic causes to explain capitalism in the Occident implies the absence of such causes elsewhere. Furthermore, it is not entirely obvious that dependency theory or some notion of 'underdevelopment' will success-fully account for the absence of autonomous capitalist development out-side Europe. The second solution would appear to rule out any law-like statements about the general characteristics of capitalism conceived as an abstract model of society in favour of empirical descriptions of particular developmental processes. The outcome of both positions might be that the notion of capitalism is a purely contingent development or that the very concept of 'capitalism' should be abandoned, because it is too vague and too general. The alternative to Althusserian structuralism would be the position 'that industrialism was not written inevitably into the destiny of all agrarian society, but only emerged as a consequence of an accidental and almost improbable concatenation of circumstances which, it so hap-pened came together in the West' (Gellner 1980: 296).

However, it is difficult to see how 'methodological accidentalism' could be accepted as a general basis for a sociology of capitalism, which attempts to provide causal statements about the necessary connections between social structures, while also recognising that empirically these connections may be very complex and subject to contingent local vari-ations. The conclusion must be that Weberian sociology, on the one hand, and structuralist Marxism, on the other, have not developed entirely satisfactory responses to the accounting procedures of orientalism.

As we have seen, much of the debate about pre-capitalist modes of production in English-speaking Marxism was initiated by an interest in the French philosopher Louis Althusser. The academic reception of Althusserian Marxism was in the context of various attempts to provide a structuralist explanation of economic processes which did not involve restrictive economic reductionism and to provide a scientific alternative to the Hegelian idealism of the humanistic interpretation of Marx. It was not until this debate was well established that it became clear that Althus-ser's emphasis on the proper 'reading' of Marx's texts was part of a more general movement in French philosophy emerging out of literary criticism, semiology and discourse analysis. One of the crucial figures in the French context was Michel Foucault whose analysis of the relationship between power and knowledge subsequently became important in the critique of orientalism. Foucault's ideas are notoriously difficult to summarize, but one important aspect of his general position is that any extension of systematic knowledge also involves an extension of power relations in society, which is manifested in more subtle and rigorous forms of social control over the body. Foucault's argument thus differs radically from a conventionally liberal perspective in which the evolution of knowledge out of ignorance requires a similar evolution of freedom out of oppression. In the liberal view, the conditions for achieving knowledge through open debate involve fundamental political freedoms. For Foucault, the growth of penology, criminology, demography and other social sciences in the late eighteenth and the nineteenth century corresponded to the increasing need to exercise political and social control over large masses of people within a confined urban space. More generally, these separate 'discourses' of the body constituted a dominant 'episteme' by which separate individuals could be categorised as different – as criminals, madmen, sexual perverts and so forth. All forms of language presuppose or create fundamental categories of sameness and difference, and the application of these categories is an exercise of power by which one social group excludes another. The growth of systematic reasoning can be measured or indicated by the growth of time-tables, examinations, taxonomies and typologies which allocate individuals within a theoretical space just as Bentham's panopticon, the asylum, the classroom and the hospital administer bodies within an organized social space. Historically speaking, the growth of scientific psychiatry corresponded with the growth of asylum, the growth of penology with the prison, the development of clinical medicine with the hospital and the discourse of sex with the confessional.

Within the perspective of Foucault's analysis of knowledge, we can now treat orientalism as a discourse which creates typologies within which characters can be distributed; the energetic occidental man versus the lascivious Oriental, the rational Westerner versus the unpredictable Oriental, the gentle white versus the cruel yellow man. The notion of orientalism as a discourse of power emerging in the context of a geo-political struggle between Europe and the Middle East provides the basis for one of the most influential studies of recent times, namely Edward Said's *Orientalism* (Said 1978a). Orientalism as a discourse divides the globe unambiguously into Occident and Orient; the latter is essentially strange, exotic and mysterious, but also sensual, irrational and potentially dangerous. This oriental strangeness can only be grasped by the gifted specialist in oriental cultures and in particular by those with skills in philology, language and literature. The task of orientalism was to reduce the bewildering complexity of oriental societies and oriental culture to some manageable, comprehensible level. The expert, through the discourse on the Orient, represented the mysterious East in terms of basic frameworks and typologies. The chrestomathy summarized the exotic Orient in a table of comprehensible items. The point of orientalism, according to Said, was to orientalise the Orient and it did so in the context of fundamental colonial inequalities. Orientalism was based on the fact that we know or talk about the Orientals, while they neither know themselves adequately nor talk about us. According to Said there is no comparable discourse of occidentalism. This is not to say that there have been no changes in the nature of orientalism, but these changes tend to mask the underlying continuity of the discourse. The early philological and philosophical orientations of Sacy, Renan, Lane and Caussin have been replaced by an emphasis on sociology and economics in the new programme of 'area studies', but much of the underlying politics of power remains.

While orientalism is an especially persistent discourse, Said believes that, given the changing balance of power in the modern world, there are signs of a new appreciation of the Orient and an awareness of the pitfalls of existing approaches. He thus pays tribute to such writers as Anwar Abdel Malek, Yves Lacoste and Jacques Berque and to the authors associated with the *Review of Middle East Studies* and the Middle East Research and Information Project (MERIP). These groups are both sensitive to the damaging legacy of orientalism and to the need for new beginnings and different frameworks. Unfortunately, Said does not offer a detailed programme for the critique of orientalism or for the creation of alternative perspectives. To some extent, he is content with a general rejection of ethnocentric frameworks:

> The more one is able to leave one's cultural home, the more one is able to judge it, and the whole world as well, with the spiritual detachment and generosity necessary for true vision. The more easily, too, does one assess oneself and alien cultures with the same combination of intimacy and distance.
>
> (Said 1978a: 259).

The problem of Said's attempted solution depends on how closely he wishes to follow Foucault's analysis of discourse. The point of the critique of official psychiatry, established clinical medicine and contemporary discourses on sex is not, for Foucault, to present alternatives, since these would simply be themselves forms of discourse. In Foucault's perspective, there is no, as it were, discourse-free analysis. Given the nature of the modern world, we are constrained historically to: 'the patient construction of discourses about discourses and to the task of hearing what has already been said, (Foucault 1973: xvi). For example, Foucault's analysis of medicine does not propose an alternative medicine or the absence of medicine; instead he attempts an archaeology of discourse, of the historical layers that are the conditions of discourse.

An adherence to Foucault's perspective on discourse as a critique of orientalism might, therefore, result in somewhat negative and pessimistic conclusions. The contemporary analyses of Islam and the Middle East to which Said approvingly alludes turn out to be themselves discourses, corresponding to shifting power relationships between West and East. The orientalist premise remains largely intact: I know the difference, therefore I control. There may, however, be one starting point which would be compatible with Said's universal humanism and Foucault's pessimism about discourse on discourses. It has been noted that language is organised in building blocks of sameness and difference, but the main characteristic of orientalism has been to concentrate on difference. In the case of Islam and Christianity, there is a strong warrant for looking at these aspects which unite rather than divide them, for concentrating on sameness rather than difference. We can then observe how common elements or themes are handled by orientalist discourse as themes which are not 'really' the same or which in fact constitute departures and differences. As we have already commented, Islam and Christianity can be regarded as dimensions of a common, Semitic-Abrahamic religious stock. They have also been involved in processes of mutual colonization, having common traditions of Jihad and Crusade. Islam and Christianity not only have important religious and geographical features in common, they also to a large extent share common frameworks in philosophy, science and medicine. Despite these overlapping cultural traditions, the general direction of orientalism has always been to stress differences and separations. One particularly interesting illustration of this tendency is provided by the history of Western philosophy.

Islam and Christianity as religions of prophetic revelation were not initially equipped to provide a philosophical framework within which to present and discuss the theological problems of orthodoxy. Furthermore, they were both early on confronted by a powerful tradition of secular logic and rhetoric which was the legacy of Greece. The philosophy of Aristotle which became the major Christian framework for the philosophical formulation of Christian beliefs was transmitted by Islamic scholars – Averroes, Avicenna, al-Kindi and al-Razi. Here, therefore, is an area of common experience and historical development, where mediaeval Christian culture was dependent on Islam. The orientalist response to this historical connection has been to argue that Islam was merely a medium between Hellenism and the Occident. Islamic scholarship neither contributed to nor improved upon Greek heritage which eventually found its 'true' home in fifteenth- and sixteenth-century European science and technology. The notion of an Islamic contribution to Western culture was attacked, for example in the nineteenth century by the French orientalist and philosopher Ernest Renan. He argued that Islamic civilisation was incompatible with scientific advance:

> All those who have been in the East, or in Africa, are struck by the way in which the mind of the true believer is fatally limited by

the species of iron circle that surrounds the head, rendering it absolutely closed to knowledge, incapable of either learning anything, or being open to any new idea.

(Renan 1896: 85).

By extension, Renan suggested that science in Islam could and did only flourish when the prescriptions of orthodox theology were relaxed. One illustration of this position was Renan's sympathetic response to the Muslim reformer Jamal al-Din al-Afghani, whose overt orthodoxy was matched by a covert, elitist rationalism. Finally, Renan claimed that the great majority of so-called Arab scientists and philosophers were in fact 'Persians, Transoxians, Spaniards, natives of Bokhara, of Samarcand, of Cordova, of Seville'.

This view of Islam as merely the sterile transmitter of Greek philosophy and science to European civilisation has subsequently been re-affirmed, although often with more subtlety and less prejudice. Bertrand Russell dismissively commented in his *History of Western Philosophy* that Arabic philosophy was not significant as original thought. A similar line of argument was taken by O'Leary in *How Greek Science Passed to the Arabs* (O'Leary 1949), where it was argued that Islamic philosophers were mainly important as translators of Greek culture. Although he recognized the importance of Muslim scientists in such fields as medicine, optics and chemistry, he treated Islamic thought as the property of a 'privileged coterie'. The great attraction of seeing our philosophical, cultural and scientific inheritance as based upon Greek culture and of seeing Islam as simply a neutral vehicle for the transmission of those values is that it allows us to connect scientific freedom of thought with political democracy. The major contribution of Greek society to Western thought was logical and rhetorical modes of argumentation, permitting the systematization of debate and enquiry. These modes of analysis arose because of the need in the Greek polity for open, public dialogue. Once more it is possible thereby to contrast the oriental despotic tradition of closed, centralized authority with the Greek model of democracy requiring open, uninhibited discourse. The association of freedom and truth has thus become a central theme of Western philosophers occupying very different positions within the political spectrum. While in other respects in profound disagreement, there is an ironic agreement between Karl Popper and Jürgen Habermas that valid and critical knowledge requires an open society.

The problem with this emphasis on Hellenism and democratic enquiry is that, as we have seen, it ignores the fact that Greek society was based on slavery and that the majority of the population was, therefore, precluded from these open debates between citizens. The debate about the ultimate origins of occidentalism and the connections between Islam and Christianity via Greek philosophy raises the question of whether the dynamism of Western culture lies within a Christian legacy or in Hellenism. To illustrate the point of this observation it is enough to recall that, against writers like Werner Sombart in *The Jews and Modern Capitalism* (1962), Weber sought the origins of ethos of modern society in Protestant asceticism, whereas Marx traced the secular/critical content of Western thought back to Heraclitus. In general, those writers who are indifferent or critical towards Christianity are likely to underline the Greek roots of western society; in addition, they often take a sympathetic view of Islam as the basis for their criticism of it. This position is characteristic of, for example, Friedrich Nietzsche. While orientalism has so far been treated as a form of negative accounting stressing the absences within Islamic society, it is also possible to detect forms of positive accounting which adopt certain features of Islam as the means for a rational critique of Christianity. The contents of oriental society may therefore not be the central issue for orientalism, but rather it raises questions about the constitutive features of occidental society. While what we may call theistic orientalism adopted Christian values as the counter-weight to Islam as a deviant religion, agnostic orientalism treated Greek culture as the true source of Western values, often incidentally treating Islam as a more rational form of monotheism than Christianity.

It is possible to indicate the complexity of these relationships between occidentalism, orientalism and Hellenism in Western philosophy by a brief comparison of Hume and Nietzsche. While there has been much disagreement over the nature of Hume's philosophy of religion (Capaldi 1975; Gaskin 1976; Williams 1963), it will be sufficient for this present argument to concentrate on his celebrated contrast of the virtues of polytheism and monotheism. In the *Natural History of Religion*, Hume argued that polytheism is the ancient religion of all primitive people and that monotheism developed later with the advance of rationalism, especially in the argument from design. While there is this historical development from polytheism, there is also a constant swing backwards and forwards between these two types of theistic belief, since the vulgar and ignorant tend, in any society, towards polytheism. On the whole, the advantages to mankind of polytheism are greater than those arising from monotheism. The latter is associated with intolerance, exaggerated asceticism and abasement. When the gods are only marginally superior to mortal men, a more open, friendly and egalitarian attitude towards them is possible: 'Hence activity, spirit, courage, magnanimity, love of liberty, and all the virtues which aggrandize a people' (Hume 1963: 68).

The principal advantage of monotheism is that it is more 'comfortable to sound reason', but this very fact brings about an alliance between theology and philosophy which in turn leads to a stultifying scholasticism. Since Hume holds that Islam is a stricter form of theism than is Christianity with its trinitarian doctrine, it follows that Islam is 'comfortable to sound reason', but this also means that Hume regarded Islam as an intolerant, narrow religion. In regard to rationality, therefore, Islam is favourably contrasted with Christianity and, furthermore, Hume humorously refers to Islam as a means of illustrating the absurdity of Roman Catholic doctrines of the Eucharist. A Turkish prisoner was once brought to Paris by his Russian captor and some doctors of the Sorbonne decided to convert this captive to Christianity. Having been catechized and having taken first communion, the Muslim prisoner was asked how many gods there were and replied that there were no gods, since he had just eaten Him! The point of this Humean illustration is to show that, while Said largely treats orientalism as a negative accounting system, in the hands of a rationalist philosopher like Hume, Islam can be used as a positive critique of the 'absurdity' of Christian doctrines.

This critical attitude towards Christianity was especially prominent in Nietzsche's philosophy. In *The Genealogy of Morals*, Nietzsche claimed that Christian morality had its social origins in the resentment of the Jews against their oppressors; the doctrine of turning the other cheek and altruistic love are in fact moral doctrines of a slave class giving vent to feelings of inferiority and suppression. Christian morality has its location in the psychological revolt of slaves against masters:

> It was the Jews who, in opposition to the aristocratic equation (good = beautiful = happy = loved by the gods), dared with a terrifying logic to suggest the contrary equation, and indeed to maintain in the teeth of the most profound hatred (the hatred of weakness) this contrary equation, namely 'the wretched are alone the good; the poor, the weak, the lowly, are alone the good'.
>
> (Nietzsche 1910: 30)

Nietzsche regarded the critical spirit of Socrates as the supreme root of the true virtues of self-development, criticism and heroic independence. While Nietzsche compared favourably the self-sacrifice of Socrates and Jesus for an ideal, he regarded Christianity as a system of conventional morality which destroyed individual creativity and critical thought (Kaufman 1950). It was from this perspective that Nietzsche came to see the slave morality of Christianity as the negation of the heroic virtues of Socrates and Muhammad. In the *Anti-Christ*, Nietzsche declared that:

> Christianity robbed us of the harvest of the culture of the ancient world, it later went on to rob us of the harvest of the culture of Islam. The wonderful Moorish cultural world of Spain, more closely related to us at bottom, speaking more directly to our senses and taste, than Greece and Rome, was trampled down ... why? because it was noble,

because it owed its origins to manly instincts, because it said Yes to
life even in the rare and exquisite treasures of Moorish life.

(Nietzsche 1968: 183)

Nietzsche's positive evaluation of Islam in general and of Islamic Spain
in particular cannot be readily understood in terms of Said's view of
orientalism, but it is comprehensible within a scheme of positive, secular-
ist orientalism which employs Islam as the basis for a critique of Christianity. Nietzsche employed otherness as a major lever of criticism against
the comfortable world of Protestant Germany.

The problems of translation and comparison which lie at the heart of
sociology and religious studies, have been implicitly resolved by the
creation of accounting schemes, which establish hierarchies of sameness
and difference. In the study of Islam and Asiatic society, the dominant
accounting procedure of orientalism seeks to explain the nature of Islamic
culture by negation so that Islamdom is constituted by its absences. In
recent years the orientalist tradition has been heavily criticized, but no
radical alternative has yet emerged and, in terms of a pessimistic perspective on the nature of discourse, it is difficult to see how any valid alternative could emerge. The critique of orientalism has largely neglected two
possible routes out of the conventional discourse on the Orient. Alongside
negative accounting schemes, there has also been a positive view of
oriental rationality on the part of secular philosophers who have
employed Islam as a mirror to indicate the absurdity of Christian faith,
but this option is merely accounting in reverse. Following Foucault's
analysis of the archaeology of knowledge, Said has studied the various
ways in which a persistent orientalism has been founded on a contrast of
differences, but a language of the Orient could also generate, in principle,
an account of sameness. One solution to theological ethnocentrism, on
these grounds, would be to emphasize those points of contact and sameness which unite the Christian, Jewish and Islamic traditions into merely
variations on a religious theme which in unison provide the basis of a
global culture.

Part II

Orientalists

Chapter 4

Conscience in the construction of religion

INTRODUCTION

While Marshall G. S. Hodgson, who died in 1968, was influential in the United States as professor in charge of the history of Islamic civilization course at the University of Chicago and as author of a series of scholarly articles on Islamic history, art and religion (Hodgson 1955a, 1955b, 1960, 1964), he has been aptly described as 'a lesser-known giant among better-known scholars' (Smith 1974: ix). Although this is unfortunate, the appreciation of the true stature of Hodgson may well be corrected by the reception of his three-volume, posthumous work *The Venture of Islam* (Hodgson 1974). This study is certainly worthy of close scrutiny since its intention is to criticize and transcend the presuppositions of traditional 'Islamics' – to use Hodgson's terminology – which rest on Arabism and philology. By 'Arabism', Hodgson meant the tendency to treat pre-Islamic Arabian culture as somehow native to Islam so that Bedouin culture was regarded as 'lost' if it was not carried into the Islam of the Fertile Crescent. By contrast, Arabism regarded Persian, Syriac and Greek cultural components as 'foreign' to the genuine Arabian core of Islam. In order to counteract such assumptions, Hodgson attempted to give what he regarded as an appropriate weight to more central Islamicate regions and cultures. By the philological bias, Hodgson pointed to the exaggerated emphasis given to 'high culture, to the neglect of more local or lower-class social conditions; and within high culture, to be preoccupied with religious, literary and political themes, which are most accessible to a philological approach' (Hodgson 1974, vol. 1: 41).

In this discussion, it will be useful to regard philological approaches as merely a minor feature of a more general form of orientalism. In *The Venture of Islam*, Hodgson attempted to overcome traditional philological approaches to Islam by giving full consideration to the variety of ways in which Islam was determined or influenced by sociological, economic and geographical factors. While these intentions may be laudable, Hodgson's approach still fails to extricate itself fully from the asociological pitfalls of traditional orientalism. The sub-title of Hodgson's study was 'Conscience and history in a world of civilization'. Islam as a religion and social system was treated as an adventure of the inner, personal conscience which created an external, impersonal civilisation. The conscience was treated as a creative, irreducible activity in history of private individuals for whom social, political and economic factors ('ecological circumstances') operated 'Merely (to) set the limits of what is possible' (Hodgson 1974, vol. 1: 26). The consequence of such an approach was to provide, so to speak, a religious niche or hiding-place within which 'faith' could remain sociologically immune. My criticism of Hodgson's treatment of Islam will consist in providing a causal account of 'conscience' as a sociologically explicable phenomenon.

There is an additional reason for paying close attention to the arguments put forward in *The Venture of Islam*. In order to buttress his orientation to the problem of understanding Islam, Hodgson deployed a variety of relatively established traditions within Islamic studies and more generally within the sociology of religion. For example, his distinction between Islam as personal faith (*Islam*) and Islam as a social system (*nizam*) depended explicitly on Wilfred Cantwell Smith's 'special case' theory of Islam. Hodgson's treatment of the problem of the commitments of the researcher and the relationship between 'spiritual interests' and 'material interests' follows implicitly the philosophy of social science of Max Weber. My criticism of Hodgson's approach to Islamics will consequently have much wider implications for the attempt to replace the philology of Islam for a sociology of Islam.

CONSCIENCE AND RELIGION

In *The Venture of Islam*, Hodgson introduced a number of new terms for defining various dimensions or regions of Islam. This discussion of terminology was not simply contingent to his main purpose since it pinpointed the fundamental structure of his approach. Thus, 'Islamdom' was used as a direct analogy with 'Christendom' to denote a complex of social relations within which Muslims and their religion were dominant politically and culturally. Within Islamdom, of course, a range of other cultures may be present just as Jews and their institutions were part of European Christendom. 'Islamdom' does not refer to a specific culture; it is rather the channel which bears a culture for which Hodgson provided the term 'Islamicate'. Islamicate culture may be shared by both Muslims and non-Muslims insofar as the latter are at all integrated within the institutional nexus of Islamdom. 'Islam' refers specifically to the religion of the Muslims. By 'religion' is meant 'any *life-orientational* experience or behaviour in the degree to which it is focussed on the role of a *person in an environment felt as cosmos*' (Hodgson 1974, vol. 1: 362).

Such a focus will contain some element of experience of the numinous or transcendental on a cosmic level. Furthermore, such religious responses to the numinous may take three modes. In the 'paradigm-tracing' mode, the ultimate is sought in 'enduring cosmic patterns'. In the kerygmatic mode, ultimacy is located in the 'irrevocable datable events' of history. Finally, in the mystical mode, the faithful have looked for ultimate reality in 'subjective inward awareness', in transformed selfhood. These life-orientational schemes are, however, not the rock on which Islamicate culture and Islamdom ultimately rest. Personal piety ('a person's spiritual devotion') is a person's 'manner of response to the divine' whereas 'religion' includes 'the diverse ramifications of those traditions that are focused on such responses' (Hodgson 1974, vol. 1: 360). Religion is the complex of institutions and practices which embody or focus personal responses to the divine; religion is the social cult which encases piety.

This encasement is partial and variable. Hodgson argued that the piety of the agents who happen to belong to religious communities may vary considerably. Similarly, piety cannot be reduced to ethics or to 'zealous acceptance of myth and ritual'. Piety, the individual conscience, the personal response to God – these are in 'some ways but a small part of religion (as a set of institutions and orientations). Yet it is the core of it' (Hodgson 1974, vol. 1: 360). Piety is thus treated as the ultimately irreducible and creative core of religion. Religion is the sociologically explicable outer husk of which piety or conscience is the interior, sociologically inexplicable kernal.

The implication of this scheme is that the closer one draws to the inner circle of faith, the further one withdraws from sociological forces. The inner religion of faith is independent of society as an irreducible 'pious fact' – to give a reverse twist to Durkheim's notion of 'social facts'. Hodgson accepted the fact that religion is channelled into social traditions which are supported by 'group interests' reflecting 'ecological circumstances in general'. These sociologically determined channels and contexts, however, provide merely the location within which piety can play an historically crucial and creative role, a charisma operating within 'the interstices of routine patterns' (Hodgson 1974, vol. 1: 25). The creative acts of history must, to some extent, satisfy latent group interests otherwise they would have no social and historical effect. Yet, these creative acts of conscience 'do not merely fit into an existent pattern of interests as it stands; they lead back not to the ecology as such but to some thrust of autonomous integration within an individual' (Hodgson 1974, vol. 3: 6). Sociological factors are written into this account of the nature of religion as merely limitations on piety.

It is possible to obtain a more comprehensive view of Hodgson's treatment of piety by considering the analogy he draws between styles of art and styles of piety. Traditions in art, fashions in aesthetic appreciation and schools can be seen as analogous to the institutional and cultural network of religion, while personal piety is analogous to individual, artistic genius or creativity. Just as the existence and transformations of schools of art might be sociologically explained by reference to patronage, for example, so changes in religious institutions might be explained by reference to the decline of the feudal mode of production, but religious piety and artistic genius are not reducible to 'ecological circumstances'. At most, we could see the impact of traditions on personal creativity, as cramping the creative expression of the individual. Within the broad limits set by style and tradition, an enormous range of sociologically undetermined creativity is possible.

In conclusion, Hodgson's treatment of piety/religion results in the sociological immunity of faith. This immunization could be located within an implicitly Kantian view of human affairs in which people inhabit a noumenal world where the private conscience is free to operate. While the outer, phenomenal world of religious institutions may be causally determined by ecological laws, the inner world of noumenal conscience knows only 'the thrust of autonomous integration' of the private individual. Hodgson's most direct statement of this position is contained in the following: 'Ultimately all faith is private . . . We are primarily human beings and only secondarily participate in this or that tradition' (Hodgson 1974, vol. 1: 28). Islamdom, Islamicate culture and even Islam as a religion are public and can be sociologically explained; piety, faith and conscience are private, having an integrity uncontaminated by sociological factors.

COMPARATIVE RELIGION

Comparative religion has been riddled by problems of methodological neutrality. As Hodgson notes, it has been all too easy for scholars with a Christian commitment to regard Islam as a 'truncated' version of Christianity. Muslim scholars, by contrast, are likely to view Christianity as a perverted form of Islam. A scholar with no overt religious predilection cannot easily ignore the truth-claims of either religion. If Hodgson is committed to the view that piety is the irreducible locus of religion, this does raise difficulties for anyone attempting to understand Islam from outside. This problem is compounded by the fact that Hodgson himself was a committed Christian – a point I shall return to in detail at a later stage. Hodgson's final answer to the issue of understanding alien belief systems seems unsatisfactory because it is inconclusive, but it has the merit of being epistemologically honest and unsentimental.

Hodgson rejected any attempt to pick out of Christianity and Islam certain isolated elements which could be regarded as equal and comparable. For example, the idea that moral behaviour should be based on divine revelation could be held to be common to both religions. Yet behind these superficially common elements lie profound differences in theology, relating to the moral challenge of the Qur'ān and the redemptive nature of Christianity as a sacramental community. Any attempt at syncretism, or any notion that ultimately all religions are the same since they rest on a common human response to the divine, is rejected by Hodgson. Christianity and Islam should be treated as independent, and to some extent irreconcilable, structures which give different emphases to a range of religious elements within them. Comparative research would explore what elements within independent religious structures get subordinated or emphasized. By this method, the two religions can be seen to be in a state of tension, of productive dialogue. Persons with or without religious commitments can join in this form of analysis provided they maintain 'a sensitive human awareness of what can be humanly at stake' (Hodgson 1974, vol. 1: 30). It appears that with this sort of structural approach, religious commitments on the part of the researcher can be regarded as irrelevant, or at least inconsequential, but it is well known that religious and other commitments have played a major role in the work of many of the great scholars of Islam (Waardenburg 1963). Hodgson recommends that the scholar should attempt to avoid the pitfalls of idiosyncratic commitments while also learning 'to profit by the concern and insight they permit' (Hodgson 1974, vol. 1: 27). Furthermore, since 'all faith is private', committed scholars in Christianity might be able to communicate far more easily with 'congenial temperaments' in Islam than with colleagues in their own culture, but the role and importance of religious commitments in scholarly research remains unsettled and ambiguous. Hodgson recommended that those commitments on the part of researchers should be explicitly and deliberately examined in order to specify what was possible within the limitations set by those commitments. One minor criticism of Hodgson which has far wider implications for the concluding sections of this chapter is that he did not face his own commitments squarely and systematically. On the contrary, he informed us in one footnote that he was 'a convinced Christian, of the Quaker persuasion', but went on to assert that his viewpoint on modern religious studies owed far more to Rudolf Otto and Mircea Eliade than to his private religious inclinations. One contention could be that Hodgson's whole view of conscience was a specifically Quaker interpretation.

SUPPORTING TRADITIONS

Hodgson's primary distinction between the inner creative faith and the outward social system of religion depends heavily on the approach of Wilfred Cantwell Smith's *The Meaning and End of Religion* (Smith 1964). For Smith, the notion of religion as a social system developed relatively late in human history, whereas the idea of a personal faith was established long before the rise of religious systems. Thus, he contrasted the terms *din*, *daena* and Islam with *Islam* and *nizam*. Islam is a 'special case' in the sense that it emerged in a social setting where the idea of religion as a social system was already developed and established. Muhammad set out to create Islam as a systematic religion in a manner that differentiated him clearly from either Jesus or Buddha. Islam has a special awareness of itself as a religion and in particular as a religion named by God as Islam. Nevertheless, the notion of Islam as a personal submission to God was originally more significant and central than outward submission to rituals, beliefs and customs. In the Qu'rān, for example, the terms '*aslama*' (to submit), '*iman*' (faith), '*din*' (piety) are far more prevalent than 'Islam' and '*nizam*'. The Qu'rān refers to '*islamukum*' as a personal Islam, as your 'islam' and Smith notes that there are passages which attack the idea of exclusive religious boundaries in favour of 'a direct and uninstitutionalized moralist piety' (Smith 1964: 103). The notion of an uninstitutionalized faith directly corresponds to Hodgson's own emphasis on the pious kernel, partially encapsulated within the cultic outer husk. This orientation to the problem of 'what is religion?' is combined, on the one hand, with Otto's theory of the holy as the numinous and, on the other hand, the treatment of religion as a public system as elaborated by the incorporation of the sociology of Emile Durkheim (1961) and Clifford Geertz (1966).

However, Hodgson's indebtedness to the sociology of Max Weber is far more implicit and diffuse. For one thing, Hodgson comments that it is unfortunate that Weber 'said so little about Islam' (Hodgson 1974, vol. 1: 133). It is possible to identify at least three major areas in which Hodgson's approach depends fundamentally on the theoretical and methodology position elaborated by Weber. The first relates to Weber's sociology of power in terms of charisma, tradition and rationality. Hodgson's argument that piety is creative, working within the 'interstices of routine patterns', parallels Weber's view of charisma as a creative force, a threat to the stability of social relations based on tradition and rationality: charismatic devotion and enthusiasm cannot be reduced to merely economic forces. By extension, Weber's distinction between virtuoso religion based on pure charisma and mass religion based on mere custom and routine parallels Hodgson's view of the pious as a holy hard-core within the tepid religiosity of mere cultic allegiance. Similarly, Weber spoke of himself as 'religiously unmusical', thereby implying an analogy between charismatic gifts in music and religion. The virtuosi of religion and music stand in constant opposition to the mass routinization of public practice and task. Unlike Hodgson, however, Weber regarded Islam as a religion in which the exterior commitment to routine practices predominated over the possibility of interior piety. Weber spoke of Islam's distinctively feudal characteristics in which one finds an 'essentially ritualistic character of religious obligations ... the great simplicity of religious requirements and the even greater simplicity of the modest ethical requirements' (Weber 1966: 264).

Clearly, Hodgson's account of the piety which lay inside these ritualistic obligations is a direct challenge to Weber's whole position. Second, Hodgson's view of the independence of religious (pious) interests from group interests, specifically socio-economic features (the ecological context) depends on Weber's attempt to show the relative autonomy of political, ideological, legal and religious factors from the economic base of society. Weber's emphasis on the moral challenge of monotheistic/salvation religions in shaping human institutions and attitudes is precisely Hodgson's view of conscience as a causally significant factor in history. The basic methodology of *The Venture of Islam* could be summarized in Weber's words, namely, 'Not ideas, but material and ideal interests directly govern men's conduct' (Gerth and Mills 1991: 280).

Finally, Hodgson's treatment of the problem of scholarly commitments closely relates to Weber's treatment of the issues of value relevance, neutrality and objectivity. For Weber, a scholar's values determine the object of his or her research and the range of problems that are to be identified. A social scientist, however, must exercise ethical neutrality by not taking advantage of his or her social prestige to make value judgements about empirical evidence. As a neo-Kantian, Weber accepted the importance of a radical divorce between facts and values, between the phenomenal and noumenal worlds. Knowledge about the real world did not entitle the sociologist to make authoritative ethical pronouncements about the moral quality or ethical significance of that world. The use of value-interpretation of the meaning of social actions was crucial if the meaning of social behaviour was to be adequately conveyed, but this method should not be confused with the general requirements of scientific objectivity. Once a sociologist had declared his or her values and selected the object to research, the usual criteria of objectivity in the selection and evaluation of data applied automatically. In this way, it was possible to claim that sociology was both value-relevant and value-free. Hodgson's notion that the values of the scholar, while contributing as it were to the 'richness' of historical understanding sets limits within which the scholar can delve deeply into the selected topic of research. Similarly, for Weber, since 'causality is infinite', the value-commitments of the researcher are in fact crucial, not only for selecting the object of research, but for the researcher's total orientation to this subject matter. Values are not so much embarrassing obstacles, not a painful encumbrance, but a positive asset in the full appreciation of the meaning of religious and other human activities. From this point of view, Hodgson's Quaker commitment would set limits to his understanding while enriching his perspective at a deeper level.

CRITICAL ASSESSMENT

One problem with the Weber–Hodgson position on values is that it is by definition impossible to choose between ultimate values which are thereby rendered wholly irrational. This problem is particularly significant in comparative religions scholarship where conflicting values are paramount. Values are sharply divorced from facts in terms of the Kantian is/ought dichotomy. No empirical evidence can ever guide, let alone dictate, moral positions. It follows that no objections can be raised against a scholar who declares that he will interpret Islam within the limitations of Quaker Christianity, but it also follows that no objections could be mounted against the interpretation of Islam from the point of view of fascism, utilitarianism, Taoism or any other belief system. Hodgson, of course, wants to deny that his Quaker convictions are central to his theoretical comprehension of Islam. As we have seen, he explicitly claims that his orientation is derived from Eliade and Otto. It is difficult, however, not to read *The Venture of Islam* without an awareness of the prominence of Quaker theology dominating certain key issues.

It could be argued that the view that religion is merely the outer structure of an inner, private faith is a specifically Protestant, nineteenth-century view of the relationship between ritual and faith. For Hodgson, piety is quite literally the inner light that animates the outward forms of religion. At the end of Volume 3, Hodgson writes that in a society dominated by 'technicalist specialisation' it is very difficult for individual values to find an effective expression, but small groups of inspired individuals may yet shape critical areas of social change. He refers specifically to the social impact of 'the tiny Quaker Society' (Hodgson 1974, vol. 3: 434). This minor comment in fact characterizes Hodgson's whole interpretation of the relationship between faith and religion, individual and society. Hodgson writes in terms of piety/individual *versus* religion/society. For example, Hodgson consistently treats the *Shari'a* as 'essentially oppositional', as an expression of the autonomy of society against political absolutism (Hodgson 1964). The effect of *Shari'a* was 'to stress the rights of the individual as such' (Hodgson 1974, vol. 1: 344). Just as the Quaker acted as a gadfly within Christianity, so the pious of Islam constantly threatened the routinization of religion by forming an oppositional group in the midst of the cultic community. In short, Hodgson's emphasis on the autonomy of religious ritual and of religion itself, the oppositional nature of piety – all of these elements playing a central role within his orientation to Islam – bear decisive marks of a Quaker commitment.

The problem with the Weber/Hodgson approach to the role of value commitments, as we have noted, is that in one sense it is closed to external critical inspection. For example, from a liberal perspective one might adduce evidence to the effect that Islamic ethics as expressed in the *Shari'a* were not oppositional at all, but specifically conservative and ineffectual as a point of criticism of political control (Lewis 1972). Hodgson could, however, easily counter such an objection by arguing that, while it is true that his value commitments lead him to a particular position, the same can be said of all value commitments. Every researcher has a value-position; *ergo*, all research has limitations. The cost of this value-relativity is, however, inflationary in that it would ultimately silence all debate. Hodgson could have no easy objection to an entirely contrasted interpretation of religion, namely a Catholic viewpoint. It could be argued that ritual is not an optional extra that can somehow be tacked on to the conscience. Without ritual, sacrament, myth, community, and an objective religious law, the isolated, individual piety would not only fade away, it could not exist at all. It is religion that nurtures piety, not vice versa. Once it is conceded that there is no way of arbitrating between ultimate scholarly commitments, there is total impasse. The two positions are equally valid and equally incompatible.

Behind Hodgson's phenomenological approach to piety as the irreducible inner core of religion is, one suspects, a fairly common assumption that to give a causal account of religion is to 'explain it away', thereby leaving the committed scholar of religion without a subject matter. If religion is not entirely explained away by sociology, then it is felt that a sociological explanation of religion in some way casts doubt upon the truth-claims of authentic religion. To these notions is added a sense of methodological injustice in that, while the science of politics leaves politics as a phenomenon intact, the science of religion would demolish its own subject matter. These three anxieties may to some extent explain the popularity of hermeneutics and phenomenology of religion amongst sociologists of religion who are 'religiously musical'. Hermeneutics provides a method which is congenial because it does justice to religion in its own terms. At least on one score, these anxieties seem paranoid in that the causal explanation of a set of beliefs has no necessary bearing on the truth or falsity of those beliefs. That allegiance to certain minority sects by American poor whites might be explained by the theory of relative deprivation does not prove that sectarian beliefs are false. Causal explanations are appropriate in the case of true and false beliefs indiscriminately (MacIntyre 1971). What I want to show is that a sociological explanation of 'conscience' can indeed be provided. The point of this exercise is to demonstrate that one cannot distinguish between piety and religion on the grounds that there can be no sociological explanation of the former.

Such an historical/sociological treatment of 'conscience' does not, however, in some way call into question the validity of 'conscience'.

To my knowledge there is no existing sociological analysis of the concept of 'conscience' as it has been developed within Islam. In the absence of such a study, doubts can be raised against Hodgson's view of the irreducibility and universality of conscience in Islam by briefly commenting on studies of Christendom. These studies raise a number of general theoretical problems for any Islamicist wishing to take up Hodgson's general orientation into the sociology of Islamic piety. Since Hodgson does not define or discuss 'conscience' in any depth or with any precision apart from general statements to the effect that piety is the human response to the divine presence, the implication is that piety is commonsensically obvious, uniform and transcultural. No attempt is made to spell out the difference between the Christian and Islamic notions of 'conscience' – such an omission is distinctively odd, given the centrality of the concept to his scheme of analysis. 'Conscience' is in fact a highly complex, if not ambiguous concept, implying 'private thoughts', 'self-accusation', 'self-awareness' and also knowledge of consciousness. While 'unconscientious' means not regulated by moral principles, the 'unconscious' may mean simply something forgotten (unaware) or an actual terrain within the psychic structure. Paul Tillich comments that the Roman language,

> following popular Greek usage, unites the theoretical and practical emphasis in the word *conscientia*, while philosophers like Cicero and Seneca admit it to the ethical sphere and interpret it as the trial of one's self, in accusation as well as in defence. In modern languages the theoretical and practical side are usually expressed by different words. English distinguishes *consciousness* from *conscience*, German *Bewusstsein* from *Gewissen*, French *connaisance* from *conscience*.
>
> (Tillich 1951: 153)

Aquinas distinguished between *synderesis* (habitual knowledge) and *conscientia* (application of moral rules). In Christianity, 'conscience' had a juridical quality about it ('trial of the self') which found a specific expression in the idea of a 'Court of Conscience'. If 'conscience' can be taken as a human response to the divine, then it appears to have been a typically guilty response. This sense of guilt seems to play little part in Hodgson's interpretation of conscience and piety. Hodgson treats 'conscience' as oppositional, whereas, in pre-Reformation Christianity in particular, the guilty conscience was an element of ecclesiastical control of the faithful. Conscience acted within a culture of guilt in which the task of religious confessors was 'to represent law in the forum of penance and make conformity to the regulations of the hierarchy a strict matter of conscience' (Tentler 1974: 117).

In Christianity, conscience was institutionalized within the sacrament of penance, controlled and monopolized by an ecclesiastical elite. As Michael Gilsenan has observed, confession (*'itiraf*) is uncommon in Islam and, where it does occur, it remains distinguishable from Christian penance in having no associated act of absolution or forgiveness (Gilsenan 1973: 107). In short, Hodgson ignores the whole hermeneutic problem of the relativity of the meaning of 'conscience'.

This omission leads to much more serious difficulties. 'Conscience' in Christianity not only has a clear history, but its origins and development have clear sociological, or more generally 'ecological', causes. Father Chenu has shown that the twelfth century prepared the way for a radically new psychology of man in which the importance of subjective intention began to replace the more traditional emphasis on exterior, objective morality (Chenu 1969). The major figure in this transformation of moral philosophy was Pierre Abelard (1079–1142). One consequence of Abelard's treatment of moral intention was to shift the whole emphasis within the confessional away from the external, ecclesiastical absolution towards the subjective, individual contrition. Chenu argues that these changes within theology were also exemplified in the emergence of platonic affection for women as persons rather than sex objects within 'courtly love'. The main sites of these new themes concerning the centrality of 'conscience' were the guilds, the universities and urban communities. 'Conscience' arose once the commercial market created new social conditions which were incompatible with feudalism. The new psychology was the product of market relations which required freedom from feudal restrictions of travel and exchange – 'there is freedom in town air'. The market produced 'the individual' who found an interior self not present under feudalism. Chenu's argument can be supported by, for example, comparing the Irish penitentials of the feudal period with the *summas* of later theologians. It is also supported by the research of Rosenwein and Little on mendicant spirituality. One might also note Goldmann's argument that the growth of an exchange economy produced characteristically a belief system based on the notions of individualism, freedom of contact and contract. There is a sense, however, in which my objections to Hodgson would stand even if these causal accounts of the rise of 'conscience' under market, urban conditions were proved inadequate or false. The point is that causal explanations of 'conscience' are neither improper nor implausible; there is no *prima facie* reason for regarding 'conscience' as immune from sociological investigation.

It is somewhat odd to note that Hodgson himself seems fleetingly aware of the possibility of a causal account of the rise of 'conscience' in Islam. He suggests one himself which parallels the theses of Chenu, Goldmann and others. Hodgson observes that in the Axial Age (800–200 BC) new markets for inter-continental trade began to emerge alongside the development of cities culture in which merchants arose as significant social classes. As a result, 'the Cuneiform literatures of the time reflect a growing sense of personal individuality which most probably catered to the tastes of the market more than to either temple or court' (Hodgson 1974, vol. 1: 11).

The problem of the relationship between the private individual and the social order, argues Hodgson, increasingly came to exercise the religious speculations of the prophets of the Axial Age, particularly Zarathustra and the Hebrew prophets. While one might accept this assertion as at least the beginnings of a sociology of the conscience, it is incompatible with the main thrust of Hodgson's position that piety is the uncaused origin of religion, that social groups might be explained sociologically while the individual faith remains entirely independent, and that piety is private while religion is public and dependent on social factors. Hodgson almost unwittingly acknowledges that both piety and religion can be explained sociologically, while explicitly maintaining that the conscience belongs to noumena not phenomena.

Hodgson's treatment of piety is ambiguous in one further crucial respect. The general impression of Volume 1 of *The Venture of Islam* is that everyone has an inward conscience, a personal piety, by virtue of being a human being. The quality of piety is also extremely variable: 'Devotional response is inevitably a highly personal thing. As in the case of aesthetic appreciation, every individual has his own bent' (Hodgson 1974, vol. 1: 361). However, Hodgson also recognizes that the quantity, so to speak, of piety also varies from one individual to another in the obvious sense that some are more pious than others. The result of these variations in the quality and quantity of personal, devotional life is to produce a definite religious stratification between the mass and the virtuosi. Hodgson recognizes that the Sufi saints, for example, developed a clear stratification system which separated the mass from the pir. One could think of Sufism as a religious pyramid linking dead saints, pirs, disciples, novices and the mass. Hodgson's view of the relationship between 'material interest' (ecology) and inward conscience commits him to the notion that the hierarchy of charismatic qualities varies independently of the secular status order. This relationship, involving the autonomy of charisma, was precisely what Weber had in mind when he wrote about the differences between mass and 'heroic' religiosity.

Since charisma is in great demand but in short supply,

> all intensive religiosity has a tendency towards a sort of *status* stratification, in accordance with differences in the charismatic qualifications ... By 'mass' understand those who are religiously 'unmusical'; we do not, of course, mean those who occupy an inferior position in the secular status order.
>
> (Weber 1966: 287)

In Hodgson's treatment of religious 'talent', charisma, breaking out of established routines, cannot be explained 'away' by sociology, because the 'proper' object of sociological scrutiny is public routine not private virtue.

There are difficulties with such an interpretation which can be illustrated by developing the analogy between musical talent and religious piety ('individual bent'). Even if we grant that there is, as it were, a pool of talent in any population, this talent (whether it is religious or musical) has to be trained, developed and practised. It follows that any person who wishes to develop a talent must be withdrawn in some fashion from direct, productive labour. Religious charisma, on these grounds, would be more common among widows, retired men, young people or the ruling class. Where charisma appears among those actively engaged in labour, they are likely to retire from productive tasks or they must become in some way supported by their disciples. Charisma must be paid for by offering, tribute, rewards or direct cash. Those without charisma (the religiously unmusical) must be brought to support the small elite, so that charismatic services (healing, magic, divination, prophecy) are exchanged for various payments which support the elite in office. For this reason, the religious stratification system is closely connected with the secular status system. On the one hand, there is a tendency for the religious elite to be over-recruited from the secular elite. For example, between the sixth and twelfth centuries over 90 per cent of Christian saints were recruited from the ruling class. On the other hand, religious virtuosi who 'retire' from labour in order to cultivate their talents form an unproductive class in the same way that, in Marx's terms, the ruling class is unproductive because it creates no surplus value. This difficulty in relation to Hodgson's attempt to preserve the autonomy of piety from sociological explanation is directly connected with his version of Weber's separation of 'material' and 'spiritual' interests.

We have already commented on the consequences of believing in the methodological argument that value-commitments are totally independent of empirical facts; it leaves one with no criteria for selecting between competing interpretations. I have attempted to undermine part of that position by claiming that all social beliefs, indeed all beliefs as such, are determined. There is no residual category of beliefs which are not causally determined, but the causal determination of beliefs should not be confused with questions of rationality, truth and authenticity. That is only one aspect of the issue. The idea that politics, religion, law and all other social institutions are partly autonomous from economic forces very easily slides into the platitude that 'everything influences everything else'. This attempt by sociologists or Islamicists (like Weber and Hodgson) to adopt this theoretical and methodological approach is ultimately connected with the rejection of Marx, but the rejection involves a particularly crude 'economist' and/or 'technicalist' interpretation of Marx. This is not the place to launch into the debate about the relationship between Marx and Weber. Suffice it to say that for Marx, the economic (the mode of production) determines which of the major institutional orders (political, ideological, state, educational 'instances') is dominant within any given social formation. Thus,

> that the mode of production of material life dominates the develop-ment of social, political and intellectual life generally is very true for our own time, in which material interests preponderate, but not for the middle ages, in which Catholicism, nor for Athens and Rome, where politics reigned supreme.
>
> (Marx 1970, vol. 1: 82)

The appearance of the dominance of 'spiritual interests' should not be confused with the determination of religion by the particular stage of the development of a mode of production. In this way, Hodgson falls into the trap implied by Marx's fundamental question about Islamdom, namely, 'Why does the history of the East appear as a history of religions?'. In *The Venture of Islam*, we are presented with a history of Islamicate societies determined by the inner history of personal piety. The institutionalized shell of law, economics, political organization is thereby secondary to the sociologically unfettered dynamics of man's inner response to God. Because Hodgson wants to protect piety in this way and because he wants to treat the main articulation of piety as art, poetry and philosophy, Hodgson is in fact forced into the arms of phil-ology and orientalism from which he wants to extricate the study of Islam. Social science cannot be held at arms length by forcing it to analyse the merely external, the circumstantial. In particular, sociology is not simply a science of 'ecological circumstances in general'. Such a treatment of social science leaves orientalism to reign supreme or, as Hodgson himself admits, it is to abandon the study of Islamdom to 'the "pre-historic" period of scholarship' (Hodgson 1974, vol. 1: 47).

Chapter 5

Gustave von Grunebaum and the mimesis of Islam

The orientalist version of Islam is defined by a limited, but highly persistent, bundle of interpretative themes which have the effect of bringing into question the authenticity of Islam as religion and culture. First, there is the dominant theme of historical decay, retreat and decadence, because of which the explosive rise of Islamic society was followed by an equally rapid and total decline. The consequence is that Islam is a religion which either fails to fulfill some latent promise or which represents some retardation of the prophetic monotheism of the Abrahamic faith. Second, the 'failure' of Islam is located within a broadly teleological conception of history in which the unfolding of Islam and its interruption are explained by reference to certain innate and ineradicable features of the 'Muslim mentality', the favoured characteristic being Leibnitz's 'Mahommedan Fate'. In its sociological version, this conception of an inherent flaw in Islamic social structure concentrates on alleged gaps in the 'civil society' of Islam. The social stationariness and economic stagnation of Islamic society are thus connected with the absence of autonomous urban communities, a bourgeois capitalist class, achievement motivation and a systematic, but flexible, legal system. Third, there is the orientalist notion that Islam, if not exactly a defective form of Pauline Christianity, is then at least a parasitic and arid religion. The expansion and appeal of Islam can be partly explained by its alleged simplicity, both in theological formulation and ritual practice. While Islam is typically held to be merely dependent on the Judaeo-Christian tradition in spiritual terms, Islamic philosophy and natural theology are themselves highly dependent on Greek philosophy. In addition, Islamic philosophy is dependent on decadent forms of Hellenism, namely the Neo-Platonic compilations of Plotinus. Finally, while the orientalist is professionally immersed in his or her subject, there is characteristically an emotional gap and cultural hostility which alienates the orientalist from Islam, producing a covert antipathy towards the Orient. The personal distance between orientalist and Orient serves to reinforce the notion of the uniqueness of the West and the unbridgeable gulf separating Orient and Occident. These persistent themes within the orientalist tradition by which 'Islam' is constructed and represented were deeply embedded in the diverse scholarly work of Gustave von Grunebaum, who has become the object of both academic glorification and critical scorn (Banani 1975; Waines 1976).

G. E. von Grunebaum (1909–72) was born in Vienna on 1 September 1909 and received his Ph.D. from the University of Vienna in 1931. Having taught at the University of Vienna, he emigrated in 1938 to the United States, where he subsequently taught at the Asia Institute, New York (1938–43), the University of Chicago (1943–57) and, as Director of the Near Eastern Center, at the University of California, Los Angeles (1957–72) (Rosenthal 1973). The early publications of von Grunebaum were primarily concerned with issues in Arabic poetry (Grunebaum 1937) but, while he never abandoned his interest in Arab literature, he became known as the author of a number of influential studies of macro-cultural problems relating to the unity of Islamic history and society. These macro-cultural studies included *Medieval Islam* (1946), *Islam* (1955a), and *Classical Islam* (1970). He was also editor of and contributor to *Unity and Variety in Muslim Civilization* (1955b) and *The Dream and Human Societies* (1966). A bibliography of his scholarly publications lists 172 items covering the years 1936 to 1970 (Tikku 1971). Gustave von Grunebaum can therefore be regarded as a typically productive member of the European migration to the United States in the period of fascist ascendancy (Fleming and Bailyn 1969).

Unlike the majority of academic orientalists steeped in the scholastic minutia of such problems as Averroes' interpretation of Aristotle's view of tragic poetry, von Grunebaum came to appreciate the relevance of anthropological and sociological studies into the analysis of Islam. He was, for example, perceptively critical of Max Weber's commentary on the role of Islamic towns in *Economy and Society* (1968). It was, however, the cultural anthropology of A. L. Kroeber which von Grunebaum adopted as a perspective on his favourite theme, that of Islamicate cultural diversity and integration.

Kroeber (1876–1960), in developing the geographical notion of *Kulturprovinz* in his studies of the North American Indian, concentrated on the notion of 'culture' as a superorganic entity which was largely independent of material culture and developed according to processes which were immanent principles (Laroui 1973). Kroeber, whatever his views on the Plains Indians of North America, was not exactly a sympathetic student of Islam which, according to Kroeber, 'lacks some of the most significant features of other great civilizations. It had no infancy and no real growth ... There is nothing new, nothing specific to it ... Ideologically, the peculiarities of Islam are restrictions' (Kroeber 1952: 381).

Von Grunebaum also adopted the conceptual apparatus of Robert Redfield's studies of folk society which distinguished between the 'great tradition' of the scribes and the elite, and the 'little tradition' of the village and the illiterate mass; this dichotomy made an appearance, for example, in von Grunebaum's commentary on the adjustments in Islamic society of the orthodox culture to the local cult tradition (Grunebaum 1955b: 28). While there are those overt interests in cultural anthropology, von Grunebaum's work appears to depend more on Hegel's idealism than on Kroeber's culturalism.

As with many nineteenth-century philosophers and historians, Hegel was impressed by the vigour and vitality of early Islam, but impressed also by its 'failure' to fulfill that early promise. Islam lacked that dialectical process by which human communities could in history achieve self-consciousness. The result was that 'Islam has long vanished from the stage of history at large, and has retreated into Oriental ease and repose' (Hegel 1956: 360). Like Hegel, von Grunebaum was the historian of Islamic decadence and retreat. In the preface, for example, of his *Classical Islam* von Grunebaum informs us that its very title 'implies a judgement. The classical represents a model. It is, in fact, a model whose reconstruction is by definition an obligation and an impossibility' (Grunebaum 1970: 7).

Islamic history is the history of the divergence of an ideal community, based on holy law, prophetic guidance and uniform commitment to certain religious norms from the reality of its imperial fragmentation, the separation of legal prescription from everyday social practice and the loss of a state legitimated by sacred principles. The decline of Islam from the ideal embodiment of religious virtue was, in von Grunebaum's view, crucially bound up with the problem of its sacred law tradition which could not be rapidly developed to meet entirely new circumstances and exigencies of social development. Thus,

> The steady decay that, beginning as early as the ninth century, ate away the strength of Islam and had, by the middle of the tenth, ruined the central authority of Baghdad beyond repair compelled acquiescence in conditions only too far removed from those postulated by political theory. It may be doubted whether the caliphate as designed by the legists ever had any real existence, but in the eleventh century the discrepancy between reality and ideal had become so flagrant it could not longer be overlooked by the body of believers... The believer was thought under obligation to obey whosoever held sway, be his power *de jure* or merely *de facto*.
>
> (Grunebaum 1946: 168)

This alleged hiatus between religious ideal and power politics as manifest in the gaps in the *Shari'a* has been a constant theme of orientalism and closely related to the argument that in Islam there is no sound principle of opposition to illegitimate government. It was, for example, fundamental to Max Weber's view that the gap between legal ideal and empirical reality could only be plugged in the legal system by irrational *fatwa*; the same orientalist thesis emerged in Bernard Lewis' argument concerning the absence of all oppositional principles of Islam. For von Grunebaum, the rigidity of law and the gap between norm and practice manifests, not the absence of a principle of legitimate resistance, but, rather, the teleological failure of Islam. Islam suffered from conservativism and lack of cultural integration:

> Arrested in its growth during the eleventh century, it has remained an unfulfilled promise. It lost the power of subjecting the innumerable elements to an organizing idea more comprehensive than the desire for individual salvation. It stagnated in self-inflicted sterility.
>
> (Grunebaum 1946: 322)

While von Grunebaum has been characterized as the theorist of decay, in fact his 'Islam' is an endless repetition of the same, an unchanging religious reality of failure and decay. As a fixed cultural form, Islam constantly erected barriers and defences around itself in order to maintain its sacral identity against external intervention. Hence 'the adjectives that von Grunebaum unites with the word Islam (medieval, classical, modern) are neutral or even super-redundant: there is not difference between classical Islam and medieval Islam, or just Islam' (Laroui 1973: 27).

Illustrations and examples can, therefore, be taken indiscriminately and at random from any Islamic society and from any point in history to demonstrate the unchanging nature of Islamic reality. The indiscriminate selection of evidence and total disregard for precise periodization perfectly illustrate this Hegelianized version of Islam in which any one item of culture is expressive of the totality (Althusser and Balibar 1970: 17) One single poem can illuminate the whole of Islamic culture. The endlessly repetitious nature of Islamic history is, for von Grunebaum, one further aspect of Islam's capacity for cultural mimicry and social imitation. Islam is consequently treated as an endless borrowing from its pagan Arabic past, from Judaeo-Christian monotheistic theology, from Hellenistic logic and from Chinese technology. On the whole, Islamic society was completely uncreative and almost without influence. Byzantine iconoclasm was not the product of Islamic influences (Grunebaum 1962) and the conventions of Arabic composition in poetry have made for 'repetitiousness and a certain lack of invention' (Grunebaum 1944: 234). The need to maintain the authority of revelation over reason put definite limits on the impact of Greek science and philosophy on Islamic thought:

> Where theory ran no risk of becoming dangerous, investigation went ahead: optics, botany, pharmacology and empirical medicine were all deeply indebted to Islamic research. But the conceptual framework of

late classical thought, and even Galen's anatomy and Hellenistic astrology, remained untouched though certain parts were known to be superseded.

(Grunebaum 1970: 135)

In philosophical matters, the Islamic theorists remained entirely mimetic. Rational thought was confined to the elite; the philosophers were essentially translators, merely a vehicle of Greek thought (O'Leary 1949). Islamic history is thus the history of failure, unfulfilled promises and cultural limitation. In terms of three fundamental criteria of civilization, Islam can be seen to be a major failure:

> Mastery of nature, public morality and the condition of the common man have been suggested as measures of backwardness or achievement of a civilization. It does not require elaborate demonstration that, by these standards, the Islamic world has but a small contribution to make. There never has been a concerted effort in Islam to put natural resources to such use as would insure progressive control of the physical conditions of life. Inventions, discoveries, and improvements might be accepted but hardly ever were searched for.

(Grunebaum 1946: 343)

Despite the fact that orientalists normally hold that despotism in Islamic society was the product of large scale irrigation works designed to insure 'progressive control over the physical conditions of life' (Bailey and Lobera 1981), von Grunebaum here decides to ignore those developments in experimental science and technology which were apparently characteristic of Islam.

When von Grunebaum turned to problems of Islam in terms of religious belief and practice, we find once more the notorious charge that Islam is arid, simple and emotionally unsatisfying. In his study of ritual, it is interesting to note that von Grunebaum employed the somewhat contemptuous notion of 'Muhammadan festivals'. In this discussion of the 'five pillars of Islam', von Grunebaum's main argument was that the simplicity of Islamic practices creates a gap within which saint worship and the cult of the Prophet could develop to satisfy the emotional needs of the laity. From the point of view of a cultured scholar, however, Islam appears somewhat underdeveloped, liturgically and ritually. The reason for this is not hard to discover.

> Islam was born in one of the backward areas of the ancient world. The radical monotheism of its doctrine and the puritanism of its mood, combined with the aesthetic limitations of the Muslim cultural heritage, left the believer satisfied with an arid, if physically exacting liturgy.

(Grunebaum 1958: 3)

Because Islam had no clergy, there was no social group of liturgical specialists with an interest in ritual elaboration and innovation. Islam, from inception, was intended to be a 'layman's faith' and, therefore, the beliefs and practices of the religion are 'few and simple' (Grunebaum 1958: 5), namely *shahada, salat, saum* and *hajj*. The implication of this view is that Islam is an undemanding religion, placing few psychological burdens on the religious consciousness. Islam lacks, therefore, precisely that social leverage which is held to be characteristic of the Protestant ethic. Islam is a religion of cultural and psychological containment. Hence, in a passage which reads like a copy of Hegel's comments on the orient in the philosophy of history, von Grunebaum concluded his study of medieval Islam with the authoritative pronouncement that

> The Muslim's world is at rest, and he is at rest within it. His immediacy to God and his acceptance of the divine order were never, during the Middle Ages, seriously disturbed. Resignation and submission to the inevitable and abdication of searching reason before the inscrutable were rewarded by the consciousness of fitting perfectly and naturally into the great preordained scheme of things that embraces mankind as it embraces the genii, the angels and the stars. The Muslim knows and accepts man's limitations.
>
> (Grunebaum 1946: 346)

In short, von Grunebaum leaves us, as the conclusion to his study of medieval Islam, with a thesis that the failure of Islam was in the last analysis a failure of mind and will. This sense of fatalism, in a world determined by the iron laws of divine omnipotence, conditioned the human spirit to 'peace and repose' (Grunebaum 1946: 347). In the West, the emergence of the modern world was marked by a declaration of the active knowing mind, namely, 'I think, therefore I am'. The Cartesian revolution of philosophic scepticism paved the way towards modernization, which was based on values of achievement and action.

A range of criticisms could be mounted against the Kroeberian perspective of von Grunebaum. There are, for example, problems associated with the privileged status he accords to the analysis of poetry in the understanding of the Islam; despite references to the 'little tradition', there is in fact no space in his history of Islam for everyday life and the world of the common people. Rather than considering detailed criticisms, there are two very general objections to von Grunebaum's analysis which can be addressed. First, he examines Islam from the outside and indeed regards it as an academic duty to sit in judgment over Islam. It is not simply that he brings external criteria to Islam, but that he considers Islam in terms of elitist, normative and exacting Western criteria. The standards which signify the 'failure' of Islam would in fact also signify the failure of Christianity. The gap between the ideal of a Christian community and the realities of political life as indicated in the controversy surrounding the church–sect typology and the compromise with state power and political violence would be a case in point. Put simply, von Grunebaum's perspective is coloured by prejudice and ultimately by an 'almost virulent dislike of Islam' (Said 1978: 297).

Second, there is a striking relationship between von Grunebaum's style and the repetitious, mimetic character which he ascribes to Islam. His discourse is peppered by erudite references, by quotations from a variety of philosophical and linguistic sources and by a curious mixture of social anthropology and philology. Despite his apparent commitment to social science, there is curiously little significant intellectual development in his work, little change in his account of classical Islam and little moderniz-ation of his views on Islamic literature. Von Grunebaum not only repeats himself, but reproduces all the mimetic themes of orientalism. The station-ariness of von Grunebaum's discourse is ironically a facsimile of the social stationariness which allegedly characterizes Islam and a mimicry of that very intellectual repose which supposedly characterised the Muslim mind.

Part III

Globalism

Chapter 6

Politics and culture in Islamic globalism

From the perspective of sociology of religion, there are two separate but related processes in modern Islamic cultures. The first is the emergence of a global Islamic political system and the second is the cultural reaction of Islamic fundamentalism against Westernism and consumerism. These processes are analysed in this chapter in terms of a sociological framework which embraces, somewhat eclectically, a number of theoretical perspectives.

The issue of Islamic modernization may be understood initially within the framework of Max Weber's sociology of the process of rationalization which focused on the paradoxical relationship between the process of rationalization and the problem of meaninglessness. The argument here is that Weber's sociology provides an anticipation of the current contrast between the programme of modernization and the condition of postmodernism. Within this framework, Islamic fundamentalism is seen as a reaction against cultural and social differentiation and fragmentation. More specifically fundamentalism is an attempt at de-differentiation. However, it is important to avoid a sociological orientation which considers Islam in isolation from other world religions, because the major religions are necessarily involved in global processes. The emergence of universalistic standards in cultural and political life is consequently analysed in relation to the world religions (more specifically the Abrahamic faiths).

In order to understand the recent political and cultural history of Islamic societies, two related arguments must be considered. The first argument attempts to recognize the profound problems of having, within a world cultural system, competing world religions which claim exclusive and largely absolutist truths or values. At present, there seems little possibility of global ecumenism on a fundamentalist basis. Previous research into national forms of ecumenism has drawn attention to the profound difficulties of securing agreement between churches of the same religion, claiming separate versions of truth. The problem on a global level, when dealing with exclusive fundamentalist religious movements, is clearly more difficult and the future relations between the Abrahamic faiths in particular is uncertain. The poignancy of the relationship between the Abrahamic faiths is nowhere better illustrated than in their separate, exclusive, and largely incompatible claims to Jerusalem. The first problem then is how to contain, within a single global environment, absolutist religious positions presented by mutually conflictual religious systems. In the case of Islam, the relationship between the Household of Islam and the sphere of war gives rise to particularly profound political problems.

The second argument is concerned with the problem of relationship between the cultural, aesthetic, and stylistic pluralism of postmodernity and fundamentalist commitment to the coherent and unified world organized around values, styles and beliefs which are held to be incontrovertibly true. The problem of meaningfulness arises from consumer culture on a global scale which makes alternative lifestyles, beliefs, and attitudes appear as a set of commodities for sale on a world cultural market. However, against Weber and his followers, Islam was perfectly compatible with the modernization project involving, as it did, a high degree of secularization of traditional religious cultures, but Islam cannot deal satisfactorily with postmodernity which threatens to deconstruct religious messages into mere fairy tales and to destroy the everyday world by the challenge of cultural diversity. The problem of cultural perspectivism is an effect of the pluralization of life-worlds brought about by the spread of a diversified, global system of consumption.

The debate about contemporary fundamentalism has to see these social movements as attempts to secure political hegemony within the global political structure, while at the same time securing at the local level a degree of control over the life-world by attempting to exclude the pluralism of contemporary patterns of consumption. Modern fundamentalism is a two-pronged movement to secure control within the global system and also to maintain a local regulation of the life-world. Fundamentalism in both Islam and Christianity can therefore be analysed as a value-system which actually promoted modernization, because modernization was an attack on magical beliefs, local culture, traditionalism, and hedonism. Fundamentalism is therefore the cultural defence of modernity against postmodernity.

POLITICAL MODERNIZATION: MAX WEBER'S THEORY OF SOCIAL CHANGE

Weber has often been interpreted very narrowly as being interested in the relationship between religion and capitalist development. More recent interpretations of Weber's sociology have, however, drawn attention to the concept of rationalization as the core theme of Weber's entire sociological concern (Brubaker 1984; Hennis 1988; Roth and Schluchter 1979). Even this theme of rationalization was merely an aspect of Weber's more general interest in the origins of modernity and modernization. Briefly, modernity is the outcome in cultural, social and political terms of the broad process of rationalization by which the world is controlled and regulated by an ethic of world mastery, involving the subordination of the self, social relations, and nature to a programme of detailed control and regulation. The modernization project is the imposition of rationality (in terms of means–ends schemes) to the total environment. The history of modernization is the history of reason as the instrumental regulation of society and environment as described classically in the *Dialectic of Enlightenment* (Adorno and Horkheimer 1944).

Weber's account of modernity and modernization can be understood initially in terms of his model of social relations outlined abstractly in the introductory section of *Economy and Society* (1968), where he distinguished, first, between social relations which are either open or closed to outsiders. This involves social closure to secure the monopolistic advantages of resources against unqualified intruders. Second, following the comparison (Tönnies 1957) between *Gemeinschaft* and *Gesellschaft*, Weber distinguished between communal and associational relationships. Communal relations are based upon traditional or affectual forms of interaction, involving dense reciprocities between people linked together by customs and local practices. By contrast, associational relations are more impersonal, fleeting, and contractual. By combining these two dimensions, we can form an ideal type of social relations as shown in Table 1.

Table 1 Weber's typology of social relations

	Open	Closed
Communal	church	village
Associational	market	political party

If we interpret Weber's typology in a dynamic and historical fashion, then we can argue that the process of modernization was from social relations which were predominantly closed and communal to relations which were primarily open and associational. In terms of social stratification, this was a movement from estates, communities, and castes to classes, organized in terms of market principles (Turner 1988a). Rather like Sir Henry Maine in *Ancient Law*, Weber saw the development of modern societies as a process from status to contract. As a jurisprudential theorist (Kronman 1983), Weber saw the progress of modern societies as a transition from status arrangements involving the total personality in a set of magical and traditional bonds to a social system in which impersonal contracts of a legal character linked persons together into open associational relations. He argued that originally contracts were magical acts binding persons together through a form of fraternization, but contemporary contracts are 'purposive contracts' which are important for the development of modern market places. We may note in passing that Weber's conception of the emergence of modern capitalism in these terms was not unlike that of Marx for whom the cash nexus in modern societies is the primary bond between persons (Turner 1988b).

If we examine Weber's typology within the context of the historical development of modern societies, then it is clear that the classical sociological tradition saw this evolution from village to market, or from *Gemeinschaft* to *Gesellschaft*. In this transition to an 'open society,' Protestant Christianity (specifically Calvinism) provided a crucial cultural level. Of course, there were empirically many alternative historical processes whereby various combinations of social relations were maintained which are in principle incompatible with open-associated relations. The historical continuity of ethnicity and gender as features of social stratification are the primary illustrations. This model of social relations has two major contributions for this analysis of Islamic fundamentalism in a global perspective.

First, while conventional theories of secularization often assume that religion and modernization stand in a contradictory relationship, Weber's study of the Protestant ethic suggests an alternative interpretation. Ascetic fundamentalism, far from being incompatible with modernity, actually pushed societies from closed-communal to open-associational relations. In this respect, Protestant denominations emerged as the religious counterpart of trading associations. However, as the consumer market threatens to break out into a new stage of fragmented postmodernity in late capitalism, fundamentalism now acts as a brake on the historical development of world capitalism. Fundamentalism appears now in a 'reactionary' guise as the defender of the project of modernity against the disjointed pluralism of postmodernity. The second aspect of the argument is that Weber's model provides some clues about the possible range of the images of the globe. For example, the image of the world as a global system may be presented in terms of a global supermarket (open-associational space) or as a super-church (open-communal) or as a global village (closed-communal). As the world-system moves towards modernity and then beyond into the postmodern age, fundamentalism pulls this process back towards a more traditional mode, but in particular towards the trajectory of either the global 'church' or the global 'party'. In terms of the Islamic system, fundamentalism points towards a genuinely global Household of Faith which must place some limits on membership and which must retain some element of conflict with other absolutist systems (such as communism in the post-war period).

This discussion of Islam and modernization is not concerned with the specifically economic or historical features of these developments. The aim here is to focus on the cultural and religious implication of this transition from a society grounded in traditional and affectual relations to societies based more and more upon economic contracts of an open and impersonal or associational character. While it was the Calvinistic sects which made possible the transition from closed, communal societies to contemporary capitalist or industrial civilization, Weber had argued that because there was no dynamic contradiction between the sacred and the profane, Buddhism, Confucianism, and Hinduism were unable to provide the social and cultural leverage for the emergence of the modern world.

Given this emphasis on Calvinism, Weber was forced to argue that the other Abrahamic faiths (Islam and Judaism) were unable to provide the historical leverage (via ethical prophecy and the critique of society and human relations) for a transition to modernity (Turner 1974b, 1978a, 1987b). In Judaism, the inner-worldly quest for mastery was turned outward into dietary and other exclusively social practices. In Islam, the inner-worldly salvational quest was turned outward and externalized into a quest for land and military dominance. Even within Christianity, the emotional sectarian movements associated with pietism and Methodism translated the salvational problem into personal emotion. It was the stern ascetic discipline and theology of the Calvinistic sects which, through their irrational inner quest for meaning, produced an external world of discipline, vocations, and rational mastery. As we know from Weber's own work in *The Protestant Ethic and the Spirit of Capitalism*, he argued that once the treadmill of modern rationalization had been set in motion, capitalism no longer required the supportive foundations of spirituality, since modern rational systems have a logic of their own.

What were the implications of these religious and cultural changes for political doctrines and social systems? The historic evolution of the market place corresponded in an important fashion with the gradual evolution of an emphasis on the individual and in later historical epochs with an emphasis on individualism as a specific doctrine of social rights (Abercrombie, Hill, and Turner 1984). Indeed, the liberating impact of impersonal, open, associational relations within the exchanges of the market place can be seen in terms of transition from holistic conceptions of reality to individualistic cultures (Dumont 1983, 1986). For Weber, the emergence of modern capitalism (or more generally the emergence of rational market places) created the conditions for the emergence of the autonomous, self-directed personality. This also had its roots in the emergence of the abstract, religious soul, linked to an abstract monotheistic God by a series of connections of rational belief and religious faith. While the God of Christianity was a personal God, the individual in modern society emerges as an abstract and general, public character. This impersonal dimension is specifically important in the political realm or the public arena, where the particularistic characteristics of individuals (such as age, sex or race) become, from a political point of view, increasingly unimportant, given the legal and political emphasis on abstract egalitarianism.

Following the work of T. H. Marshall, the expansion of social citizenship rights entails an expansion of the definition of the social and the social arena, with the consequence that the individual citizen constantly emerges as a more abstract, universalistic, and free agent within political space (Turner 1978a). The political citizen within a modern democratic culture is no longer defined in terms of property-holding, gender, racial characteristics, or any such particularistic dimension, but rather emerges as the abstract bearer of general rights of social participation and membership. Another way of expressing this argument is that modern social systems are dominated by the principles of egalitarian citizenship and by the quest for political and social equality (Prager 1985). This development of the abstract citizen is the political counterpart to the historical transition from *Gemeinschaft* to *Gesellschaft*; citizenship can be regarded as an index of secularization in which the City of God gives way to the modern polity of abstract strangers linked together by legal entitlement and abstract exchange relationships. The expansion of political citizenship in terms of this abstract framework can also be connected with the notion that the growth of a money market produces the idea of the abstract individual user of financial facilities (Simmel 1978). There is therefore a certain interpenetration of the economic development of abstract individualism and the long-term historical implications of the individualism of the Abrahamic faiths. The idea was also taken up by Talcott Parsons (1963) who noted that the contractual nature of the relationship between man and God, and the individualism of the Christian tradition created the conditions for a radical egalitarianism which liquidated the notion of religious bonds based upon ethnic particularism. The importance of Christianity for the emergence of a political community was that it undermined fundamentally the particularistic relationship of blood in favour of a community based upon a universalistic faith (Weber 1958a). The logical extension of this sociological argument is that the abstract citizen must emerge eventually as a global agent within a world political system, since the individual (within the logic of the process of rationalization) can no longer be contained within the nation-state. The paradox of the emerging, egalitarian individualism of nineteenth-century capitalism, especially in England, was that the growth of the abstract individual also followed historically the emergence of the nation-state as a closed and particularistic entity in which social membership was ultimately located in one particular language or dialect. There is, as both Marx and Weber implicitly recognised, a potential conflict between the abstract, globally located, citizen-individual and the local requirements of the nation-state as the political encasement of the individual.

It is possible to link this argument about individualism and globalism to the world-system theory of Wallerstein (1974, 1980). Wallerstein has argued that globally the world has moved from a system of large-scale empires (based upon local economies) to a world, structured by one global economy but articulated through particular or local political systems. If we transpose this argument into the context of the world religious systems, at least Islam and Christianity conceptualized themselves or thematized themselves as world religions, and therefore they have a particularly problematic relationship to local political systems.

In the pre-modern period, the world religious systems had little opportunity to realize themselves globally, because the systems of communication and transport were wholly underdeveloped or nonexistent. Prior to the emergence of modern communication systems, the world religions operated on a largely localized basis with tenuous linkages to their cultural centers and articulated at a global level by an underdeveloped and fragile system of trading relationships (Mann 1986). In the modern period, the possibility of achieving global religious systems has been facilitated by the emergence of modern forms of transport, communication, and integration. This produces a number of tensions and paradoxes between the abstract individual and the demands of nation-state political commitments, and between the universalism of the religious system in a competitive world cultural environment, where fundamentalist versions of the Abrahamic faiths are forced to conflict with each other over local sites and sources of recruitment, and geo-political influence.

Weber also had a negative, pessimistic, and demonic version of the modernization project which in some respects anticipated modern debates about anti-modernism and post-modernism. Following the work of Nietzsche, Weber recognized that with the death of God, the pluralization of life-worlds, and the secularization of culture, we live in a world which is relativized and which forces social theorists to adopt perspectivism as their primary orientation to cultural facts. For Nietzsche, the therapeutic capacity of art and music had been undermined by the growth of cultural nihilism. In Nietzsche's epistemology, languages are merely metaphorical accounts of reality; he proceeded to de-construct the underlying metaphors of religion and science. While Nietzsche himself rejected nihilism, his philosophical views had a profoundly disturbing effect on subsequent German philosophy. Nietzsche was received as a great nihilist of culture, whereas the primary emphasis in Nietzsche's own solution lay on the re-evaluation of values. In response to the problems of secularization, Weber converted Nietzsche's philosophy into a sociology of social action and personality, which gave a primary emphasis to the ethic of responsibility and a vocation in science (Stauth and Turner 1986, 1988).

Weber's theory of rationalization provides a basis in sociological theory for an analysis of contemporary movements in culture which are either fundamentalist or neo-conservative and which attempt to restore moral coherence as the basis of modern religious and social practices. On the one hand, Weber recognised a profound process of rationalization and modernization in society leading to the differentiation of religious, scientific, and moral realms and a profound secularization of values. On the other hand, Weber recognized, following Nietzsche, that the project of reason always discovers its own unreasonableness by exposing the arbitrary character of all forms of rationalization. While rationality can select appropriate means for action, it cannot provide a rational ground for ends.

Fundamentalism can be interpreted as a response both to modernization and to postmodernity since fundamentalism is a process of de-differentiation (Lechner 1985a, 1985b; Robertson and Chirico 1985). We might also treat these social movements of fundamentalisation as forms of collective nostalgia which seek to restructure the world in terms of more simple entities and communal cultural relations (Turner 1987a). In political terms, fundamentalism attempts to create a set of boundaries which will contain political pluralism and the abstract generalization of the citizen on a global scale, but in terms of some notion of community or household. In the cultural arena, fundamentalism is an attempt to impose certain boundaries on modernization, and more particularly on postmodernism and postmodernity. It attempts to reverse the historical process towards a hyper-secular consumerism and pluralism by providing paradoxically a traditional defence of modernity. We can consider these developments through a brief sketch of the evolution of contemporary Islam.

THE POLITY OF THE HOUSEHOLD OF FAITH

In theological terms, Islam is based on a idealistic construction (or reconstruction) of the *umma* (community) which Islam has never completely institutionalized. The idealistic conception involved an integration of politico-religious authority, a terrain or household in which Islamic practice is uniformly followed, and an outward religious thrust or *Jihad* involving a struggle against unbelief. While Islam normatively considered itself as a universalistic faith, it is important to recognize the Arabism of Islam, since for example the Qur'ān as an Arabic expression of divine revelation has a crucial part to play in the authoritative structure of Islamic cultures. In addition, the Prophet's Arabic lineage has been of enormous significance, and finally Islam is rooted in a holy space (Mecca and Medina) which is obviously profoundly Arabic. This ideal community could never entirely resolve the problem of authority, especially the problems of political control through either the claims of lineage or those of elected leaders, a tension which contributed in part to the emergence of two distinct forms of Islamic faith, namely Sunni Islam and Shi'ism. More importantly, Islam was unable to impose its authority on minor or subordinate groups within the household of faith, and there developed throughout Islam a millet system which permitted internal pluralism and ethnic diversity to continue. Finally, we should note an important variation within Islam between the ascetic traditions of literary Islam within the urban tradition and mystical Islam which flourished in Sufism, permitting the development of saintship, local cults, and hierarchical forms of practice which conflicted with, or at least stood in contradiction to, the egalitarian principles of the core tradition (Gellner 1969, 1981). The history of Islam in part revolves around these problems of local and global authority, giving rise to the periodic social movements of Islamization in which the ascetic and literary codes were imposed upon localist forms of Sufism. The reform of Islam has normally assumed a recurrent pattern in which strong political leaders attempt to impose political control over the hinterland in the name of a monotheistic conception of Islam against the polytheistic tendencies of the periphery.

However, before the emergence of modern forms of communication and transportation, the imposition of unitarian control around a monotheistic culture had always been limited by certain technical-military problems and by the inability of dynastic power to secure its control through time and space (Mann 1986). While in Weberian terms the Household of Islam was patrimonial, the political structure was in fact decentralized into local, dynastic authorities which competed with the patrimonial core of authority. We can therefore conceptualize pre-modern Islamic politics in terms of a constant tension between patrimonial centres and local sources of political authority (Turner 1981b).

There is some general agreement among historians that Islamic cities in the pre-modern period lacked feudal estates and there was no significant development in Islam of urban centers like the urban communes or municipalities of Europe. Islamic imperial rule depended upon local notables who were either scholars (*Ulama*), or notables (*A'yan*), or commanders of local garrisons who provided political skills at the local level for the imposition of Islamic authority. There was a certain integration or structural symbiosis between the state, merchants, and *Ulama* who provided clerical services for the state bureaucracy. The achievement of local autonomy on the part of towns developed in Islam through two channels, either by the weakening of imperial control (for example, Timbuktu in West Africa), or by local rebellions (for example, Seville in Muslim Spain or Tripoli, or Tyre) (Shoshan 1986).

It is important to understand this pre-modern structure in order to comprehend the character of modern fundamentalism as a political movement. Despite the truism that Islam requires the unity of religion and politics, in pre-modern times, that is before the emergence of European colonialism, Muslim rulers were unable to impose their political authority on religious leaders. Within these empires, the ruling elites were forced to depend on the intermediary role and functions of local notables, who claimed to be descendants of the Prophet, or were the *Ashref*, merchants and local garrison leaders. It is the availability in modern times of effective global communication systems which makes possible for the first time a globalization of Islam which in fact is the Islamization of cultures through the norms and practices of Islamic fundamentalism. While Islam had always claimed a universalistic status, it was, prior to the emergence of contemporary communication systems, actually unable to impose this type of uniformity and universalism. The paradox of modern systems of communication is that it makes Islam simultaneously exposed to Western consumerism and provides the mechanism for the distribution of a global Islamic message.

FROM COLONIZATION TO FUNDAMENTALISM

Between Napoleon's invasion of Egypt and the end of the nineteenth century, three separate but related social and economic processes transformed the Islamic regions. First, the Ottoman Empire was broken up by colonialism into relatively separate nation-states. Second, the economies of the old Islamic world were gradually incorporated into and subordinated by a world capitalist system as highly dependent units and, third, there was a significant cultural response to these changes through various religious reform movements. The development of colonialism called forth, as it were, a new local intelligentsia of clerical workers who were often Western-trained and adopted Western attitudes but never achieved full integration into the Western system. The result was an intense ambiguity as to the relationship between secular Westernization and anti-colonial nationalism (Enayat 1982; Hourani 1962). We can regard these three processes as forms of cultural and structural differentiation of the Islamic world.

One response to Western colonialism was to adopt a deliberate policy of secularization which was legitimized by a return to Islamic sources. Islamic reform involved an attack on traditional and popular forms of Islam (in particular Sufism) which was associated with political decay and social stagnation. By returning to primitive Islam (defined as an ascetic and disciplined form of Islam), it was argued that Islamic societies could be modernized while also becoming more Islamic. One has therefore a somewhat paradoxical relationship between secularization and reformism in the liberal response of Islam to Westernism. These developments were probably most explicit in the Turkish case where Kemalist reforms involved a direct confrontation with traditional populist Islamic lifestyles (Shaw and Shaw 1977). As a reformist regime, the Kemalist government was deeply influenced by Western ideas about, for example, education and nationalism. Educational reform (under the leadership of Ziya Gokalp) was directed in terms of Durkheim's concept of social solidarity. Secularization involved the creation of new legal systems which typically relegated Islamic holy law (the *Shari'a*) to the personal sphere, leaving public relations under European legal codes; and, second, secularization involved the separation of religious and secular institutions of education. Third, secularization involved changes in dress and custom, such as the introduction of the Turkish Hat Law of 1925. These changes in custom involved the differentiation of Islam culture and social structure on the model of Westernization.

The central theme of modernization was, however, legitimized in terms of a return to classical Islam, that is the Islam of ascetic, literary monotheism. Once Islam was liberated from its folk traditions and from foreign accretions, Islam could emerge as a dynamic and progressive component of the reform of society. The return to the Qur'ān was in practice used to bring about profound changes in Islamic life. We can regard this as the liberal age of Islam and its major spokesmen were Jamal al-Din Al-afghani, Muhammad Abduh, and Rashid Rida (Esposito 1984). The liberal reforms are often referred to collectively as the *Salifiyyah* movement which embraced the classical dogmas of 'primitive' Islam in order to bring about a political program of liberal reform.

Islam also came to play a crucial role in the development of anti-colonial nationalist movements in North Africa, India and Indonesia. Within these ethnically diverse and culturally complex societies, Islamic symbols were important as components of nationalist integration in Morocco, Tunisia, and Indonesia (Esposito 1984; Geertz 1968). It is important to recognize, however, that in this period Islam was seen to be a foundation for Arab nationalism; consequently, there was less emphasis on Islami unity and global Islamdom. Since Islam was one foundation of anti-colonial nationalism, some writers have detected a movement away from Islam in the post-independence period toward more secular and nationalist ideologies which attempted to modernize and legitimate separate nation-states (Smith 1974; Wolf 1971). In the 1950s and 1960s many Muslim countries adopted a program of political nationalism, democratic sovereignty, the creation of parliamentary rights, the adoption of secular legal codes, and most importantly the development of Western-style educational systems (Gellner 1981). As national ideological systems became more and more orientated towards secularism, Islam appeared to be increasingly confined to the area of personal belief and practice. Many of these nationalist movements assumed a distinctively socialist program. In Egypt, Iraq, and Syria, the old liberal regimes were overthrown, and nationalist and socialist programs were developed under Nasserism in Egypt, and under the Baath Party in Syria and Iraq. For these regimes modernization was to be brought about by Arab socialism under the charismatic influence of Gamal Abdel Nasser (Berque 1972). Under the Baath Party, religion was often mobilized to create a populist set of slogans for social change; but there was little in the nationalist ideology to promote Islam as a global strategy.

Alongside these rationalist/secularist political movements, we can also detect important fundamentalist Islamic reactions to secularization and Westernization, especially in the emergence of the Muslim Brotherhood, founded in 1928 by Hasan al-Bamma (1906–49) (Mitchell 1969). The Muslim Brotherhood sought the unity of the Muslim community, denounced foreign intervention in Egypt, and opposed the establishment of Israel. The relationship between the Brotherhood and the Egyptian nationalist movement has always been characterized by tension and con-flict, resulting eventually in the assassination of Anwar Sadat, and in recent years the Muslim Brotherhood has increased its political represen-tation within the Egyptian political system. Despite these examples of Islamic resurgence, the 1960s were largely dominated by more secular nationalist movements in the Middle East and South-east Asia.

The emergence of fundamentalism and militant Islam is a striking feature of the 1970s and 1980s with the Iranian revolution under the influence of Ayatollah Khomeini, the political emergence of the late Zia ul-Haq in Pakistan, the Muslim resistance movement in Afghanistan, the growing importance of Shi'ism in the Middle East and the development of an Islamic resurgence in Malaysia (Nagata 1984). Islamic fundamentalism, while different in its national and local manifestation, shares a common rejection of the modernist secular period on a variety of grounds. These include the perception that modernization has failed because its secular character could not offer coherent values. In addition, modernization failed because too rapid urbanization and inadequate agricultural policies produce gross inequalities of wealth and power, leaving the peasantry often in a precarious economic situation. In addition, there is the notion that liberalism has failed because the policies of the nationalist, Arabic, state systems did not allow genuine political expression and democracy. For example, it is suggested that Egypt, despite radical changes, remained dominated by traditional elites who manipulated the electoral system to maintain political power under the slogan of political participation.

While the Western secular program was seen to be in ruins, traditional Marxism also had little to offer in the way of either ideology or successful economic programs. Marxism remained the ideology of an elite and failed to appeal to the masses through a popular discourse which mobilized traditional Islamic themes. It was also too closely associated with the USSR, atheism, and foreign domination. Fundamentalist ideology also regards the Islamic absolutism of the Saudi regime as incompatible with the genuine message of pure Islam, since the Saudi government has been corrupted by Western consumerism and adherence to the foreign policy objectives of Western societies. The great appeal of ideological and intellectual leaders like Ali Shari'ati was that he combined traditional Islamic themes with modern political and cultural critiques derived from Marxism and French philosophy (Shari'ati 1979). Shari'ati was able to translate the implicit political philosophy of classical Islam into a modern idiom.

At the ideological level, Islam has been able to fill the gap (or at least the experience of a gap) between the promises of Westernization and/or Marxism and the actual reality of social change at the everyday level. Islam has an egalitarian appeal, an ascetic world-view, a dynamic conception of social change and through its history provides an alternative therefore to the Western model which was imposed by colonization. Islam through its prayer meetings and other religious institutions provided an alternative political and social platform to state institutions, expression of oppositional and critical viewpoints which governments could not silence, because religion had deep popular roots in the broader community. Fundamentalist beliefs of Islamic leaders had a direct appeal to the social experiences of everyday life.

Although there are major differences in the various movements of religious revitalization in contemporary Islam, 'they all share the experience of recent, rapid and sometimes uncontrolled urbanisation and industrialisation, pervasive western influence, and the spread of literacy with the burgeoning of a crucial, educated class without precedent in traditional society' (Nagata 1984: 236). Under the influence of writers like Shariati, Islam was transformed into a modern doctrine of radicalism and opposition to Westernization, promoting Islamic ideals of equality and change against Western liberal democratic views of political and cultural participation. Islamization under the fundamentalist umbrella therefore involved a redefinition and re-allocation of institutions and values within an Islamic state. In particular, it involves a re-organization of educational institutions to ensure that Islamic values, beliefs, and practices are inculcated in children and young adults. This involves changes to both secondary and tertiary education systems, pulling the universities away from their Western orientation. In terms of economic systems, Islamization requires a greater emphasis on the traditional Islamic objectives of an equal redistribution of income and wealth and the creation of certain welfare institutions for orphans, the needy, and the poor. In terms of legal systems, it demands the reinstitution of the *Shari'a* as the only source of legal thinking, thereby deprivatizing Islamic regulations and excluding secular Western forms of legal organization. This would also involve of course the co-option of the *Ulama* and the promotion of religious scholars into the system. From our perspective, probably a more interesting development is the reintroduction of Islam into the mass media and the regulation of broadcasting and advertising by Islamic institutions and norms. In this area Islamization is distinctively anti-consumerist and therefore anti-postmodernist. The growth of a global system of communication has made possible for the majority of Muslims the ritual necessity of pilgrimage to Mecca, thereby reinforcing the concept of Islam as a global system. At the same time, these institutions of global communication spread the message of pan-Islamic unity:

> Ironically, the technological tools of modernisation have often served to reinforce traditional belief and practice as religious leaders who initially opposed modernisation now use radio, T.V., and print to preach and disseminate, to educate and proselytize. The message of Islam is not simply available from a preacher at a local mosque. Sermons and religious education from leading preachers and writers can be transmitted to every city and village.
>
> (Esposito 1984: 212)

Islam is now able to self-thematize Islamic religion as a self-reflective global system of cultural identity over and against the diversity and pluralism involved in the new consumer culture (Luhmann 1984).

ISLAM AND CONSUMERISM

While sociologists of religion have regularly commented on the problem of meaningfulness in contemporary society, seeing the crisis of meaning as a direct consequence of the secularization of religious values, it is more appropriate to start at the level of the pluralization of life-worlds with the proliferation of consumer lifestyles as the basis for the fragmentation of religious belief and values. Consumerism offers or promises a range of possible lifestyles which compete with, and in many respects, contradict the uniform lifestyle demanded by Islamic fundamentalism. We can see the emergence of consumerism as a consequence of the evolution of capitalism as a world cultural and economic system. Within this perspective, early capitalism involved the rationalization of production systems and the discipline of labour through the imposition of religious asceticism or alternatively the imposition of Taylorism. In the twentieth century a further development of capitalist culture and organization has emerged, namely the rationalization of distribution and consumption. The development of a global distribution system was based upon certain technical developments (such as efficient refrigeration) and as a consequence of the development of global systems of transport and communication, creating a mass market for travel and tourism. In the mid-century, capitalism was further developed with the rationalization of consumerism and consumption through the development of debt financing, credit systems and the improvement of mass banking, hire purchase, and other arrangements for extended consumerism. The lifestyle of the middle classes with its emphasis on leisure, gratification, and hedonism has now become a global normative standard, shaping the aspirations and lifestyles of subordinate classes who, while they may not directly consume, consume at the level of fantasy.

In sum, the development of a global mass culture has now begun to shape and condition the lifestyles of the third world, developing societies and post-Soviet states. These developments in mass culture have also made a major impact on the world of Islam, representing for Islamic religious leaders a new form of indirect colonial penetration, a form of internal cultural invasion. Many of these cultural changes in everyday life, which are the unanticipated consequences of mass media usage, were anticipated in Lerner's *The Passing of Traditional Society* (1958).

These developments of global mass consumerism can be seen as a further extension of westernization and symbolic penetration, providing a problematic mixture of localist cultures and mass universalism (Stauth and Zubaida 1987). In the case of Sadat's open door policy in Egypt, critics of Sadat's regime argued that this economic policy involved not only complete capitulation to Western economics but also involved the further undermining of Egyptian values, or more precisely Islamic values by the spread of consumerism and western lifestyles. The critical evaluation of this situation suggested that at the level of peasant life, American consumerism stood for a further erosion of traditional values.

> As the peasant sits in the evening with his family to watch the TV that his son has purchased from the fruits of his labor in Saudi Arabia the intrigues of J. R. Ewing and Sue Ellen in Dallas strip him of what is left of his legitimacy as a culture bearer in his own culture. Between programmes, he is told in English that he should be drinking Schweppes or in dubbed Arabic that he should use deodorant, and that all his problems are caused by having too many children – a total package of imported ideas.
>
> (El Guindi 1982: 21)

Of course, the symbolic meaning and functions of consumer items are complex and unstable. For example, during the Iranian revolution against the Shah, the wearing of the veil by women signified opposition to the regime, adherence to Islam, and political commitment to Shi'ism. The veil however also had a practical function, since it was difficult to identify women individually on the part of the secret service while they were veiled. In the aftermath of the revolution, on a global scale, the veil has come to signify a general commitment to Islamic fundamentalism. However, in Egypt poor and economically deprived university students often

found veiling to be the most practical solution for avoiding sexual harass-
ment, since the veil signifies purity, but also these students are unable to
buy the very expensive Western clothes which the upper classes of the
Egyptian society buy to demonstrate their own personal distinction. In
recent years there has also developed a more fashionable upper middle-
class form of veil and associated dress which has become fashionable in
some areas of Cairo. Again on a global perspective, it is possible to refer
to these strata as 'an Islamic bourgeoisie' (Abaza 1987). Even within
Islamic fundamentalism, the multiplicity of the meanings of symbolic
cultures can never be entirely contained.

CONCLUSION

Following Jameson (1984), we can associate the emergence of a postmodernist culture with the development of consumerism and post-industrialism.
While Islam responded to modernization through the development of an
ascetic ethic of hard work and discipline, contemporary Islam has
responded to postmodernity through a fundamentalist politics of global
community and through an anti-consumerist ethic of moral purity based
upon classical Islamic doctrine. These processes involve an apparent paradox: the emergence of a global system of communication made a global
Islam possible, while also exposing the everyday world of Islam to the
complication of pluralistic consumption and the pluralization of life-
worlds. While the Abrahamic faiths successfully survived modernization,
there are profound problems for religious absolutism in the area of
postmodernity. In epistemological terms postmodernism threatens to
deconstruct all theological accounts of reality into mere fairy tales or
mythical grand narratives which disguise the metaphoricality of their
commentaries by claims to (a false) authorship. These threats of deconstruction emerge out of the pluralization of lifestyles and life-worlds
making perspectivism into a concrete everyday reality. Postmodernization
of culture is a significant issue at the level of consumption and everyday
lifestyle, and it is for this reason, as I argued in Chapter 1, that Gellner
fails to see the real importance of postmodernism in his *Postmodernism,
Reason and Religion* (1992).

There are various solutions to postmodernism. In terms of the Weberian
model (Table 1) one solution to postmodernism is a nostalgic quest
for holism through fundamentalist traditionalism, whereby the village is
opposed to the global market place. Another solution is nationalism which
involves an associational but closed relationship in which the nation-state
is opposed to the egalitarian abstraction of globalist citizenship (Table 2).
Within this second model, ecumenicalism is a market place of beliefs
which is more compatible with globalism, but which still attempts to

retain some credibility in terms of truth by acknowledging that there may be variations on truth in the theological market place.

Table 2 Religio-social movements

	Open	Closed
Communal	Islamization	Traditionalism
Associational	Ecumenicalism	Nationalism
	Individualism	

Islamization is an attempt to create at the global level a new *Gemeinschaft*, a new version of the traditional household which would close off the threat of postmodernity by re-establishing a communal ideology. Islamization is a political movement to combat Westernization using the methods of Western culture, namely a form of Protestantism within Islam itself. Islamization equals political radicalism plus cultural anti-modernism. Within this perspective, Islamic fundamentalism is a defense of modernization against postmodernism. The outlook for global ecumenicalism does not appear to be a realistic option since, for example, the Abrahamic faiths in their fundamentalist mood claim an absolute truth. The problem is that the Islamic Household must view alternative global households as threatening and dangerous and therefore Islam constantly finds itself forced up against 'lands of war'. It is difficult to imagine how one can have several universalistic, global, evangelical, religions within the same world political space. How can one have mutually exclusive households within the same world cultural system? There are in a sense two problems for Islam. First, there are the problems of external relations with other faiths and traditions or households where the traditional millet system will no longer work. Second, there are internal relations with 'deviations' such as the Copts in Egypt, or the Bahai faith in Iran, or there are the complications of the Islamization of women and the conflicting interpretations, for example, of egalitarian relations between men and women.

While in this chapter I have specifically been concerned with the conditions that have promoted fundamentalism in contemporary Islam, it is clear that similar pressures operating on other world religions have produced political movements to redefine secular national boundaries in religious and traditional terms. For example, in Israel the Haredin have called for the reactivation of a pre-1948 law governing changes in religious status which would enable the Rabbinate to determine the precise religious status of converts to Judaism emigrating to Israel. One consequence of such a change of political involvement of the Rabbinate would be to block off the migration of reform or conservative Jews from North America and Europe attempting to enter Israel as Israeli citizens (Friedman 1987). In Islam, the Muslim Brotherhood aims to establish not simply an Islamic order, but an Islamic state (by force where necessary) as a political program against, not only secularism and nationalism on the part of Arabic governments, but against Western intrusion and against the state of Israel. In terms of the Brotherhood's political philosophy, only a war against such alien forces will bring about the re-unification of the spiritual and political world within Islamic culture. Because the Abrahamic faiths share the same spiritual space, the development of global fundamentalism promises to make the Middle East increasingly unstable in political and economic terms, but on a wider global level it is difficult to see how fundamentalist religious movements could tolerate an ecumenicalism of ideas.

Chapter 7

From orientalism to global sociology

The problem of 'Other Cultures' has been, as I have argued in the previous chapters, a persistent aspect of Western social philosophy since Herodotus pondered on the fact that all forms of socio-cultural difference raised a question over the distinction between the natural and the conventional. Consciousness of difference was an inevitable consequence of the social differences (especially between slaves and free men) which has been brought about by Greek trade and military imperialism (Finley 1980). The theological conflicts between Abrahamic faiths produced the first set of systematic and global theories of 'otherness' as the morally and ontologically corrupt. With the rise of Christianity to political hegemony, the 'Islamic Question' was eventually added to the 'Jewish Question' as a political debate which came to define the contours of human society. 'Difference' is an inevitable and necessary feature of all human societies *qua* human societies as a consequence of the functional importance of the development of a moral core (Durkheim 1951). It follows that all human societies are racist, because they are stratified by the dual process of differentiation and evaluation (Dahrendorf 1968). While these processes of separation and judgement are a necessary feature of collective life as such, the issues of 'otherness', of outsider-culture and of the threat of 'alien belief systems' (Peel 1969) they become prominent and pressing only under special circumstances of national crises and social disruption. In the twentieth century, the problem of otherness has been increasingly associated with the political necessity to understand Islam. The oil crisis, the Iranian revolution, the war in Afghanistan, the Gulf War and the global resurgence of Islamic fundamentalism have transformed not only the map of the world, but the global consciousness of the precarious nature of intersocietal and inter-religious stability. The pressing awareness of cultural globalism has brought with it a necessary consciousness of regional opposition, fundamentalist faith and anti-modernism (Robertson 1987; Robertson and Lechner 1985). It was in the political vortex of this global conflict that the intellectual debate over orientalism originally arose.

Following Edward Said's formulation of the problem, we can define 'orientalism' in three rather separate ways (Said 1978; Mani and Frankenberg 1985). First, orientalism can be regarded as a mode of thought based upon a particular epistemology and ontology which establishes a profound division between the Orient and the Occident. Second, orientalism may be regarded as an academic title to describe a set of institutions, disciplines and activities usually confined to Western universities which have been concerned with the study of oriental societies and cultures. Finally, it may be considered as a corporate institution primarily concerned with the Orient. In this comment on global sociology I shall be concerned exclusively with the first definition, namely as a discourse for the production and constitution of the Orient as the object of a particular form of colonial power and knowledge.

The central component of Said's argument was that orientalism as a discourse arose initially in Christianity as part of a missionary interest in the control of the Other by knowledge. This discourse has proved to be remarkably resistant to change and transformation despite its antiquity. In fact the evolution of the concept of religion itself was a consequence of colonial exploration and a product of the need to create the anthropology of religion as a special discourse (Asad 1993). A discourse may be regarded as a combination of power/knowledge which produces objects of knowledge; such an approach to epistemology undermines the conventional foundationalist view of the relationship between concepts and objects. In linguistic structuralism it is argued that language is a totally self-referential system, there are no phenomena outside of language and therefore the character of orientalism is that it produces the Orient as a object of knowledge and as the outcome of certain relations of power (Bhatnagar 1986). There is, in short, no alternative to the metaphoricality of the world in which science is merely one mode of reality-appropriation alongside many other alternatives.

The principal component of the critique of orientalism was to argue that the orientalist paradigm was a persistent feature of social science which constructs the Orient (as stagnant, irrational and backward) as a contrast case to explain the Occident (as changeful, rational and progressive). These orientalist components generate an essentialist concept of 'Oriental society' which becomes the object of colonial discourses of knowledge and power. First, orientalism can be seen as a theory of despotic power. Despotism was primarily explained by the absence of social differentiation within the social system of oriental societies. We can locate much of the origin of this theory in the work of the French philosopher Charles Louis de Secondat Montesquieu (1689–1755). His *Lettres persanes* (1721) was a critical investigation of the institutions of the *ancien régime* which used the Orient (specifically Persia) as a foil for an enquiry into European despotism. Montesquieu's argument was in fact quite complex (Hulliung 1981), but we may summarize his position quite briefly. Montesquieu argued for a separation of powers, and for an intermediate stratum between the monarchy and the people in order to maintain a progressive political system. In Montesquieu's analysis, the Orient provided the backcloth of a nascent sociology of political institutions. However, the theme of despotic powers constantly reappeared in European social science wherever a discussion of the Orient was at issue. As we have argued in social science, the debate about absolutism in the Orient became specifically identified with the theory of the 'Asiatic mode of production' and hence with the work of Karl Marx (Anderson 1974). This argument about despotic power was not, however, peculiar to Marxism, being adopted by writers from a variety of ideological positions. In the twentieth century, this theory came for example to be closely identified with the writings of Karl Wittfogel (1957) who was primarily concerned with the nature of Russian despotism. However, his comparative study also embraced the study of the political system of Islam. These analyses of oriental despotism shared a common view that political absolutism and arbitrary power were associated with the absence of structural differentiation, the absence of an autonomous middle class and finally by the absence of a tradition of civil rights within a stable legal framework. Of course, the German terminology for civil society or *burgergesellschaft* clearly indicated the nature of civil life as a function of bourgeois culture and institutions. Civil society was the historical product of the bourgeois revolutions of the seventeenth century in England and Holland.

The second major aspect of orientalism as a discourse is a theory of social change (or rather a theory of the absence of social change). Perry Anderson has in *Lineages of the Absolutist State* (1974) examined the theory of despotism and the theory of social stagnation. He traced the origins of the theory of oriental stagnation back to Aristotle's *Politics*, Montesquieu's *Lettres persanes* and *De L'esprit des lois*, Adam Smith's *An Inquiry into the Nature and Causes of the Wealth of Nations*, and Hegel's *The Philosophy of History*. These theories of stagnation suggested, with special reference to China, that uniformity equally demands despotism because administrative levelling is incompatible with freedom and individualism; the result was social and political stagnation. The utilitarian tradition of James Mill, J. Bentham and J. S. Mill perceived an obvious connection between the dead hand of tradition, religious authority, arbitrary power and despotism as the roots of 'Chinese stationariness' (Turner 1974a). In this theory, the Orient was a mirror in which to consider the threat of mass democracy to political leadership in Britain and America. In his analysis, J. S. Mill had been powerfully influenced by the publication of Alexis de Tocqueville's *Democracy in America* (1835) where he had speculated pessimistically on the possible future of democracy in a society where the universal franchise was a radical component of the constitutional arrangements. The absence of a democratic tradition in oriental society was used here as an ideological objection to the process of democratization then underway in Britain and America. The revolutionary doctrine of equality of opportunity in the American revolutionary struggle against Britain and later southern slavery had profound implications for class inequality in British society, and for the continuity of an educated elite. Despite Mill's commitment to liberal politics, he assumed an authoritarian and negative position with respect to full democracy.

Third, oriental discourses involve a theory of sexuality and sensuality in the disguise of a theory of asceticism. Said (1978) has in particular drawn close attention to the emphasis on sexuality, sensuality and irrationality in the discourse of French orientalism. The jacket cover ('The snake charmer') of Said's *Orientalism* by Jean-Leon Gerome was a perfect illustration of this theme of sensuality in the traditional vision of oriental society as one dominated by the irrationality of the senses. In the work of Gerome (as in the painting of Victorian romanticism generally), we have many of the dominant symbols of the orientalist concern with the body of the Orient. In 'The snake charmer' the snake itself was a profound symbol of sexuality. Within the British orientalist tradition, there was also a persistant emphasis on sensualism (Turner 1984a). In Victorian Britain the indolence of the Orient was explained by its sensuality; in turn the sensualism was associated with climate and religion. The central illustration of this theme would be drawn from Edward Lane's *The Manners and Customs of the Modern Egyptians* and E. Warburton's *The Crescent and the Cross* published in 1845. This tradition would also include the work of Richard Burton, W. S. Blunt and A. W. Kinglake. These writers revealed through the literary gaze the mysteries of the Orient to their middle-class English audiences, without the inconvenience of travel. The relationship between the feminine, the Other and the Orient continued in the nineteenth century as a theme in decadent art (Buci-Glucksmann 1984). Because the Orient in Western imagination is often perceived as the fantastic, it is associated with sexual fantasies. Apart from conventional themes of secret harems, the Orient was populated by androgynes, slave traders, lost princesses and the degenerate patriarch. The Orient was a world of excess.

While there is clearly a literary and artistic version of this theme of sexuality, within sociology Max Weber presented a similar argument in his studies of Protestantism and capitalism, namely *The Protestant Ethic and the Spirit of Capitalism* (1930) in 1904/5. In his comparative sociology of religion, Weber developed a global theory of asceticism in which the sensuality of Islam was contrasted with the denial of luxury and the ascetic demands of Protestant spirituality (Schluchter 1987; Turner 1974b; Turner 1981a). The rational discipline of the senses was a necessary basis for the emergence of capitalism, since denial was the psychological root of economic accumulation. The sensuality of the Orient ruled out such disciplines and thereby removed the possibility of a breakthrough from the traditional economy into a society dominated by free-market principles. A similar theme (although with an entirely different purpose) was to be found in Friedrich Nietzsche's commentary on the merits (or otherwise) of Christianity and Islam in *The Anti-Christ* of 1888. For both Weber and Nietzsche, there was also a negative critique of asceticism in relation to the theme of resentment. Nietzsche regarded the ascetic ideal as a no-saying philosophy whereby Christianity represented a form of institutionalized resentment by its refusal of the life of the senses (Stauth and Turner 1986). By contrast, Nietzsche celebrated the heroic-masculine virtues of Islam over the life-denying forces of ascetic Protestantism, and in this respect, Nietzsche treated Islam as an active force, whereas Christianity was merely reactive (Deleuze 1983). The idea that Christianity represented a denial of sensuality and furthermore that this denial became the basis for rational capitalism became a common theme of Western cultural analysis. We can perceive this framework very clearly in the cultural theories of the Frankfurt School, especially in Max Horkheimer and Theodor Adorno's *Dialectic of Enlightenment* (1972) (van Reijen 1987). However, because Nietzsche had such a deep impact on Freud's theory of sexual repression, it is not surprising that Freudian psychoanalysis treated sexual suppression as a causally important feature of neurosis. Ascetic control of the sexual life contributed to human sickness.

The fourth component of the orientalist construction of oriental society involved a theory of discipline and rationality. This theory of rationality was closely related in Weberian sociology to the argument concerning asceticism. In Weber's sociology, the theory of rationalization as a process of cultural change peculiar to the West was in fact the basis of his sociological perspective as a whole. Weber identified two institutional locations for the rise of discipline. First, the requirements of an infantry to move in unison provided a strong pressure towards the rational control of men. Weber said that 'the discipline of the army gives birth to all disciplines' (Gerth and Mills 1991:26). Second, Weber argued that the monastic tradition of Europe created the basis for routine in everyday life as a consequence of its development in Calvinism which transported the monastic cell into the secular household. The process of secularization in this particular approach to the emergence of instrumental reason was analysed as primarily a transfer of religions functions, especially the confessional, into the private sphere. Weber saw this process of rationalization as somewhat self-defeating in terms of the contradiction between Western bureaucracy and regulation, and the life of the autonomous individual. While discipline was necessary for the rise of Western systems of control, these very systems eventually created an iron cage which undermined the individuality of each social actor. By contrast, oriental societies had patrimonial bureaucracy, arbitrary law and *ad hoc* decision-making procedures. The Orient therefore did not develop the stable, routinized and disciplined life necessary for strong government and the effective administration of capitalism (Turner 1974b). In fact the failure of the middle class to achieve political dominance and consequently the continuity of aristocratic culture can be seen as a key issue in the theory of Western democracy.

In this volume I have discussed various components of the orientalist discourse, namely a theory of power, an argument about social change, a perspective on sexuality, and a theory of rational bureaucracy. This discourse in social science has two consequences. First, it provided a general perspective on social and historical difference which separated the Occident and the Orient. Indeed, in this framework the Orient became the negative imprint of the Occident. Secondly, it generated a moral position on the origins of modern culture, despite the fact that this social science language was couched in terms of value neutrality.

The orientalist discourse was ultimately about the origins of the West, not the origins of the East. Social theorists took very different positions on this issue in the nineteenth century. We have seen that Weber in his sociology of religion identified the origins of rationality in Western culture in the Christian tradition which he clearly regarded as occidental. By contrast, Nietzsche in *The Birth of Tragedy* in 1872 sought the origins of contemporary society in a Greek or classical legacy (Silk and Stern 1981). In this respect, Nietzsche shared in the enthusiasm for Hellenism which dominated German thinking in the nineteenth century, but Nietzsche's interpretation was also a radical departure from the conventional romantic position, since he argued that modern culture had its origin in the violence of the Greek tradition, not in its tranquillity and sanity (Stauth and Turner 1988). The question of origins raises serious difficulties for the orientalist tradition, since much of contemporary science and technology arose within Chinese civilization. Since China was, within the orientalist discourse, apparently a stagnant and stationary society, it was difficult to see how China could have produced major technological changes and scientific developments. This question about China has never been satisfactorily resolved and continues to be a major problem within the sociology of science (Needham 1954; Turner 1987b). There is a similar debate about the origins of Japanese capitalism and its possible relation to Confucian values which has been central to recent attempts to rethink capitalism as a system.

The critical evaluation of orientalism has produced a new awareness of the underlying general assumptions of Western social science, history and literary criticism. The process of de-colonization clearly cannot be separated from the de-colonization of thought. However, there are a number of unresolved issues within the critique of orientalism itself. First, it is simplistic to see the Western analysis of oriental society in a completely negative light because the notion of 'oriental society' was not always used merely as a negative stereotype. We have seen for example that Nietzsche used Islam as the basis for a critique of Christianity and regarded the Greek legacy as a legacy of extreme violence. In fact, the orientalist tradition was often ambiguous in its assessment of oriental cultures, especially where orientalism adopted a romantic perspective on non-Western societies. The actual role of the oriental scholar in relation to both colonial authorities and subordinate cultures was often highly problematic. Thus conflicting interpretations of Christian Snouck Hurgronje's contribution to Dutch colonial policy in Indonesia provide a good illustration of these issues (Benda 1958; Niel 1956; Wertheim 1972). Snouck Hurgronje, whose study of Mecca deeply influenced Weber's views on Islam, especially on the role of the city in Islamic culture, posed as a Muslim scholar to study the holy places. His advice to the Dutch Government during the Acheh War was regarded by his informants as a terrible betrayal. While he advised the Dutch authorities that Islam was not a fanatical collection of 'priests' under the control of the Ottoman caliph, he had no doubts as to the superiority of Western values. This confident belief in the superiority of the West served to justify the betrayal.

We can note that the critique of orientalism often somewhat naïvely criticizes orientalism as racist. This critique of racism would be true for example of V. G. Kiernan's *The Lords of Human Kind* (1972). Racism, however, is endemic to human society, since it is part of a basic 'we–other' problematic. That is, the problem of 'other cultures' is a universal problem, given the very existence of norms and values in human society. There are good reasons for believing that all societies create an 'insider–outsider' division and in this sense orientalism is not a problem peculiar to the Occident.

The issues are however somewhat trivial. As we have argued, the main problem with the critique of orientalism is a problem around epistemology. It is difficult for critics of orientalism to confront the issue of the 'real Orient', particularly if they adopt an anti-foundationalist position on discourse. Postmodern epistemologies do not promise an alternative orthodoxy and reject the possibility of 'true' descriptions of the 'real' world. This epistemological scepticism does not lend itself either to political action or to the development of alternative frameworks (Rorty 1986). If discourse produces its own objects of enquiry and if there is no alternative to discourse, then there is little point in attempting to replace oriental discourse with some improved or correct analysis of 'the Orient'. There is no neutral ground from which to survey the possibilities of an alternative analysis. This problem seems to be a particular difficulty for Said since he often appears to be merely recommending an improvement in our account of Islam. This appeared to be his position in *Covering Islam* (1978b). Do we want a better description or an alternative description? Or is it the case that contemporary theories of epistemology would rule out such a set of questions? These difficulties are not confined to the study of Islam. One finds that similar attempts to develop new, postcolonial frameworks for the study of Indian history have not proved to be especially productive or significant (O'Hanlon and Washbrook 1992).

We clearly need a more positive and less pessimistic outcome to the critique of orientalism. By way of conclusion to these chapters on orientalism, I shall suggest four intellectual responses which might point to a more conclusive outcome to this debate. First, it appears to be obvious that the sociological value of the concept 'oriental society' is zero. The ideal type of oriental society is too limited, too prejudicial and too shallow in historical terms to be of any value in contemporary social science. However, the debates which have surrounded this conflict and the critique of orientalism have been theoretically productive and beneficial, regardless of its moral merits. One can detect in contemporary writing on Islam, for example, a far more self-reflexive and self-critical attitude towards Western constructions of Islam. In particular, there is now far greater awareness of the diversity and complexity of Islamic traditions which preclude an essentialist version of a monolithic 'Islam' (Lubeck 1987). Second, we should also note that the orientalist discourse was based upon the problem of difference (we *versus* them, East *versus* West, rationality *versus* irrationality). Perhaps an alternative to orientalism is a discourse of sameness which would emphasise the continuities between various cultures rather than their antagonisms. For example, in the case of Islam it is clear that we may regard Islamic cultures as part of a wider cultural complex which would embrace both Judaism and Christianity. We need therefore a new form of secular ecumenicalism. This type of historical and moral sensitivity clearly underlined the work of Marshall G. S. Hodgson, whose *The Venture of Islam* (1974) is a magisterial contribution to the historical sociology of religions, despite my criticism of his view of conscience and piety. Third, and following from this comment, we should recognize the fact that the most recent developments in historical sociology have been focused on the idea of a world-system or the political and cultural importance of globalism. We live culturally and economically in a world which is increasingly unified in terms of the emergence of a world-system by common forces, at least in the economic field. Our awareness of globalism should begin to transform the character of social science. There is now an important body of literature focused on the idea of the obsolescence of the nation-state and the growing self-consciousness of the world as a world-system (Chirot 1986; Mann 1986;). While the theory of a global order has theoretical and moral problems of its own, it does represent a significant shift away from the traditional ethnocentricity of the orientalist debate. Indeed, these cultural developments (specifically the emergence of a global communications system) make 'the development of a form of global sociology' (Robertson 1987b: 37) increasingly important. The traditional forms of 'society-centred' analysis in sociology are hopelessly out of date. Equally the sharp contrast between Occident and Orient is an anachronism of the nineteenth-century imperial legacy. Fourth, there is considerable intellectual merit in the methodological strategy of treating our own culture as strange and as characterized by a profound otherness. One practical technique here is to turn the anthropological gaze onto the history of our own religions and cultural practices. Since anthropology emerged originally as a response to cultural colonization of other cultures, the application of anthropology to modern industrial society and to the Western forms of modernization has a radical effect on the consciousness of Western scholars. Perhaps the primary example of this approach is to be found in Talad Asad's *Genealogies of Religion: Discipline and Reasons of Power in Christianity and Islam* (1993). Asad argues that in order to understand how local peoples enter or resist the process of modernization, anthropology must also study the West. In applying anthropology to Western processes of development, Asad explains how religion was fundamental to the emergence of disciplines and rational values in the West. In modern times, he also demonstrates how the reaction to the Salman Rushdie affair has been crucial for a defence of Britishness in a society which is increasingly multicultural. Here again, the reaction to Islam has been a major part of the reshaping of British conservative thought.

One problem for contemporary scholarship is that, if orientalism was itself part of a project of modernity which has now terminated (Kellner 1988), it is difficult to establish a clear alternative. The dominance of postmodernist perspectivism tends to make one nervous about definite or universalistic stand points. It is clear that banal recommendations to merely scrutinize our own value positions when conducting empirical research on alternative cultures are pointless. The critique of orientalism leaves us open to two dangers. The first is a naïve trust in the 'native' or the pre-modern as a form of humanity which is not corrupted by Westernization or modernization. Basically there are *a priori* no privileged moral positions. It would be nice however to follow the recommendation that the social researcher has one, prior and decisive commitment, namely 'solidarity with the wretched of the earth' (Wertheim 1972: 328), but we also have to take note of the problem of excessive anthropological charity when understanding alien beliefs in their context (Gellner 1962).

Another problem is that the critique of orientalism leaves us open to a peculiar form of indigenous conservatism posing as progressive anti-Westernism. In some Arab intellectual circles, Foucault has been stood virtually on his head. The argument goes like this. If the critique of orientalism is true, then all Western observations are a distortion of the real nature of Islam. Therefore, our own version of ourselves is true. While it is clear that what Muslims say about themselves, 'must have a central role in the enquiry' (Roff 1987: 1) into Islam, the 'internal' evidence cannot have an exclusively privileged position. We do not want to exchange an outdated orientalism for an equally prejudicial occidentalism. The importance of the current epistemological scepticism is that it precludes such discursive privileges.

Four lines of development are important as an alternative to orientalism. The first is to abandon all reified notions of 'Islam' as an universal essence in order to allow us to study many 'Islams' in all their complexity and difference. Such a move would at least avoid the unwarranted essentialism of the old scholarly orthodoxy. Second, we need to see these Islams within a global context of interpenetration with the world-system. We need to understand Islamic debates in a deeply global context. This perspective avoids the limitations of dichotomous views of East and West, or North and South. Third, sociology itself has to break out of its nationalistic and parochial concerns with particular nation-states from a society-centred perspective. Over twenty years ago, W. E. Moore (1966) challenged sociologists to abandon their narrow nationalistic perspectives in order to develop the (largely implicit) global sociology of the classical tradition. My argument is that a satisfactory resolution to the many problems and limitations of the orientalist tradition ultimately requires a genuinely global perspective. Fourth, the anthropological gaze should be also directed towards the otherness of Western culture in order to dislodge the privileged position of dominant Western cultures.

Chapter 8

The concept of 'the world' in sociology

INTRODUCTION

There has been since the late nineteenth century an important interaction between theology and sociology in their understanding of the concept of 'the world'; in both disciplines 'the world' is simultaneously significant and equivocal. In theology, it is that which God created, but it is also the corrupt place of human habitation. As a result, it is synonymous with sin and the Devil. Thus, 'the world' expresses the alienation or homelessness of human beings. While 'the world' is the place of human beings, they are frequently regarded as rootless strangers. For example, it has often been claimed correctly that Karl Marx's idea of estrangement had its origins in the Judaeo-Christian theme of the separation of God and 'man'. Communism provided a secular soteriology for transcending this estrangement. A similar theme runs through Karl Mannheim's analysis of the utopian critique of 'the world' (Mannheim 1991); through Ernest Bloch's inquiry into utopia as an 'anticipatory consciousness' (Bloch 1986); and through Walter Benjamin's 'inverse theology' (Bolz and van Reijen 1991).

Alternatively, religious studies have traditionally recognized 'world religions' as global movements which necessarily have a conception of that world as a place and of their place in the world. Different world religions have obviously had different conceptions of the nature of the world, and our contemporary view of the globe can be seen as partly shaped by these 'primitive' attempts to think globally. The paradox of the idea of a 'world religion' is that there must be something that lies outside or beyond; it typically involves the counter-idea of a religion which resists incorporation within the Household of Faith or within the City of God. Thus, religious ideas about 'the world' have necessarily promoted the idea of the 'Other'. For example, the Islamic Household of Faith stands in opposition to the Household of War. Within contemporary poststructuralism, the concept of the Other beyond universalistic, standardized and domesticated reason, appears to be a common theme, which runs from the *Collége de Sociologie* (with its interest in Sade's anti-utopia or utopia of evil) to Michel Foucault and Jacques Derrida (Boyne 1990).

In this discussion, these complexities and ambiguities of the concept of 'the world' in the Abrahamic religions are used as an intellectual device for thinking about the complexity and ambivalence of 'the world' in recent theories of globalization. This intellectual device will also prove useful in uncovering a latent but important moral dimension to the globalization thesis: Can globalization be defined as global homelessness, or is there a place for 'man' in the world? This apparently modern question had its precursor in the theology of the Abrahamic faiths, but the debate has been carried over into globalization theory – for example, the enquiry into the inevitability of nostalgia in the contemporary intellectual scene. If this is the case, we might ask what sociology might have to contribute to the description of normative lifestyles and life-orders for global denizens.

Although much of my discussion will be directed to the work of Roland Robertson, the framework for Max Weber's sociology of religion is also employed to grapple with these ethico-sociological issues found in the globalization thesis. This strategy is appropriate since part of Robertson's work on globalization appears to arise from his own commentary in *Meaning and Change* (Robertson 1978) on the problem of soteriology in Weber's work. One additional reason is that Robertson's sociology is, I assume, generally a consequence of his debate with Weber via the work of Talcott Parsons. One might think of much of Robertson's sociology as an attempt to understand the global place of 'religion' (in the broad sense) within a Weber/Parsons paradigm. Specifically, one aspect of his globalization thesis is about the tensions between universalistic and particularistic values within global civilizations (Robertson 1989a; 1991a: 77). We can understand this project as an attempt to reflect globally on Weber's typology of associations, itself a commentary on Ferdinand Tönnies' *Gemeinschaft/Gesellschaft* dichotomy (Robertson 1991a) and Parsons's pattern variables as a model of modernization (Robertson and Turner 1991).

If we develop this line of reasoning in Weber (following his famous, and in retrospect tragic, speeches on science and politics as vocations), what might be, for a person trained in sociology, an appropriate (that is, defensible) calling in the globe? In raising these ethico-sociological questions, I am following an important theme in *The Sociological Interpretation of Religion* (Robertson 1970: 194) that sociology is 'a secularized issuance of religious Christianity, influenced very much also by Judaism'.

TECHNICAL CRITICISM

In trying to make a critical but sympathetic evaluation of Robertson's globalization theory, it is possible to identify a number of technical problems where his approach is still unresolved or uncertain. First, what set of processes or causal mechanisms bring about globalization? Robertson has in part attempted to answer this issue via a critique of the economism of the original Wallerstein version of world-systems theory (Robertson 1985b; 1991a; 1991b). It is not yet entirely clear how one is to conceptualize the processes which bring about globalization. This requirement to specify historical processes is related to Robertson's persistent claim that sociology has neglected culture terms (Robertson 1978; Robertson and Lechner 1985). Of course, this is a conventional problem: What is the relationship between culture and social structure (Robertson 1988b)? However, in the globalization debate, this problem is specifically bound up in the economistic legacy of Marx who, in his treatment of the development of capitalism as a world economic process, provided an early model of world-systems. It is not entirely clear how a multidimensional voluntaristic theory (Robertson and Lechner 1985: 103) of globalization will avoid the reductionism of the early Wallerstein.

A second problem is that it is not clear whether Robertson believes that classical sociology failed to come to terms with the globalization process. He normally points out that the take-off phase of globalization (1870–1925) corresponded roughly to the golden age of classical sociology, but classical sociologists did not easily or self-consciously transcend the nation-state paradigm. Whether this criticism would apply to Weber, who was clearly concerned with understanding social processes in terms of nation-state rivalries, we cannot tell. In Robertson's terms (Robertson 1990a), Weber adopted an international relations approach to globalization. Does the criticism also apply to Durkheim? Here again one can argue that Durkheim's interest in humanity and cosmopolitanism (Durkheim 1957) anticipated aspects of the globalism debate. Since this issue is unsettled, the exact relationship between the task of sociology as a discipline, the nature of interdisciplinary research, and the globalization process itself is unresolved. Just as sociologists have posed the question about whether a postmodern sociology is possible, so the tasks of creating a sociology which is able to theorize the world-as-a-whole, that is, to formulate a theory of the structuration of the world (Robertson 1990a: 16), are formidable. A number of classical sociologists have, of course, attempted to avoid a reified notion of the social by adopting the idea of social processes. Both Georg Simmel and Norbert Elias had a conception of sociation and process. Here again this problem is part of a traditional issue, namely, what is the subject matter of sociology? It is clear that globalization theory makes the conventional reification of the concept of society deeply problematic. This fact might be one aspect of Robertson's long-term interest (Robertson 1978) in the work of Simmel whose treatment of 'sociation' was far removed from reified notions of the society (Robertson 1982).

Finally, there are some technical problems about the uneven developments of time and space concepts in globalization. Robertson has often referred to the tensions between localism and globalism, on the one hand, and globalism and anti-globalism on the other. This emphasis appears to be related to his desire to avoid any accusation of evolutionism. He is therefore clearly conscious of the presence of strong social forces which will counteract globalization. To borrow from conventional theories of development and under-development: Are there patterns of uneven globalization, not by reference to localism and globalism, but by reference to globalization and de-globalization? Are there social processes which force groups or cultures or institutions out of the process of globalism? Is de-globalization somehow precluded by the coming into existence of global institutions (such as human rights legislation) which rule out significant reversals? How are we to think about such issues? On a related topic, how does globalization theory have an impact on critical conceptualizations of orientalism? Robertson's work on Japan, the United States, and orientalism is obvious here (Robertson 1990b). In addition, Robertson insists that globalization is a recent phenomenon, intimately related to modernization. If this is the case, what are we to make of classical conceptions of the world in Greece and Rome, or of Islamic concepts of the Household of Faith? Was the universalism of some aspects of medieval Catholicism irrelevant to the process?

While these are important questions, they might be described appropriately as 'technical'. There is nothing in Robertson's existing theory which would prevent him *in principle* from dealing with these problems. Since his work is still developing, one can anticipate that he will respond to these issues and Robertson is obviously aware of conventional criticism of existing globalization theory: It is evolutionary and teleological; it is in fact a new version of Westernization; it cannot provide causal accounts without recourse to some version of reductionism. Robertson has done much to protect his own version of globalization theory from these criticisms. Therefore, in my view it is more interesting to follow a different line of enquiry, which is to reflect upon the deep ambiguities of the idea of 'the world'. My aim is to nudge globalization theory into the domain of normative debate, partly because many of the important questions of our time lie along the interface between descriptive sociology and moral philosophy.

SOCIOLOGY AND THEODICY: FROM WEBER TO PARSONS

It is not necessary to give a full account of Weber's famous study of soteriology in the *Zwischenbetrachtung* (Gerth and Mills 1991). Robertson has examined this typology in some detail (Robertson 1970; 1978; 1985a) as has Parsons. Parsons's own treatment also remains influential and important (Parsons 1966). Suffice it to say that Weber classified major religions in terms of the radical character of their orientation to 'the world'. This classification produced the famous distinctions between inner-worldly and other-worldly orientations and between asceticism and mysticism. These orientations were solutions to the soteriological problems associated with theodicy. Calvinism was fundamentally radical because it sought an inner-worldly ascetic mastery of the world and since Calvinistic monotheism produced a solution which was so powerful and demanding in terms of faith, Calvinists sought confirmation of their election through worldly success. This aspect of Weber's historical sociology produced the famous essays on the Protestant ethic thesis, but unfortunately Weber's project on the economic ethics of the world religions (*Die Wirtschaftsethik der Weltreligionen*) was never completed; his commentaries on Islam (Turner 1974b) and Catholicism are merely fragments, but Weber's typology of salvational orientations had a major impact on the subsequent sociology of religion. It was particularly significant in Parsons's contribution to the study of modernization (Parsons 1966; 1971), and to the development of the sociology of knowledge (Berger 1969; Luckmann 1967). However, it is only recently that sociologists have seriously attempted to understand Weber's ontology in relation to his conceptualization of personality, meaning, and life-orders (Hennis 1988).

One crucial difference between Weber on the one hand, and Parsons and Robertson on the other, centres on their evaluations of future possibilities in soteriological responses to 'the world'. It is well known that Weber's social philosophy was intensely pessimistic. He shared with many German thinkers of his time a profound sense of the fatefulness of our time (Liebersohn 1988; Turner 1981b). There was a strong current of nostalgia in classical sociology (Holton and Turner 1986: 207–34). Robertson has noted similar nostalgic themes in sociological writing on fundamentalism, secularisation, and globalism (Robertson 1989b; 1990a). Weber read Nietzsche's death-of-God theme not in the positive sense of a time for the revaluation of values, but negatively as implying that people can no longer live in a world of coherent beliefs, because social pluralization has created a conflictual cultural context of polytheistic values (Stauth and Turner 1988). The concept of an ethic of responsibility can be regarded as a minimalist soteriological response to a world which is secular and pluralistic.

It is also well known that, while Parsons was profoundly influenced by Weber's sociology of religion, his social philosophy was by contrast liberal, optimistic, and progressive and in the post-war period, one can even describe Parsons's political sociology as triumphalist. Radical critics, especially C. Wright Mills and Alvin W. Gouldner, loathed this aspect of Parsonian sociology, which they saw as part of the cold-war ideology. There are, of course, more sympathetic readings of Parsons which emphasize his liberalism, his New Deal commitments, his opposition to totalitarianism and in retrospect his clear-sighted belief that communism would not survive as a social organization against inevitable democratic pressures from within. Robertson's own interpretation of Parsons has over the years supported this particular view of Parsons's political sociology (Robertson 1982; Robertson and Turner 1991). Some aspects of this optimistic view of politics and the world-order have been injected into Robertson's globalization theory.

Robertson had already rejected Weber's rather closed view of soteriology in *Meaning and Change*:

> Why did Weber not confront fully the possibility of new and diverse forms of theodical solutions and/or 'rational metaphysics' in modern societies? . . . on the whole the comments he made about the cultural trends of his own time were very much of the negatively critical type.
> (1978: 73)

This negative reading of cultural possibilities was related to features of Weber's personal intellectual development and to his negative interpretation of rationalization as the only significant feature of social change. Thus, both Parsons and Robertson have a more open view of the prospects and dangers of modernization, but this openness is precisely the point at which they are typically challenged by critics.

Just as Robertson has argued that it would be naive to interpret Parsons as simply a theorist of social integration via coherent, consensual values, so it would be a mistake to read globalization theory as merely an optimistic analysis of social change. My proposal is to examine how Robertson views the negative dangers and problems of globalization in order to begin the task of moving towards a soteriology of 'the world' which might transcend the fatalistic reading of social change we find in Weber. If we examine Ulrich Beck's (1986) concept of 'risk society', what are the problems and prospects of globalization?

TOWARDS WORLD OPENNESS

In outlining the problems and prospects of global society, it is appropriate to follow Robertson's own schema which he has developed in terms of the Simmelian question: How is the globe possible? In a framework which he has consistently followed, Robertson has argued that a theory of the global complex must address individual national societies, a system of national societies, individual selves, and humanity (Robertson and Chirico 1985). Globalization theory will have to consider the problem of the nation-state society within a context where its characteristics are increasingly determined from outside. Of course, globalism renders many of these conventional notions of internal and external redundant. There is the problem of establishing some basis of global order. Finally, these global transformations constantly problematize the idea of the self and humanity.

It is not yet clear whether Robertson has systematically elaborated the principal processes which operate within this paradigm of society, societies, individual, and humanity, but they are referred to in many of his recent publications. The two major issues which face the global circumstances in Robertson's paradigm are the problems of complexity and commitment. The complexity problem relates to meaning; the commitment problem relates to the possibility of society. We can see these issues as versions of the *Gemeinschaft/Gesellschaft* dichotomy. In a global-*Gesellschaft*, how can stable meanings be secured and how can individuals be motivated or committed to global conditions? In simplistic terms, one can understand the commitment of a peasant to the village in which he and all his ancestors were born, but can we imagine commitment to the global village? I shall try to summarize the processes which introduce complexity into the global complex: differentiation, relativization, and socialization.

Robertson has frequently and correctly drawn attention to the problems of polyethnicity and multiculturalism in the global scene (Robertson 1991a). As the world moves towards a single place, there is a corresponding increase in cultural complexity. Inter-ethnic conflicts are now an inevitable feature of global politics. The possibilities for estrangement are literally related to the fact that one's neighbors are strangers. Whereas the problem of the stranger within a Simmelian world still had a scarcity value, in the global village all participants are likely to be strangers (Harman 1988). As societies become more differentiated by global forces of tourism, world labour markets, and surplus populations of refugees, problems of political and cultural coherence will increase dramatically. The conventional Hobbesian problem of order becomes necessarily a problem of global order.

By 'relativization', Robertson means the global contextualization of cultures and a corresponding emphasis on reflexivity (Robertson and Chirico 1985: 234). In his recent work, Giddens has also turned to this issue of self-reflexivity as a project (Giddens 1991) but it is interesting that he has not referred to Robertson's work on identity and authority (Robertson and Holzner 1980), or to his general discussion of how the project of the person is an essential aspect of globalization (Robertson and Chirico 1985). The idea that modernization is a process which brings about the institutionalization of doubt is common to much contemporary commentary on modern social change, but Robertson is one of the few sociologists to have perceived this development as a global issue. It is also common in sociology to doubt whether this intense and constant self-reflexivity can evolve without containment or restraint and without undermining social order and personal security. Berger and Luckmann (1967: 232), drawing on Helmut Schelsky's notion of 'permanent reflectiveness' (*Dauerreflektion*) as a method of describing the modern condition where a 'market of worlds' prevails, have suggested that we live in pluralistic societies in which there is a relativization of all worlds. We subjectively view our place as merely 'a world' rather than 'the world' (Berger and Luckmann 1967: 192). Their view is that a market-place of possible worlds lacks subjective plausibility; hence, there must be some strategy for closing off the infinite openness of the contemporary scene. Robertson has seen the implications of these processes for global existence, but he does not advocate a closure of global reflexivity. In other words, he rejects a fundamentalisation of the global condition, because along with Parsons, Robertson wants to argue that it is the task of sociology to take 'complexity as a moral issue in its own right' (Robertson 1989b: 71).

The socialization problem is concerned with 'tertiary mobilization' which relates to 'the relativization of citizenly involvement' (Robertson and Chirico 1985). Globalization brings into question the autonomy and sovereignty of nation-states, and thereby relativises conventional conceptions and conditions of citizenship participation and motivation. Robertson has shown how the emergence of human rights concerns is a feature of the globalization of citizenship concepts. Recent debates about the instability of the polity through the alienation of social actors have taken the nation-state as their focus, but little research exists about the political commitments of social actors who are also (or primarily) players within a global political framework. If this represents a major shift away from primary loyalties to nation, or state, or party, what will be the nature of political commitment within a global context? How will local and global loyalties be reconciled or combined?

One can identify a number of areas in which Robertson is openly conscious of the societal problems which emerge from globalization processes. These problems center around a number of questions: (1) How is society possible in a context of increasing global multiculturalism? (2) How is a stable self possible when 'permanent reflectiveness' is a necessary consequence of global relativisation? (3) How will individuals be committed to the global *Gesellschaft*? As Robertson has often indicated, these are modern versions of questions which grew out of Simmelian sociology. One crucial difference, however, between Robertson's treatment and the development of these classical questions in the analyses of German social theorists, especially Weber, Tönnies and Troeltsch, is that Robertson's *Weltanschauung* is relatively free from nostalgia, existential *Angst*, and nihilism. There is nothing in Robertson's sociology to match Weber's comment that what lies before us is an icy night of polar darkness. Can Robertson's version of globalization be criticized as simply utopian?

An alternative view might argue that the problems facing the globe are sufficient to lead any reasonable social scientist to a sense of inevitable global catastrophe: global warming, destruction of the rain forests, global epidemics, global recession, starvation and crop failures, and a growing tide of refugees, nationalistic wars, and international political instability.

As a brief and therefore inadequate defence of Robertson's globaliz-ation thesis, one might note that he tries to show in many cases that the risks which are created by globalization are also opportunities, and that global circumstances often constrain social actors to behave in terms of other-regarding acts. While citizenship loyalties might be undermined by globalization, and as a result the stability of the nation-state called into question, the existence of human rights legislation as a global legal process puts constraints on governments and other agencies to respect the person. While globalization involves relativization and brings about a profound secularization of cultures, globalization also thematizes new, ultimate, 'humanistic' (Robertson and Chirico 1985: 233) concerns such as the environment, the person, and health, which in turn bring about a re-sacralization of reality. The very idea of the world-as-a-single-place implies some constraint because social problems (crime, alienation, and unemployment) can no longer be tackled on a local basis; they are consequences of global changes. Similarly, the AIDS epidemic and the ecological crisis will require global solutions which will compel govern-ments to act in concert. There are no national solutions to world problems, precisely because it is difficult to imagine what a 'national problem' would look like.

As a consequence, one can argue that Robertson's globalization thesis is a form of Simmelian sociology and that many of the underlying themes of globalization theory are related to ideas which preoccupied Simmel: How is society possible? What is the social role of the stranger? What is the nature of mental life in the metropolis? In particular, Robertson's optimistic evaluation of the risks and possibilities of global life is not unlike the position adopted by Simmel in his analysis of money. It is wrong to read Simmel's philosophical account of money as simply repro-ducing Marx's view of the alienating character of money. While Simmel was aware of how money contributed to exploitation and alienation, he also thought that money created new opportunities. Simmel (1991: 21) saw money as 'opening up a particularly wide scope of individuality and the feeling of personal independence'. If this interpretation of the relationship between Simmel's sociology of the cosmopolitan, uprooted, and commercialized culture of the city, and Robertson's view of the complex opportunities and dangers of globalization, is correct, then we should expect that Robertson will not conceptualise global social actors as other-directed, *declassé*, cosmopolitan, cynical *flâneurs* of the world-as-one-place. It is important for any sociology which wants to avoid nostalgia and *fin-de-siècle* nihilism to look at the opportunity side of rootlessness, complexity, and diversity. In terms of a Weberian sociology as a vocation, it would be more valuable to analyse the human opportunities which might arise from the difficulties presented by the loss of local *Gemeinschaft*. Behind this proposal is in fact a plea to read Arnold Gehlen's concept of human world-openness (*weltoffenheit*) within a perspective of global optimism. One way of developing the globalization thesis would be in terms of an ethical sociology of vocations in the world.

Part IV

Intellectuals and postmodernism

Chapter 9

Nostalgia, postmodernism and the critique of mass culture

Most sociological explorations of mass culture, especially those under-taken within a Marxist or critical theory perspective, tend to be elitist in their cultural and political assumptions. This cultural elitism furthermore rests upon a position of high culture, requiring discipline and asceticism which can only be acquired by the professional intellectual through years of withdrawal from everyday labour and everyday realities. More impor-tantly, an elitist criticism of mass culture presupposes, not only the distinc-tion between low and high culture, but also the availability of some general or absolute values from which a position of critique can be sustained. Following Alasdair MacIntyre's justifiably influential study *After Virtue* (1981), we can argue that a coherent system of values as the basis of criticism presupposes a relatively coherent community as the underlying social fabric of moral systems and ethical arguments. Since in contemporary society the underlying communal reality of values has been shattered, there can be no clear position of hierarchical values in order to establish a critique of mass culture. In any case, the consequence of postmodern cultural pluralism is to undermine the basis for the privileged claims of high culture to be the criterion of aesthetic supremacy (Featherstone 1987a; Lyotard 1984). Therefore, the predominant meta-phor or mode of thought in contemporary critical theory is necessarily nostalgic, since critical evaluation must be backward-looking.

In an earlier treatment of nostalgia (Holton and Turner 1986; Turner 1987a), it was shown how the nostalgic metaphor was the leading motif of both classical sociology and the Frankfurt School, especially in the cultural critique of Theodor Adorno. Nostalgia is historically speaking a primary disease of 'melancholic scholars'. It is well-known that the critical theorists were, in their attitude towards contemporary capitalism, typically melancholic in their evaluation of modern culture and contemporary capitalism (Rose 1978). While we focus on Adorno and critical theory, the Frankfurt School did not, of course, invent the notion of a revolt of the masses. Critical evaluation of 'the masses' can be traced back to the whole conservative tradition, especially the German rejection of the 'levelling', apathetic world of the mass (Giner 1976). While the critique of mass culture is not peculiar to the German intellectual tradition, it did play an important role in the whole development of *Kulturpessimismus* (Kalberg 1987). In this particular chapter, we shall utilise the notion of nostalgic paradigm as a method of examining the underlying assumptions of the critique of mass culture. Furthermore, it is argued that, with the rise of postmodernism, we need a new perspective on mass culture, because the elitist framework can no longer be maintained; unfortunately it may be the case that academics are, as it were, congenitally committed to ontological nostalgia.

We may identify two primary criticisms of contemporary mass culture. First, there is the pervasive view that mass culture is essentially artificial because it is necessarily manufactured. For Walter Benjamin, we cannot understand a work of art which has been completely extracted from its historical and productive basis. In an age of mechanical reproduction, art is systemically extracted from its cultic and ritual location to become a commodity on a mass market. The modern cults of the cinema screen do not adequately replace or resemble their historic predecessors which enjoyed a religious aura. For example,

> the film responds to the shriveling of the aura with an artificial build-up of the 'personality' outside the studio. The cult of the movie star, fostered by the money of the film industry, preserves not the unique aura of the person but the 'spell of the personality', the phony spell of a commodity.
>
> (Benjamin 1973: 233)

In these terms, premodern art had an organic relationship to the community expressing ritualistically its natural forms of production and social relationships. Art and habitus were one. Modernization, especially in terms of the application of electric technology to the reproduction of works of art had brought about a process of secularization which was manifest in the erosion of religious aura. While in the above quotation Benjamin employed the language of Marxism to criticize contemporary art forms as a commodification of artistic activity, the underlying theme of Benjamin's critique depended also upon a classical Jewish opposition to all forms of human idolatry (Rabinbach 1985; Scholem 1981).

The second criticism of mass culture suggests that it should be regarded as an element within an incorporationist ideology or institution which has the effect of pacifying the masses through the stimulation of false needs via the 'culture industry' (to employ the language of Adorno). In his *Aesthetic Theory*, Adorno had argued that

> duped by the culture industry and hungry for its commodities, the masses find themselves in a condition this side of art. In so doing they

are in a position to perceive the inadequacy though not the untruth of the present life process of society more nakedly than those who still remember what a work of art used to be.... This is all the more true in an age of over-production, where the material use-value of commodities declines in importance, where consumption becomes vicarious enjoyment of prestige and a desire to keep up with the Joneses, and where, finally, the commodity character of consumables seems to disappear altogether – a parody of aesthetic illusion.

(1984: 24–5)

In a similar argument, Herbert Marcuse in *One Dimensional Man* (1964) argued that mass production and mass consumption were essential features of the assimilation of subordinate groups into the dominant values and practices of the ruling class within capitalist society. For Marcuse, the potentially radical character of hedonism had been stunted by the development of contemporary production processes which had restricted hedonistic happiness merely to the sphere of private consumption (Marcuse 1968). In order to sustain this critical position, Marcuse was forced to develop a sharp contrast between true and false needs which remains theoretically problematic and unsatisfactory (Alexander 1987: 366–7).

In developing a critique of critical theory's response to mass consumerism, we largely follow a position initially developed by Douglas Kellner (1983) in the special issue on consumer culture originally published by *Theory, Culture and Society*. First, we need a dialectic view of the contradictory features of all culture (both high and low), since mass culture contains within itself the potentials of an egalitarian ethic in sharp contrast to the rigid hierarchical divisions embodied in traditional elite culture (Gellner 1979). Second, we need a more positive view of consumption as a real reward for the deprivations of material production and manual labour, which would avoid the implicit puritanism of the critique of mass culture, an argument which was developed in *The Body and Society* (Turner 1984b). To these responses to the tradition of the Frankfurt School, we shall add an account of the metaphor of nostalgia as a profoundly anti-modern location of cultural criticism in order to take note of the radical implications of postmodernism.

Critical theory involves implicitly a nostalgic appeal to the past (that is, to a situation where community and values were integrated) in order to develop an anti-modern critique of mass culture, the cultural industry and modern forms of consumerism. It is useful to identify two rather separate traditions in the Western treatment of nostalgia. First, there is a medical tradition whereby nostalgia was associated with melancholy and the theory of the four humours. It is of some interest that nostalgic melancholy was a condition closely associated with intellectuals and religious, in particular with the dryness and withdrawal of intellectual and spiritual vocations. In classical times, this combination of nostalgia and melancholy came to be regarded as the occupational condition of the intellectual class (Klibansky *et al.* 1964). There was a second tradition of analysis, which from the seventeenth century regarded nostalgia as a positive moral value of the sensible and the intelligent person who, in response to the horrors of the world, withdrew into melancholic despondency. In this argument we are treating nostalgia as a particular form of the more general problem of melancholy. Melancholy had been for a long period of European history closely associated with intelligence, wit and foresight. For example, Aristotle in the thirteenth book of the *Problems* had claimed that all geniuses were melancholic. This tradition was subsequently elaborated by Eramus who attributed profound spiritual powers to all melancholic maniacs (Screech 1985). It was Kant in *Observations on the Sense of the Beautiful and Sublime* in 1764 who associated melancholy, nostalgia and sympathy with moral freedom and sensitivity. People became melancholic and nostalgic precisely because of their profound awareness of death and history; the Fall created a condition of ontological nostalgia (Fox 1976).

Putting these traditions within a sociological context, we can argue that there is an ontological problem of nostalgia, which expresses the alienation of human beings in society as a consequence of their consciousness of their own limitations and finitude. In *On the Advantage and Disadvantage of History for Life*, Friedrich Nietzsche expressed the view that human beings must be necessarily melancholy because only human beings are self-consciously aware of the passage of time; human beings are essentially historical animals. This idea concerning the unhomelike quality of human life was taken up by Martin Heidegger, who regarded human beings as primarily uncomfortable in their being. There is a second meaning to the nostalgic metaphor which we have identified with an elitist critique of modernity which trades upon the myth of premodern stability and coherence. The elitist critique of mass culture nostalgically presupposes a world in which there was a unity of art, feeling and communal relations. This elitist form of nostalgia we may regard as simply a version of the *Gemeinschaft/Gesellschaft* distinction.

More precisely still, we can argue that the nostalgic paradigm has four principal components. First there is the notion of history as decline and fall, involving a significant departure from a golden epoch of homefulness. There is an intellectual linkage here with the postmodern view of *posthistoire*. Second, there is the idea that modern social systems and their cultures are inherently pluralistic, secularized and diverse; this pluralization of life-worlds brings about an intense fragmentation of belief and practice. Third, there is the nostalgic view of the loss of individuality and individual autonomy, since the autonomous self is trapped within the world of bureaucratic regulation under the dominance of a modern state. Finally, there is the sense of the loss of simplicity, authenticity and spontaneity. The regulation of the individual within a bureaucratic and administered world prohibits genuine feeling and emotion. The process of civilization thereby involves the taming of savage feeling.

This nostalgic paradigm was of great significance in the development of German social theory from Marx to the Frankfurt School. We can regard nineteenth-century social thought as a response to the loss of communal relations, the emergence of associational patterns of interaction and the development of a market which maximized the naked economic tie between human beings. Marxism with its emphasis on the cash nexus thereby shared a view articulated by Sir Henry Maine in *Ancient Law* under the idea of history as a transition 'from status to contract'. Economic exchange destroyed the hierarchy of tradition in which conventional forms of distinction in taste and culture clearly demarcated the separate ranks of the social order. Economic capital became the major resource of excellence, thereby demoting conventional forms of inequality under the formal relations of exchange.

While social theory shared a common problematic which was the emergence of exchange relations in a market free from traditional regulations, we may detect quite distinctive patterns of critique and response. Marx following Ludwig Feuerbach developed a materialistic theory of praxis which in its political form promised a revolutionary alternative to capitalism. Marx was characteristically ambiguous about the problem of time; he was outspoken in his critique of village life and peasant culture, regarding it as merely the garbage of history. Marshall Berman in *All That is Solid Melts into Air* (1982) had correctly identified Marx's commitment to modernity as an historical project, since Marx regarded capitalist production as a revolutionary system which liquidated all previous cultural forms. However, Marx's description of a future socialist society looks profoundly nostalgic, since this socialist utopia involved the absence of differentiation, the erosion of the division of labour and ultimately the removal of human inequalities. Marx's description of the activities of future socialist society might be regarded, so to speak, as a forward-looking nostalgia, as a description of the homelikeness of socialism. Socialism undermines the alienation of human beings who are committed to nostalgia by virtue of a troubled consciousness.

If we can regard Marxism as a materialistic version of Hegel's teleology, then we can consider the leading thinkers of the nineteenth century as critics of the Hegelian system which sought to reconcile human beings to history, that is to reconcile men to the state. In this perspective, Kierkegaard's existentialist version of anti-system nostalgia developed a theological view of alienation in which, against Hegelian reason, Kierkegaard insisted upon the absurdity of Christian faith. In a similar fashion, Schopenhauer, against Hegelian historical optimism, asserted the centrality of the pessimism of will as the essential condition of human beings. Schopenhauer's solution was a form of Buddhist reconciliation with the world, involving a secular nirvana. It was within this intellectual movement that we can best understand Nietzsche's rejection of nostalgia, his proclamation of the emergence of modernity and his commitment to a pessimism of strength. Kierkegaard, Schopenhauer and Nietzsche were philosophers of the will who laid the philosophical basis for the emergence of a nineteenth-century sociology in Germany which was itself a sociology of the will, that is an analysis of meaningful action. The theme which linked together Tönnies, Simmel, Weber, Lukács and finally Adorno was the notion that we constantly create life-worlds which, through alienation and reification negate the spontaneity and authenticity of the will and its conscious subject, Man.

To understand the problem of modernity, therefore, we need to turn specifically to the arguments of Nietzsche concerning the characteristics and conditions of the time in which we live. The argument here is that Nietzsche was primarily a prophet of modernity. The single element of nostalgia in his theory was a strong commitment to the classical world of Greece through his theory of tragedy. In *The Birth of Tragedy*, Nietzsche lamented the loss of the unifying and generative experiences of the ancient Greek cults which, through the god Dionysus, provided a healthy outlet for the violent passions of Greek actors. Dionysus combined with Apollo represented a dynamic component within Greek society which was ultimately swept aside by the emergence of a new culture, namely that represented by Socratic rationalism. This ascendency of rationalism was the genesis of nihilism and human pessimism, since it involved an individuation of persons, the loss of innocence and the collapse of strong emotions. Civilization required the sublimation of feeling and violence in the interests of an orderly society which celebrated the values of the mediocre. This resentment theme in history found its final expression in the Christian culture of the West which turned the moral world of Greece upside down, disguising resentment behind the theory of brotherly love.

Nietzsche perceived and analysed various forms of nihilism in modern society; these included the negative effect of the German state and its ideologies, the continuing life-denying philosophy of Christianity, the ideal of asceticism, and the emergence of decadence in art and culture represented primarily by Wagner and Baudelaire (Mann 1985). Nietzsche's philosophy was turned against the reactive forces in society, namely against resentment, the ascetic ideal and nihilism as modern forms of cultural decay and human sickness (Deleuze 1983). His solution involved the revaluation of values, the reintegration of life against individuation, the assertion of the sensual body as a value against intellectual rationality, the refusal to replace 'God' by 'society', and finally by aesthetics.

For Nietzsche, the only justification for life was art (Nehemas 1985). In addition, Nietzsche sought to condemn the separation of feeling and thinking, of mind and body, of the world of experience and the world of cultural distinction as expressed in the life of the professional philosopher and university academic. Nietzsche saw rationalization and reason as life-denying processes insofar as professional life had become separated from the dominance of the everyday world. In *Ecce Homo*, Nietzsche (1979) argued that the men of culture had ignored the 'little things' of everyday life such as taste, food, climate and recreation in favour of entirely artificial properties such as 'God', or 'the soul' or 'virtue'. Nietzsche's response to the nihilism of professional culture was to assert the centrality of the everyday life-world in shaping the thoughts and emotions even of cultivated academic persons (Stauth and Turner 1986).

Nietzsche's legacy in social science, and more generally in social philosophy, has only recently been fully recognized. It is now clear, following the Nietzsche revival in Germany and France, that Weber, Simmel, Horkheimer, Marcuse and Adorno were fundamentally influenced by Nietzsche's views and methods of analysis (Dews 1986; Stauth and Turner 1988). This legacy may be summarized as follows: With the death of God, we are necessarily committed to perspectives, which we may regard as a form of value pluralism ruling out absolute ethical standards. This problem of perspectivism was particularly important in the development of Max Weber's philosophy of social science.

Since we live in a world of mere perspectives, the absence of stability in ethics and values results in a certain loss of direction which in turn leads to pessimism, disenchantment and melancholy. The world has become unhomelike, because we have lost all naïvety and all certainty of values. The result of this philosophy was a profound cultural critique, especially against the pretensions of bourgeois values and culture. Nietzsche was particularly hostile to what he regarded as the idols of bourgeois culture and politics. The final legacy of Nietzsche was the idea that reason, far from being the liberating practice which frees us from unnecessary constraints, is in fact an essential component of the iron cage and the administered society.

While Weber's response to this crisis involved the ethic of responsibility (Roth and Schluchter 1979), we shall argue that the critical theorists in their response to the culture industry represented a return to Schopenhauer's pessimism of the will, namely a response involving resignation and nostalgia. In the absence of any genuine possibility of political reform let alone political revolution, Adorno and his colleagues turned to an aesthetic reflection on modernity which was largely pessimistic and elitist. The Frankfurt School was a response to the negative consequences of instrumental reason which had been institutionalized in a capitalist system of exploitation and found its final outlet in the gas chambers of fascist

Germany. The project of enlightenment in history had turned in on itself through the rational imposition of knowledge in the administered society which ruled out the autonomy of the cultured and separate individual.

While these theorists drew overtly from the work of Marx, their project was in fact covertly a debate with the legacy of Nietzsche and Weber. While the presence of Nietzsche was generally muted in critical theory, the *Dialectic of Enlightenment* was clearly a debate with Nietzsche. The Frankfurt School sought within the enlightenment tradition a critical alternative to the norms of instrumental rationality which had become the dominant mode of cognition in the technical sphere of contemporary capitalism. However, for the critical theorists, the progressive enlighten-ment project was still a viable option as a model to stand against the emptiness of modern consumerism, the nihilism of the culture industry and the disguised predatory character of Western democracy. The critical theorists therefore blocked off the possibility that even progressive enlightenment might be merely the resentment of politically marginal intellectuals who were in any case ultimately the servants of the state. From the perspective of Nietzsche, resistance to the world of capitalism based upon the enlightenment project still contained the perspectives and prejudices of reason which must assume unity, causality, identity, sub-stance and being. Against this world of being, Nietzsche had always opposed the world of becoming. The critical theorists tended therefore to diminish the critical scope of Nietzsche's philosophy by treating his aphorisms as merely clever psychological insights into knowledge and reality. Furthermore, the critical theorists were essentially pessimistic with respect to the possibilities of radical change, whereas Nietzsche had always attempted to avoid the pessimism of will through a pessimism of strength. That is, Nietzsche had rejected Schopenhauer's solution in the resignation of the ideal of nirvana. In any case, Nietzsche regarded art, science and religion as ultimately merely illusions by which we attempt to comfort ourselves. In a world in which God is dead, Nietzsche proposed an entirely new platform, that is, the project of a re-evaluation of all values.

In summary then, we may identify four primary solutions to the prob-lem of modernism. First, there is the aesthetic solution through artistic creation which Nietzsche regarded as a particularly powerful expression of all yes-saying practices, since art, especially in the pure form of music, was free of the immediate constraints of nihilism and resentment. It is in art that we appear fully to realize our abilities and potential to break through the limitations of our own circumstances. Second, there is the solution of the ascetic ideal which Weber embraced and developed into an ethic of personal responsibility. Within a world of polytheistic values, Weber attempted an orientation to modernity by developing the vocation of the men of science and politics. The ascetic response, however, involved a suppression of genuine emotion and feeling which drove the individual into neurotic, self-destructive behaviour. Third, there is the genuinely nostalgic negation of the present in favour of some imaginary place constituted prior to the devastating consequences of urban industrial rational capitalism. Within this paradigm, the modern is totally rejected by a nostalgic reconstitution of communities. This nostalgic paradigm was particularly significant in the emergence of sociology as a nostalgic analysis of communal relations. Weber identified a flight into the arms of the church as a typically nostalgic response to modernity. Finally, there was Nietzsche's solution, which was in two parts. Rejecting nostalgia, Nietzsche argued that we have no substitute for 'God' and therefore we should develop new values which would express rather than deny the body, emotion and feeling. Second, we should abandon the ascetic ideal which must necessarily involve a nostalgic judgment of the world based upon a distinction between sacred and profane. This solution was Nietzsche's active reconciliation with necessity in the doctrine of *amor fati*. This doctrine in association with the notion of the eternal return, was regarded by Nietzsche as his greatest formula:

> that one wants nothing to be other than it is, not in the future, not in the past, not in all eternity. Not merely to endure that which happens of necessity, still less to dissemble it – all idealism is untruthfulness in the face of necessity to *love* it.
>
> (Nietzsche 1979: 68)

This philosophical doctrine asserts that the world should not be bifurcated into a world of superior intellectual values and inferior everyday values. The *amor fati* doctrine is against the domination of men of letters and cultured persons as employees of the state, as merely servants (*Beamten*) of an order of resentment. This separation between life and knowledge, feeling and art, was for Nietzsche expressed primarily in Kant's aesthetic doctrine that the aesthetic mode was entirely opposed to feeling, that is the aesthetic perspective was disinterested. For Nietzsche, life-enhancing art must express life, not deny it or stand opposed to it. Nietzsche was therefore opposed to the new men of distinction, those bureaucrats of the Prussian state who rendered service to the new bureaucratic domination of the world of culture.

The critique of contemporary culture, especially consumer culture on the basis of mass production and distribution, presupposed an elitist position on culture, since the critique of mass society was grounded ultimately in a firm distinction between high and low culture. It has been argued that this critique of mass culture was both elitist and nostalgic, looking backwards towards a period in history when there was a greater integration between life and art, feeling and thought. The rejection of modernity in its consumer form can be regarded as a contemporary version of the opposition between *Gemeinschaft* and *Gesellschaft*. The critique itself presupposed a world of the conventional scholar and a secular ascetic whose vocation involved the production and reproduction of classical culture and knowledge. The world inhabited by the Frankfurt School had, in many senses of the word, been destroyed by the growth of consumer culture and responses to it.

In an important article by Fredric Jameson on 'Postmodernism and consumer society', it was noted that the advent of a postmodern period brings with it the obliteration of precisely the distinctions upon which critical theory depended. Jameson observed:

> The second feature of this list of postmodernism is the effacement in it of some key boundaries for separations, most notably the erosion of the older distinction between high culture and so-called mass or popular culture. This is perhaps the most distressing development of all from an academic standpoint, which has traditionally had a vested interest in preserving a realm of high or elite culture against the surrounding environment of philistinism, of schlock and kitsch, of TV series and *Readers Digest* culture, and in transmitting difficult and complex skills of reading, listening and seeing to its initiates.
>
> (Jameson 1985: 112)

While the concept of postmodernism has been much debated, Jameson employs it as an historical description of a particular stage in the development of modern capitalism. His argument is that modernism as such refers to the period which started with the post-war economic boom in the United States in the late 1940s and which brought with it the expansion of mass consumption, international travel, a new world order of economic relations and a new realm of cultural experiences for the masses. He goes on to argue that the 1960s was a transitional period involving the emergence of new forms of colonialism, the green revolution, the emergence of computerized systems of information, and the development of a global system of politics. The postmodern period therefore refers to the emergence of a new social order within late capitalism. One consequence of the development of a postmodern society, which brings with it a cultural egalitarianism liquidating the distinction between high and low culture, is the development of the 'nostalgia film' which through parody takes note of the absence of authoritative norms in aesthetic evaluation. Because we cannot achieve adequate aesthetic representation of our period, we are committed to nostalgia parody.

It is important to recognize that many of these features of the modernist/postmodernist debate were anticipated in the work of Daniel Bell, particularly in his essay 'Beyond modernism, beyond self'. Bell, giving special emphasis to the importance of Nietzsche, noted that the modern period was ushered in by the secularization of culture, namely by the death of God, the loss of a sense of hell and the collapse of traditional systems of salvation. These developments were associated with other social changes, particularly the growth of geographical and social mobility associated with the dominance of the city and the motorcar in social life. Bell noted that in the world of art this change was signalled by the disappearance of mythological creatures in artistic representation and the emergence of 'the promenade and the *plage*, the bustle of city life, and, by the end of the century, the brilliance of night-life in an urban environment transformed by electric light' (Bell 1980: 277). This period of capitalism was also associated with a growing emphasis on the reflexive self and on individualism generally. However, people are still condemned by memory and consciousness to a sense of their own limitations and ultimately to their own death. Therefore one particular feature of the modernist culture of the late nineteenth century was a growing disenchantment with reason and rationality as adequate orientations to life. Bell argued through an examination of the work of Gide, Dostoevski and Nietzsche that central to modernism is the 'derogation of the cognitive' and an emphasis on the aesthetic experience as autonomous; against reason, there was a greater emphasis on emotion and desire. According to Bell (1976: xxv) 'in the culture, fantasy reigns almost unconstrained'. However, postmodernism against modernism rejects the aesthetic solution in favour of the instinctual so that pleasure becomes more important than artistic representation. Therefore 'in a literal sense, reason is the enemy and the desires of the body the truth' (Bell 1980: 288). Like Jameson, Bell also recognized the decline of the high/low distinction in culture:

> What is most striking about postmodernism is that what was once maintained as esoteric is now proclaimed as ideology, and what was once the property of an aristocracy of the spirit is now turned into the democratization of the cultural mass.
>
> (Bell 1980: 289)

In short, bourgeois society which was the social and cultural manifestation of early capitalism is exhausted and with that exhaustion we are witnessing the disappearance of the possessive self and rugged individuality. In such a democratized mass culture, there is little role for a cultural elite or an academic caste which is separated from the herd. As a result, nostalgia is a very potent mode for a moribund intellectual elite adrift from its traditional culture and institutional setting.

As a conclusion to this commentary, we shall turn finally to a modest defence of mass culture through a consideration of the egalitarian feature of mass consumption which is associated historically with the democratization of the mass. The imposition of taste involves necessarily the cultivation of distinction which is an expression of cultural and class superiority, as Pierre Bourdieu (1984) has so profoundly shown in his book on the judgment of taste. In modern industrial capitalism, there is, in addition to the constant reproduction of social classes, also a certain drift towards an egalitarian lifestyle. Modern societies are characterized by a relatively high degree of social mobility (by comparison with feudal and premodern societies) which makes the enforcement of conventional systems of rank difficult to achieve. Modern occupational mobility is therefore incompatible with a social system grounded in the notion of hereditary rank. Both social and geographical mobility make the imposition of hierarchical authority problematic in a society committed, at the level of political constitutions, to the principle of equality of opportunity. In addition, the mass media and modern forms of consumerism have created a leisure society where conventional principles of taste and systems of cultural inequality have been threatened and challenged. The capacity for the working class to benefit from these new commodities has been enhanced by the growth of hire purchase systems and other loan facilities. The growth of a consumer society is therefore closely associated with social embourgeoisement. There has been a levelling of culture which necessarily involves a deterioration of elite standards. The emergence of a mass consumer culture was closely associated with the development of mass education and systems of uniform training providing again a certain levelling of national culture and experience. We can also argue that the growth of mass transport systems brought about a democratization of geographical movement so that the ownership of a motor car became, along with the ownership of a home, a basic objective of modern democracies. While mass culture may involve, from the point of view of an elite, the trivialization of culture, there is nevertheless embedded in these new systems of culture a certain egalitarian standard which calls into question the conventional hierarchies of traditional society (Gellner 1979: Turner 1986a). Modern systems of communication and commodity production have, of course, made the interaction between elite, avant-garde culture and mass culture especially complex and dynamic. Punk was transformed from oppositional/low culture to haute couture within the space of a few months (Featherstone 1987a; Martin 1981).

This view of the egalitarian implications of mass culture has been challenged by Bourdieu, who, through a discussion of cultural capital, has shown how there is a profound relationship between the continuity of economic inequality and cultural inequality. Each social class location has its own habitus which is a bundle of dispositions which incline its members towards particular forms of taste and particular appreciations of cultural, social and other objects. Distinction is constantly reproduced in the competitive struggle between different classes and different fractions of classes. While Bourdieu's argument is clearly supportable and important, we should see the relationship between egalitarian mass cultures and the inegalitarian implication of dispositions as an unstable cycle of processes, or as a dynamic confrontation between different principles; we can see cultural artefacts as constantly transformed in the direction of both egalitarian and inegalitarian consequences. As social classes adopt the culture of their superiors, so their superiors develop and adopt new patterns of cultural life. Both distinction and equality are thereby reproduced in the relationship between social groups and social classes.

One problem with Bourdieu's position is that it entails a total commitment to a dominant ideology thesis which largely rules out any significant possibility of resistance, change or transformation in cultural systems. Bourdieu sees the domination of cultural capital as largely unchallenged and complete in its penetration of the whole system. For example, he argues that

> there is no realistic chance of any collective resistance to the effect of imposition that would lead either to the valorization of properties stigmatised by the dominant taxonomy (the 'black is beautiful' strategy) or to the creation of new, positively evaluated properties. Thus, the dominated have only two options: loyalty to self and group (all liable to relapse into shame), or the individual effort to assimilate the dominant ideal which is the antithesis of the very ambition of collectively restraining control over social identity (of the type pursued by the collective revolt of the American feminists when it advocates 'the natural look').
>
> (Bourdieu 1984: 380)

While Bourdieu is often critical of the Frankfurt School, this view of the total domination of culture and the limitations of alternative strategies is largely compatible, at least in analytical terms, with the position adopted by writers like Marcuse and Adorno. By contrast, the analyses of the Birmingham Centre for Contemporary Cultural Studies point to the importance and presence of resistance within popular and mass culture, through, for example, the development of youth subcultures, to the dominance of the central cultural tradition (Hall and Jefferson 1976). It is not clear that modern capitalist societies either require or can achieve such overall dominance of a central cultural tradition largely owned and fostered by the upper classes. The notion of a 'national culture' is made problematic by globalization, by cultural pluralism and multiculturalism in modern states. The arguments against the dominant ideology thesis are relatively well developed in this area (Abercrombie *et al.* 1980). At the very least, we should see a tension or conflict between mass cultural systems, the cultural industry and the cultural elite, since this relationship of conflict in culture simply expresses underlying tensions which are political and economic in character. The existence of mass culture does not necessarily lead to mass incorporation in a dominant culture, since many aspects of mass culture are oppositional. Indeed, in a postmodern era, it is somewhat difficult to know what would count as 'dominant' against which culture could be 'oppositional'. The world against which Nietzsche and Freud protested is now largely obsolete. It is difficult to know which cultural tradition or which cultural groups are in fact the defenders of a dominant tradition. As Bell has eloquently noted,

> the traditional bourgeois organisation of life – its rationalism and its sobriety – has few defenders in the serious culture; nor does it have any coherent system of cultural meaning or stylistic forms with any intellectual or cultural respectability.
>
> (Bell 1980: 302)

This cultural dilemma (the disjunction between culture and social structure) creates a particular set of problems for the existence of an elite culture and for the social role of the intelligentsia. Are they to become merely the reactionary guardians of collective nostalgia, defending Wagner against the Beatles, Jane Austen against 'Dallas' or George Eliot against 'Dynasty'?

In other respects Bourdieu's analysis of culture would be compatible with these reflections on the role of the myth of nostalgic communities in the division between high and low culture. Bourdieu has shown that in many respects high culture and low culture are deeply embedded one in the other. He argues that the high culture of intellectual class is ultimately rooted in 'the primary primitive dispositions of the body, "visceral" tastes and distastes, in which the group's most vital interests are embedded, the things on which one is prepared to stake one's own and other peoples' bodies' (Bourdieu 1984: 474). We would argue that this is what Nietzsche intended by his doctrine of the little things, that is, Nietzsche's argument that intellectual life was a resentful response to the everyday world of taste, emotion, feeling and reciprocity. The cultural life of intellectuals involved both distinction and resentment. Bourdieu also goes on to note how the pure taste of the intellectual class and its rejection of mass culture involves a profound disgust with the mass and the vulgar:

> what pure taste refuses is indeed the violence which the popular spectator can sense (one thinks of Adorno's description of popular music and its effects); it demands respect, the distance which allows it to keep its distance. It expects the work of art, a finality with no other end than itself, to treat the spectator in accordance with the Kantian imperative, that is, as an end, not a means. Thus, Kant's principle of pure taste is nothing other than a refusal, a disgust – a disgust for objects which impose enjoyment, a disgust for the crude, vulgar taste which revels in this imposed enjoyment.
>
> (Bourdieu 1984: 488)

The cultural elite, especially where it has some pretension to radical politics, is thus caught in a constant paradox that every expression of critique of the mass culture of capitalist societies draws it into an elitist position of cultural disdain, refraining from its enjoyments of the everyday reality. To embrace enthusiastically the objects of mass culture involves the cultural elite in a pseudo-populism; to reject critically the objects of mass culture involves distinction, which in turn draws the melancholic intellectual into a nostalgic withdrawal from contemporary culture. Since in postmodern times probably all culture is pseudo-culture, it is invariably the case that all intellectuals are melancholics. The thesis of Erasmus (that spiritual powers of distinction belong exclusively to melancholic maniacs) appears to have been validated among middle-class intellectuals in postmodern times.

Chapter 10

The two faces of sociology: global or national?

Since its formal inception in the first half of the nineteenth century, sociology has been, generally implicitly, located in a tension or contradiction between becoming a science of particular nation-states and a science of global or universal processes. It developed ambiguously as both a science of the specific societies of the industrial world and as a science of humanity. Although the vocabulary of sociology is typically couched at a sufficiently abstract level to suggest that it is a science of universal social processes ('action', 'structuration', 'norm' or 'social system'), in practice sociology has been developed to explain and understand local or national destinies. From a sociology of knowledge point of view, we might be surprised if this nationalistic purpose were absent. Paradoxically, we might argue that the greater the sociologist, the more local the purpose, namely that sociology developed by means of brilliant insights into concrete issues of local capitalist development. I wish to explore these paradoxes through a commentary on certain classical sociologists, but the burden of this examination will focus on France and Germany up to the First World War.

Percy Bysshe Shelley once argued in his *A Defence of Poetry* in 1821 that poets were the 'hierophants of an unapprehended inspiration' because they possessed a superior imagination. Although I would not want to claim such heroic powers for sociologists, we should at least expect that sociology would reflect, if possible sooner rather than later, the major cultural tensions and developments of given societies. Since the modern world is itself subject to the contradictory tensions of globalization and localization, secularization and fundamentalization, of modernization and postmodernization, we should expect to see these contradictions reflected in the conceptual apparatus of sociology itself. My purpose in this chapter is therefore to examine the relationship between the emergence of a universalistic concept of citizenship and global notions of humanity and simultaneously to review the various ways in which sociology has been implicated in these global developments.

The idea that sociology is a product of the French and Industrial

Revolutions, mediated by the three principal ideologies of modern politics (namely conservatism, liberalism and socialism) is controversial (Nisbet 1967). However, it does provide an initially useful paradigm for considering the argument that sociology embodies a tension between a global science of humanity and a 'local' discipline in the service of the nation-state. The problem is that, while sociology may have been a response to the universalistic implications of both revolutions, it became institutionalized, often within the context of the exponential growth of national higher education systems in the post-war period, under the auspices of the state. Is it a global science of humanity or implicitly the study of local structures of the national community? Writing of the Americanization of sociology, W. E. Moore (1966) deplored the decline of a tradition of European sociology which originally regarded the discipline as the study of humanity, and noted that the development of the world into a global system might bring about a revival of sociology with a global perspective. Moore identified a number of classical sociologists who clearly had a vision of global science (Ibn Khaldun, Comte, Durkheim and Spencer), but curiously enough neglected to discuss Claude-Henri de Saint-Simon (1760–1825). From the vantage point of the emerging (re)unification of Europe and increasing awareness of modern globality (Turner 1987a; Robertson and Chirico 1985), Saint-Simon's commentary on the relationship between industrialism and human globalization has proved to be extraordinarily prescient.

As an individual, Saint-Simon was perfectly placed to experience the revolutionary implications of his own epoch. A member of the French aristocracy who served briefly in the French army during the American War of Independence, he was subsequently arrested in 1793 and financially ruined by revolutionary change. His failure to secure public recognition led eventually to an unsuccessful suicide attempt in 1823 when he shot himself in the head seven times. He miraculously survived only to die two years later after an attack of gastro-enteritis. He left behind a genuine intellectual following and a body of work which proved crucial for the foundation of both sociology and socialism because it directly influenced both Durkheim (Gouldner 1958; Lukes 1973) and Marx (Rattansi 1982).

In his philosophical works he advocated positivism as an antidote to metaphysical speculation, but the core of Saint-Simon's substantive sociology was dominated by the analysis of industrialism. In fact, Saint-Simon's conceptualization of social change anticipated Herbert Spencer's sociology because Saint-Simon wanted to draw a sharp contrast between militaristic and industrial systems. In the feudal systems of the Middle Ages, the clerical class enjoyed political and ideological dominance, because the Church was an institution which provided social cohesion. With the development of industrialism, militaristic virtues and monastic virtues of asceticism cease to be socially relevant as the social system turns from the production of war to the production of useful things, through the organization of the sciences and arts in the interests of humanity. The old style of militaristic politics was to be replaced by a system of co-operative administration in which the traditional parasitic classes would be replaced by the 'new' classes of engineers and industrialists. While Saint-Simon worked with an ideal-typical dichotomy of militaristic-theological and pacific-industrial systems, he recognized that in specific cases these two systems could overlap and continue to persist in given societies. Thus, in *De la réorganisation de la société européenne* which he published with Augustin Thierry in 1814, he criticized the militaristic dimension of England's social constitution which was combined with industrialism. In order to establish a European peace, it would be necessary to curtail this aggressive aspect of English social organization by uniting England and France under a common parliamentary system (Taylor 1975: 130–6).

These features of Saint-Simonian sociology are relatively well known. Perhaps what is far more interesting is Saint-Simon's vision of an integrated system of European states, the international spread of industrialism and the emergence of a global culture. Saint-Simon's view of industrialism creating an international order which would undermine the legacy of provincialism was important from our point of view precisely because he saw an intimate connection between the growth of globalism and a change in the nature of social science. The scholars of Europe were already forming social bonds which would challenge the archaic forms of local consciousness, he argued in *L'Organisateur* of 1819. Sociology was to become the science of the new industrialism, and at the same time a religion of humanity would replace the decaying force of Catholicism. It is this aspect of Saint-Simon's teaching which struck Durkheim forcefully. An economic industrialism would not in itself be sufficient to create a new moral basis to European societies, which were in a state of disarray with the collapse of the moral authority of the papacy. In the *Nouveau christianisme* (1825) Saint-Simon sought the principles which would provide the notion of universal unity to bring the separate European nations into a morally coherent system. In his study of Saint-Simon, Durkheim fundamentally supported this normative feature of global socialism, but he thought internationally organized professional groups would be necessary to sponsor and carry these norms.

The notion that there are important, and at times paradoxical, relations between global industrialism, secularized Christianity, cosmopolitan sociology and socialism became a persistent feature of the legacy of classical sociology. Saint-Simon's ideas about positivism and sociology were taken up by August Comte (1798–1857) in his *Cours de philosophie* where in volume four in 1838 we find the first self-conscious reference to 'sociology'. Comte elaborated the idea of developing sociology as the pinnacle of the positive sciences and a universal religion as the cohesive force of contemporary sciences. Comte wrote to Czar Nicholas, the Grand Vizier of the Ottoman Empire and the head of the Jesuit order to encourage them to accept the new positive universalism and hierarchical authority of the Roman Catholic Church as models of organization for the new order. The new religion of Humanity would have rituals, saints and calendars like the old faith, but it would be revolutionized by the spirit of positivism (Kolakowski 1968).

This simultaneous concern for a science of society and the unification of humanity (or at least as a first step the integration of a peaceful Europe) was further developed by Nemis Fustel de Coulanges and Durkheim who regarded the universalism of medieval Roman Catholicism as mid-way between the pantheism of Rome and the cosmopolitanism of the new industrial order. In *The Elementary Forms of the Religious Life*, (1961) Durkheim argued that modern societies would have to discover a new set of universally significant moral bonds. These normative elements were necessary to curb the impact of utilitarianism and individualism which were another feature of the new order of industrialism. Tragically, Durkheim, in response to German nationalism and as a consequence of the devastation of the First World War on the young men of the sociology movement or school, came to see nationalist rituals and symbols, rather than professionalism, as the key feature of the new integrative system replacing Christianity. These nationalist sentiments, especially in *Qui a voulu la guerre*? (1915) and *L'Allemagne au-dessus de tout* (1915) were also a reaction against the dangerous ideas of Heinrich von Treitschke on pan-Germanism. We can interpret Durkheim's sociology, especially his sociology of morals and education, as an attempt to provide French society with an analytical paradigm which would contribute to the restoration of social coherence, which Durkheim thought was threatened by the hedonistic materialism and anomie of rapid industrialization. In part Durkheim's interest in the problems of social order in advanced societies under conditions of organic solidarity had been occasioned by the crisis of the Franco-Prussian war. The French defeat contributed to his sense of patriotism (Lukes 1973: 41). While it is probably an exaggeration to assert that '*the raison d'être* of his scientific research in sociology was the welding of France into a well organised and well integrated nation' (Mitchell 1931: 87), it is clear that the idea of nationalism as a modern version of more traditional sources of the *conscience collective* runs throughout his work.

The involvement of many European intellectuals in the euphoria which embraced the opening of the First World War as a panacea for the crisis of European culture and as an antidote to cultural nihilism snuffed out much of the universalistic legacy of nineteenth-century positivism. But while the slaughter of 1914–18 made the prospects of international agreements look remote, over a longer period of time the twin themes of nationalism and cosmospolitanism were interwoven in Durkheim's sociology and that of his followers. In 1900 at the Exposition Universelle in Paris, Durkheim offered a lecture to a congress on problems of solidarity in modern societies in which he recognized the current force of national sentiment, but argued that there was also a new and broader social trend towards European solidarity and towards humanity as an ideal (Hayward 1959). The theme was also explored by Marcel Mauss in a development of Durkheim's ideas in 'Sociologie politique: la nation et l'internationalisme' (Mauss 1968–9, Vol. 3). In short, the theme of Saint-Simonian internationalism continued in Durkheimian sociology, despite the devastations of war.

We can define modernization in terms of the emergence of concepts of internationalism and cosmopolitanism insofar as they break with the limitations, narrowness and provincialism of tradition. Modernization is the triumph of global over local culture. In this respect, universalism is bound up with the growth of the city, with trading corporations, with universities and with the emergence of a money economy. The project of modernization is about the conditions which give rise to the abstract citizen. The disappearance of status as the primary axis of social hierarchy and the development of notions of contract were critical processes which prepared the ground for the elaboration of modern notions of universalistic citizenship (Turner 1986b; 1988). It is perfectly appropriate therefore that Jürgen Habermas should claim in *The Philosophical Discourse of Modernity* that 'With Kant, the modern age is inaugurated' (Habermas 1987: 260), and it is equally appropriate that the two essays by Kant which have drawn most attention in the recent discussions of modernity and postmodernity have been 'What is enlightenment?' and 'Idea for a universal history from a cosmopolitan point of view', which were both published in the *Berlinische Monatschrift* in 1784. As a theorist of modernity, Kant was interested in the developmental possibilities of a universalistic morality, which would function as an alternative to or replacement of (official) Christianity. These developmental possibilities also signalled major social opportunities for intellectuals as carriers of global culture.

These 'political' writings show that Kant's critical writings on philosophical issues were not remote from the social and political issues of his time. On the contrary, they may be seen as responses to the erosion of the universalism of Christian morality against the background of the American and French revolutions. In his article on universal history, therefore, Kant reflected upon the global implications of the transition of human societies from barbarism to civil society – a theme common to Enlightenment philosophers and subsequently developed of course, via Ferguson and Hegel, by Marx into a historical materialism of world society. In order to understand this aspect of Kant's article, we should perhaps note that '*Idee zu einer allgemeinen Geschichte*' can be translated as a 'general normative paradigm for world history', while '*im welbürger-liche Absicht*' could be plausibly rendered as 'from the standpoint of global citizenship'. In short, there is a parallel between Saint-Simon's vision of an integrated Europe in the context of an expanding humanity and Kant's essays on universal history, enlightenment and perpetual peace (Beck 1988). This parallel or convergence is hardly surprising, given the fact that they were both responding to the (largely implicit) ideas of global citizenship in the French Revolution. Thus, Kant argued that, while necessity compelled humanity to surrender individual (natural) freedoms in order to form a civic union, the highest goal of Nature was the formation of a perfect human community. Such a global community could only be possible in a context of international regulation of states. This idea Kant recognised was 'fantastical' (from the perspective of nationalistic objectives), but ultimately necessary, if humanity were to progress beyond the condition of perpetual war. The final solution to the Hobbesian state of nature was the creation of an international order of mutual regulation. By connecting Christianity with the spread of global politics and the ideal of a common humanity, Kantian philosophy involved a negative assess-ment of other world religions, especially Islam.

If Kant inaugurated the modern age, then according to Habermas, it was with Hegel (1710–1831) that modernity became a problem, because it was in Hegel's theory of the evolution of a world spirit that the constellation of rationality, consciousness of historical time and modernity became visible and self-consciously theorized. For Hegel 'the History of the World is nothing but the development of the Idea of Freedom' (Hegel 1956: 456), through a series of dialectical struggles towards self-realization through the Greek world, the Roman period and the German world. For Hegel, religion, and in particular reformed Christianity, played a crucial part in the emergence of modern subjectivity and individualism. For Hegel, as we have seen, Islam was in a state of repose and could not influence the course of history. By contrast, in the subjectivity of Christian spirituality, Hegel saw the origins of modern consciousness, but Chris-tianity in modern times had become fragmented and could no longer function as a common morality and a universal vision. With the growing division of labour and the competitiveness of bourgeois society, civil society lacked coherence and this alienation had separated individuals from the common realm. A new civil religion was required to replace Christianity and to express the new level of universalism and freedom which was implicit in modern society. In common with is contemporaries, Hegel combined this view of Christianity with an idealization of the Greek polis as a period in which there was no fundamental alienation between the private individual and the public arena. In his later work,

Hegel moved increasingly towards a secular view of political integration, believing that a civil religion might develop to provide the necessary integration for a developed social system (Plant 1973).

It is well known that Hegelianism had entirely contradictory implications, and as a result divided early into conservative Right Hegelians and the so-called Young Hegelians of the left. On the one hand, Hegel's ideas justified the critique of Christianity as only a partial realisation of the universal spirit of freedom and legitimized a revolutionary criticism of the particularities and limitations of modern times as an anticipation of a new leap into the future. On the other hand, Hegelianism provided a reconciliation of the present and the past, because modern institutions are the fullest realization of the course of history. Hegel's slogan 'the real is the rational' was taken to mean that what exists now (for example the Prussian state) is the embodiment of the highest form of rationality. This ambiguity permitted Popper to accuse Hegel of instigating the New Tribalism (Popper 1945: 30), while other scholars have argued that there was nothing in the text of *Philosophie des Rechts* to justify such an assertion (Knox 1940).

The fact is that we cannot understand the contradictory themes of German social philosophy without an understanding of the social structure of the German states in the period following the French Revolution. Before the Revolution, the German ruling classes and the court had looked towards France for a model of civilized taste and behaviour. Germany was still a collection of small, divided and fragmented cities, principalities and states. In cultural terms, this produced a narrow, small-town mentality which idealised the virtues of self-governing towns against the external threat of absolutism. The peculiarity of eighteenth-century Germany, however, was that this very localism also provided the social roots of a rapid development of interest in global culture on the part of officials in the bureaucracy. The German state bureaucracy also typically included teachers and clergymen, and thus there was an audience for a more universalistic culture. This bureaucratic state structure provided the institutional context for the development of the ideals of *Bildung*, of education on the part of the state employees of the middle classes. There was, however, no national cultural centre in the German states and 'it was in the absence of a national center and a national public that German literary aspirations came to focus on humanity as a whole' (Bendix 1977: 126).

After the French Revolution, the educated elites either looked towards England for a model of liberalism which might provide an alternative to revolutionary terror or they continued to develop notions about individual cultivation, self-education and aesthetic refinement as an alternative to practical politics. Their moral world-view implied a criticism of the aristocracy whose culture was thought to be based on blood sports, heavy drinking and sexual immorality, without ever rejecting social inequality as such. The literature of the middle classes reflected their *de facto* reconciliation with the world in terms of the virtues of diligence, restraint and ethical refinement. These values of the *Bildungsbürgertum* implied an ambiguity about power politics because the educated middle classes feared revolutionary terror from below and authoritarian regulation from above. Hence they 'escaped' into self-cultivation. The development of 'character' or 'personality' was an alternative to political struggle. In Germany, in response to the violence of the French terror, writers like Goethe embraced classical humanism and hoped for the development of an idealized global citizenry (*Weltbürgertum*). This context led Karl Marx to observe that what France had achieved in the field of revolutionary politics, it was left to Germany to bring about in the sphere of philosophy. Hence in the *German Ideology* and the *Critique of Hegel's Philosophy of Right*, we see Marx attempting to transcend the limitations of German idealism through the development of a materialistic interpretation of world history, which would require Marxism to go beyond the constraints of a merely bourgeois conception of a universalistic *bürgergesellschaft* or civil society.

Marx's dependence on the legacy of Hegelian idealism is too well known to require elaboration (Avineri 1968). The universal development of the absolute spirit became the historical development of the pro-duction of the material conditions of existence in which, under capitalism, the progressive character of historical development was momentarily lost in the alienation of labour from the means and objects of production. However, from the contradictions of capitalism the proletariat emerged as the universal class of historical change. However, if we look at Marx as a theorist of modernity, we can also see the continuation of Kant and Hegel. For example 'Three aspects characterise capitalism according to Marx: the rationalisation of the world, the rationalisation of human action, and the universalisation of inter-human contract' (Avineri 1968: 162). Marx's view of capitalism was as a result paradoxical. Capitalism subordi-nated the majority of the population to a life of enforced misery, but capitalism also destroyed local tradition, provincial sentiments and the enchanted garden of magic and superstition. Through its universal impulse, capitalism made history into world-history. In the *German Ideol-ogy* Marx and Engels claimed that capitalism

> produced world history for the first time, insofar as it made all civilised nations and every individual member of them dependent for the satis-faction of his wants on the whole world, thus destroying the formal natural exclusiveness of separate nations.
>
> (Marx and Engels 1965: 75–6)

This view of the world dynamism of the capitalist economy was further illustrated by the notion that Asia was characterized by its stationariness and lack of global significance. Indeed, the Asiatic mode of production precluded the possibility of internal change (Turner 1978a). Marx followed Hegel in believing that Islam was part of the pre-history and could not contribute to the shaping of modern times. It was the British Empire with its railways, private property system, newspapers and competitive commodities which would start the revolution in Asia. Because the workers have no stake in the national economy, their interests are in reality cosmopolitan. Nationalism and patriotism are thus reactionary forces, which will wither away with the global development of capitalism. National sentiment was regarded as a bourgeois device to divide the global consciousness of the workers (Davis 1965: Kolakowski 1974).

Although Marx was overtly writing about the global expansion of a capitalist world-system, we can also interpret Marx as a theorist of modernity. This interpretation of Marx has been developed recently by Marshall Berman (1982) in *All That is Solid Melts into Air*. Berman wanted to show that modernist writers and Marx converge, but also that the tensions and contradictions of modernism as an experience were produced by capitalism as analysed by Marx. Thus Berman interpreted modernism from within a Marxist paradigm:

> to suggest how its characteristic energies, insights and anxieties spring from the strains of modern economic life: from its relentless and insatiable pressure for growth and progress; its expansion of human desires beyond local, national and moral bounds ... the volatility and endless metamorphosis of all its values in the maelstrom of the world market; its pitiless destruction of everything.
>
> (Berman 1982: 121)

Marx was certainly a brilliant theorist of modernity, especially in identifying the destructive economic origins of modern progress, and thus in describing the dark side (the blood and pain) of change. However, there remains the suspicion that Marx's account of modernization was inextricably a description of Westernization, and therefore that his view of global history was a general history of the West. In this respect, Marxism may share precisely the limitations conventionally associated with functionalist theories of development. Marx had little or no appreciation for the universalism, for example of Islam, and he characteristically regarded 'Asiatic societies' as uniformly stagnant. His account of the progress of world history in developmental stages – from barbarism to civil society – was the legacy of a Western Enlightenment. Even Marx's view of European history was inescapably shaped by the German experience of historical change. Thus Marx's version of Hegel's view of the world history was a strange combination of a global vision with a distinctive orientalist perspective on the origins of rational capitalism. In this regard, there is little to separate Marx's account of a capitalist accumulation in the West from Weber's perspective on the revolutionary force of Western rational capitalism in the *General Economic History*.

In Weber the modernization of social relations by the globalization force of capitalism was translated into a theory of global rationalization. The combination of Protestant asceticism and Western rationalism has produced an irresistible force, which will slowly but surely convert the world into a regulated and organized social system within which there will be little room for tradition, magic or charisma. The de-mystification of the world will make everything in principle subject to rational calculation. Although many cultures have 'anticipated' such changes, only in post-Calvinistic Europe and in the Protestant cultures of North America has the full force of the spirit of instrumental rationalism come to full bloom.

Weber combined a vision of this global process towards a single-world rationality with a clear view of the fact that the social sciences in Germany had to serve a national purpose. In his own research, there was a continuous commitment to German nationalist objectives. In the 1890s for example he condemned the use of Polish and other agricultural workers in East Prussia which he felt represented a long-term threat to the cultural integrity of Germany (Tribe 1983). In his Freiburg address on 'The National State and Economic Policy' (Weber 1980), it is clear that economics has a direct contribution to make to the creation of a strong German state. Weber's interest in the Russian Revolution was at least partly inspired by a traditional German fear of Cossack cavalry penetrating Germany via the flat plains of Eastern Europe. Weber described the First World War as 'great and wonderful' (Käsler 1988: 18), although he did not support the expansion of Germany via for example the annexation of Belgium. Weber's persistent and overt involvement in the national politics of German life obviously raises issues about the conventional interpretations of Weber's doctrine of value-neutrality. Without entering into this epistemological issue, it is important to keep in mind the fact that Weber's statements on the issue of sociology in relation to practical politics arose in the context of his confrontation with the Minister of Education concerning the autonomy of university professors in the Prussian university system (Weber 1973). The value-neutrality doctrine was thus more a statement about university organization than about the conduct of sociological inquiry; it did not prohibit Weber from direct statements about army, foreign or domestic policy.

It could be objected that my analysis so far has merely stated an obvious proposition about the sociology of knowledge, namely that sociologists might be expected to reflect national goals and objectives, especially during periods of social crisis. In continental Europe, especially where a Germanic university system is in operation, university academics are essentially civil servants, whose research is expected, in part at least, to follow governmental objectives and assumptions. In the Netherlands, for example, 'most faculty members consider it perfectly appropriate that the government should decide the role of university research in Dutch society' (Philips 1986: 65). This situation means that the notion of 'academic freedom' will have very different meanings and implications in different university traditions and structures. In the context of government-dominated university systems, it is hardly possible to see what Mannheim's notion, following Alfred Weber, of the 'free-floating intelligentsia' or 'socially unattached intellectuals' (*sozial freischwebende Intelligenz*) could mean (Mannheim 1991). One would only expect university-based academics-as-civil-servants to reflect national, indeed nationalistic goals. In so far as classical sociology developed a global vision of reality, it may be that this view depended more on marginalized and alienated Jewish scholars (Durkheim, Simmel, Benjamin, Adorno and so forth) than on any other social group.

Yet the 'calling' of a sociologist is also to wider and broader goals, which would include in principle a commitment to the universalistic character of the discipline, the global features of intellectual life, some notion of science as a set of practices and commitments over and above national and local objectives. The very sociology of knowledge which argues that sociological knowledge will be as determined by social processes as any other type of knowledge permits us to reflect self-consciously on the vocation of a sociologist to a global picture of a science of humanity in the context of the often covert strains towards a local or 'Little England' view of social reality. Sociology should on these grounds reflect this bifurcation between a global view of sociology and a commitment to nationally specified research targets.

While this observation is introduced as an 'optimistic' observation on the limitations and prospects of sociology as a global science of humanity, it has also to be recognised how frequently sociology and sociologists have served entirely local causes. In Germany, sociology adapted relatively successfully to Nazi conditions (Rammstedt 1986); American sociology has been frequently co-opted to service nationalistic foreign-policy objectives, as in the project Camelot affair; major sociology textbooks tend to exhibit local views of the content of the discipline (Coulson and Riddell 1970); and very few major sociologists have written about sociological problems in an international, let alone a global context. For example, Parsons's sociology is overshadowed by the dilemma of his overt commitment to American democratic values (Holton and Turner 1986) and his clear intention to write a general theory of action which would be relevant to the human commitment as such. Or to take a very different example, despite the global character of the analytical questions of Habermas's social philosophy, his comments on actual societies (which are in any case rather rare) tend to be parochial in their focus on Western capitalist societies (Habermas 1979).

In conclusion, we can expect a deluge of publications in the 1990s on *fin-de-siècle* everything. Martin Jay has to some extent paved the way prematurely perhaps with *Fin-de-siècle Socialism* (1988). There are in any case certainly some interesting parallels between 1890 and 1990. There is our sense of impending doom, this time ecological rather than militaristic. It would however be foolhardy to preclude the possibility of an eco-military disaster. The greenhouse effect, the destruction of the ozone layer, the break-up of Eastern Europe, the AIDS epidemic, fundamentalist revivals in the world-religions, the greying of the industrial societies and world-wide religio-ethnic conflicts and communal violence offer a daunting picture of global catastrophe. Many versions of nihilism and/or cultural decadence are now on offer. The notion of the crisis of values, the rise of the masses and the isolation of the individual which was common as a theme in the 1890s may find a resonance today. Similarly, recent studies of the 'end of organised capitalism' (Lash and Urry 1987) might be compared (not with reference to their contents but to the scale of social change which they addressed) with Rudolf Meyer's *Der Capitalismus fin de siècle* of 1894. In our period, anxiety about the future has been summarized under the prefix 'post' as in postmodernism, *post-histoire*, post-Marxism, post-Fordism. I am assuming that even this uncertainty will give way to greater doubts, involving a comparison of our end-of-century existence with an absolutist Baroque culture.

Perhaps the crisis which drove intellectuals at the end of the nineteenth century into sociology, socialism and internationalism might, however, also find an echo in our own epoch. Durkheim's reflections on Saint-Simon's vision of the necessity for European integration, an end to English aggression against the European continent and a new science of humanity might be a valuable point of departure for contemporary social sciences to begin to engage (once again) with the tensions between our local concerns with national issues and our vocation, albeit underdeveloped and ill-defined, for a global sociology of humanity. At the very least, it would be an intellectual tragedy if the nationalistic and parochial politics of the Anglo-American world were to obscure the real possibilities which were opening up in the late 1980s with the re-unification of Germany and the democratization of Eastern Europe – possibilities which were not only anticipated but actually described by Henri Saint-Simon in his observations on the need for a European parliament in 1814.

Chapter 11

Ideology and utopia in the formation of an intelligentsia
Reflections on the English cultural conduit

English intellectuals have a peculiar relationship to global culture. As native speakers of English, they have an automatic and privileged access to the world market of intellectual production. For example, they can anticipate that their academic texts will reach a world market without the inconvenience of translation. By contrast, many of their European colleagues, especially Danish, Dutch or Swedish intellectuals, are either forced to cope with relatively small, local markets, or they will be faced with the expense of translation. In addition to this communication advantage, English intellectuals, partly as a result of British imperial history, have also enjoyed until recently a privileged access to university positions in the United States and the Commonwealth. While the process of decolonization has challenged the dominance of English literary studies in societies like India, the popularity for subaltern studies has hardly shaken the global hegemony of the English language as a means of communication. The oddity is that this global access has been combined with a remarkably complacent parochialism and insularity. English intellectuals, precisely because of the strategic importance of English as a global means of communication, are not noted for their language abilities.

English intellectuals have rarely been at the forefront or core of global intellectual developments; their main function has been rather as a global conduit of cultural exchange. If England has been a nation of shopkeepers, then its own intellectuals have been passive traders between the old and new world. They have been interpreters and purveyors of 'foreign' ideas, especially French and German ideas. Various versions of Marxism have been an essential ingredient of this foreign impact on the social sciences. Apart from the possible and dubious exceptions of anthropology and economics, they have been uncommonly uncreative. In political terms, English intellectuals who are dissatisfied with their own society have always had the option of simply leaving. They have been individual migrants and so their critical frustration has been somewhat dispersed and unfocused. Whereas other migrant intellectuals have tended to form communities, English intellectuals have merged (superficially) with their 'host' populations. They do not form a diaspora because the advantages of language and colour have meant that the English have rarely been the targets of an exclusionary process. English intellectuals simply disappear. What they leave behind is a highly fragmented intellectual deposit.

In the last decade, even this parasitic role has been threatened by a significant discharge of English academics into North American, Australian and New Zealand universities and by a further erosion of public support for the traditional independence of the university sector. Thus, the peculiarity of the English has been their high profile in the global intellectual scene by virtue of their native language ability and access to major London-based publishers, and their resilient attachment to cultural philistinism and localism. In the past, of course, English intellectual life depended heavily on a 'white migration' of (mainly Jewish) intellectuals from the continent – for example Ernest Gellner, Norbert Elias, Morris Ginsburg, Illya Neustadt, Karl Mannheim, Alfred Sohn-Rethel, Ludwig Wittgenstein, Zygmunt Bauman, Ralf Dahrendorf, John Westergaard and Bronislaw Malinowski. However, with the approach of European unification and the restructuring of higher education in Eastern Europe, many existing insular practices of British universities are being called into question. English intellectuals, rather like Westminster, will have to find a new global niche. We can expect that academic tensions between the North Atlantic and continental Europe will increase as recent reviews (Denzin 1991; Vidich 1991) of Jean Baudrillard's *America* (1988) and *Cool Memories* (1990) would appear to indicate.

With the approach of the end of the century, there is a strong smell of diagnosis, introspection and nostalgia in the air. It is a good time for taking stock and settling accounts. For some writers, the approaching end of the century has a strong apocalyptic quality, encouraging Baudrillard (1987) to declare that the new era of 2000 has already arrived. The *fin-de-siècle* combination of the end of organized capitalism, post-Fordism, postmodernity and cynical reason (Sloterdijk 1988) has suggested to other observers that we are entering a panic period (Kroker *et al.* 1989). One crucial question on the agenda is whether any form of Marxist social theory will survive into the next century, or whether the collapse of organized communism in Eastern Europe has no relationship to the intellectual problems of Marxist thought. The global role of radical Islamic thought is suddenly an urgent question for Western academics. Professional sociological celebrations of the end of the century are likely to be more sober and modest, but nevertheless nostalgic. If we define the decades of 'classical sociology' as broadly the period 1890–1930 (Hughes 1959), then there are good reasons for comparing the 1890s with the 1990s. Classical sociology was born out of a sense of crisis (essentially the transition from *Gemeinschaft* to *Gesellschaft*) which generated a parcel of concepts (anomie, alienation, community and disenchantment) by which twentieth-century social theorists have attempted to understand modernity (Frisby 1983: Liebersohn 1988). Whether or not this story is true may not be terribly interesting; the point is that sociologists see the intellectual history of their discipline within these parameters. In this respect we can analyse sociology as a primarily nostalgic discourse which recounts how authentic communities were destroyed by the ineluctable advance of industrial capitalism across urban space, leaving behind it the debris of egoistic individualism, other-directed personalities, anomic cultures and homeless minds.

The role of intellectuals in relation to this crisis has been the fascination of intellectuals over the last century. However, there are now a number of new ingredients, chiefly the relationship of intellectuals to the tension between mass and popular cultures (as potentially oppositonal forces) and high culture (as the embodiment of discipline and distinction). More precisely the current fascination with intellectuals, as manifested by Zygmunt Bauman's *Legislators and Interpreters* (1987), Russell Jacoby's *The Last Intellectuals* (1987), Alain Finkelkraut's *La Défaite de la pensée* (1987), Pierre Bourdieu's *Homo Academicus* (1988) and Andrew Ross's *No Respect* (1989), is a product of changing relations between the state, intellectuals and popular culture. The debate about postmodernism in this context of cultural struggle can be read as an attempt to discover a new social role for intellectuals in a post-literate society.

These issues which hinge upon the historical relationship of the intellectuals to high culture in the context of either state or court patronage can be illustrated through the whole field of 'cultural studies'. Although there have been a number of important contributions to the theoretical analysis of culture in Britain and North America – Robert Wuthnow's *Meaning and Moral Order* (1987), Patrick Brantlinger's *Crusoe's Footprints* (1990), Margaret Archer's *Culture and Agency* (1988), Mike Featherstone's *Consumer Culture and Postmodernism* (1991) and Jeff Alexander's *Durkheimian Sociology: Cultural Studies* (1988) – the subject has yet to find an appropriate niche within the interdisciplinary exchange between humanities and social sciences. The problem for sociology is that a sociology of culture is not an adequate answer to the issue of cultural sociology.

There are two interrelated aspects to my argument concerning intellectual communities. First, following Max Weber's epistemological views on the relationship between sociology and history, I start with a truism: there is a tension between the theoretical drive in sociology towards very general concepts and, if possible, general explanations, and the fact that all social phenomena are historically grounded, and thereby characterized by their own specificity. We want to define 'intellectual' in a very general way to permit historical comparisons which in turn would allow us to arrive at a 'theory' of the origins and social role of the intelligentsia as a social group, but we are invariably confronted by particular histories of particular intellectual strata operating under specific historical circumstances. I take Russell Jacoby's *The Last Intellectuals* (1987) to be a case in point. It is a superb account of the erosion of the public intellectual as a consequence of the rise of the professional academic in the context of university expansion. The book provokes numerous comparisons with similar processes in Great Britain, Holland, Germany and Australia, but we should also be aware that Jacoby's study is profound precisely because it is a detailed and specific study of the urban transformation of the Village and the cultural accommodation of the New York Jewish intelligentsia. The intellectual value of the study is, therefore, exactly this specificity and not its generality. However, it may be that no general conclusions about the intellectual life as such can be drawn from Jacoby's account, because this concatenation of historical conditions has been produced nowhere else.

Second, it now seems impossible to discuss the intelligentsia without some reference to the legacy of Mannheim's (1991) *Ideology and Utopia* – hence the title of this chapter. Mannheim's views on intellectuals are very widely cited in general discussion of the conditions for intellectuality; the controversy which surrounds his sociology of knowledge in the 1930s is still with us (Meja and Stehr 1990). More importantly, Mannheim raised questions, at least in his early work, about the role of utopian aspiration in all intellectual and political life. His *Essays on the Sociology of Culture* (1956a) contains one of the few serious attempts to understand the democratization of culture in modern societies with the decline or erosion of the aristocratic ethic. Thus, there are three important features of Mannheim's position. Following Alfred Weber, he attempted to locate some sociological conditions which would guarantee intellectual autonomy or at least free intellectuals from the problem of conceptual relativism – this was the famous solution of the free-floating intellectuals, and the distinction between relativism and relationalism. The second part of the legacy is the contrast between ideology as a system of belief which requires a vision of stability and permanence, and the notion of utopia which rules out any sense of the legitimacy of the status quo. Revolutionary worldviews, millenarianism and socialism are examples of utopian thought, but the deeper meaning is closer to Weber's distinction between charisma and tradition. Like charisma, utopia is a threat to established or routinized procedures of a social order. In Mannheim's sociology, utopia had originally a spiritual significance, namely that human beings cannot live meaningful lives without a utopia. Without a vision of the future, the present is meaningless. The third aspect of Mannheim's sociology of knowledge was developed during his life in England, namely a sense of the import-

ance of planning in the democratic restructuring of society. In his contribution to British reformism, Mannheim came to give a special emphasis
to educational modernization as a preparation of the population for
democratic social change and to the university as the cradle of the plan-
ner-intellectual.

For the study of intellectuals, this Mannheimian legacy leaves us with
three broad questions: (1) what is the relationship of intellectuals as a
social group to the macro social structure of the society in which they
live, specifically the relationship to patrons and audiences? (2) what is
the relationship of intellectuals to utopia or, in modern parlance, to
progressive social forces? and (3) what is the relationship of intellectuals
to the state and to the question of social reconstruction through planning
and legislation? Is planning merely the routinization of utopia, namely
ideology? The idea of the intellectual as the heroic leader of the revolutionary vanguard of the masses is, of course, scarcely credible as an
image of the contemporary role of the intellectual in relationship to
politics. To some extent, this more modest self-image has been described
and legitimized by Michel Foucault in the idea of the 'specific intellectual'
as opposed to the 'general intellectual'. The specific intellectual has to
examine the specificity of power in order to problematize taken-for-
granted knowledge, because 'the role of an intellectual is not to tell others
what they have to do' (Foucault 1988: 265). The problem of the intellectual in our time cannot be separated from the issue of democracy.

Now the legacy of Mannheim is a very general legacy; it has generated
a broad tradition of sociological inquiry about the recruitment of intellectuals, the social role of intellectuals and questions about whether intellectuals can actually direct social change. However, what we have perhaps
ignored is once more the very specificity of the historical circumstances
which produced Mannheim's theory. Mannheim inherited initially a particular tradition of Jewish intellectual life from Budapest. There were
two images of the intellectual in the Habsburg Empire. There was the
revolutionary agitator who sought to transform society by a violent
struggle which could be either nationalist or working class. It was this
romantic-chiliastic vision of the intellectual as apocalyptic leader of violent masses which Georg Lukács embraced during the Hungarian Soviet
Republic (Kadarkay 1991). There was an alternative legacy, that of the
Bildungsbürgertum, namely the educated planner of a civilized transformation. In his lifetime, Mannheim experienced both. He was closely
involved with the Soviet Republic of Bela Kun, with the radical ideas
of Georg Lukács and the cultural ambitions of the free University of
Budapest. In Britain, Mannheim switched to the idea of the intellectual
as the educated state official who, guided by rationality, attempts to
redesign society without revolutionary struggle. Here we see both the
tensions between the general and the specific, and between utopia and

ideology. It is probably no accident that Ivan Szelenyi, himself a refugee intellectual and product of the Budapest elite, should see the role of the intellectual as the rational and teleological manager of social change, whose power base is located inside the state (Konrad and Szelenyi 1979).

There are two ways of expressing this idea of the progressive intellectual. We can either argue that intellectuals produce abstract and universal thought (Nettle 1969) because they are not attached to a *particular* social group or social class, or we can say that intellectuals are progressive because they stand outside society, and therefore do not serve a specific set of social interests. The classic idea of the free-floating intellectual is in fact a version of Georg Simmel's 'The stranger' (1971), and the epitome of the Simmelian stranger is the free-floating urban Jew. It is a matter of common observation that sociology and socialism were almost entirely produced by Jews – from Marx to Durkheim, from Mannheim to the Frankfurt School, and, in our own period, the so-called New York intellectuals, the Budapest Circle in Australia and Norbert Elias. These intellectuals had very diverse institutional backgrounds and sources of patronage. The contrasts between Daniel Bell as a Harvard professor and Alfred Schutz as a banker are stark and obvious, but representative; is it possible that their Jewishness alone explains their alienation and distance from Gentile society? The idea here is that distance (whether free-floating or outside) produces the sociological conditions that generate radical and/or universalistic thought. Detachment itself is often seen as 'the platform of sociological observation' (Shils 1980: 1).

Any reference to 'progressive intellectuals' in the conventional sociological literature typically means 'socialist intellectuals', but we should not forget that Mannheim's most sustained study of the intelligentsia was in his essay on *Conservatism* (Mannheim 1991). Where conservatism was a romantic critique of capitalism, then conservatism functioned as a utopia, not as an ideology. Indeed Mannheim went out of his way to correct the assumption that an anti-capitalist utopia would be a socialist utopia. The origins of the anti-capitalist movement lay not with proletarian socialism but religious and aristocratic conservatism. We can think of many illustrations of this romantic critique of capitalism by conservative intellectuals: the English conservative intellectuals such as the (American) T. S. Eliot in *The Waste Land*, the protests against capitalist inauthenticity by the poet Rilke, the romantic philosophical anthropology of Arnold Gehlen, or the Stefan George Circle at Heidelberg. Perhaps Mannheim himself was a romantic critic, in the sense that planning was to restore order to the conflictual system of egoistic, anarchic capitalism. Finally, if we accept the arguments of Robert Nisbet (1967) in *The Sociological Tradition*, then the whole sociological movement of the late nineteenth century (including Durkheim, Simmel and Tönnies) was deeply influenced by the conservative reaction against capitalism. In the contemporary controversy surrounding Martin Heidegger's relationship to national socialism, there is a very clear illustration of this point: Victor Farias (1989) has shown all too clearly Heidegger's deep involvement in the fascist movement, especially within the German university system, and how this involvement was also part of a legacy of Catholic conservatism in South Germany which went back to the violently anti-Semitic ideas of Abraham a Sancta Clara. The principal enemies of his Swabian fatherland were American materialism and communist atheism. Whether or not Heidegger's political views during his rectorate were merely contingently related to his abstract philosophy is much disputed (Wolin 1990). What is remarkable, however, is how Heidegger's philosophy has been embraced, with the collapse of Marxism, by many sectors of the French left (Ferry and Renaut 1990). Similar issues have to be faced in the case of the politics of Paul de Man (Pels 1991). Any simple notion that being an intellectual means being a left-progressive intellectual is clearly fraught with difficulties.

Intellectuals perhaps should be defined not by reference to their relationship to 'progress' but in terms of their attitudes towards modernization. I put the question in this framework as a pretext for employing an argument by Ron Eyerman (1990) on intellectuals and progress to sketch out various approaches to the historical relationship between intellectuals and the processes of modernization. Eyerman points out that the very notion of an intellectual is a product of the Enlightenment response to modernization in the seventeenth and eighteenth centuries. The Enlightenment intellectuals, who are Mannheimian free-floating critics *par excellence*, produced the basic framework of modern analysis: social contract theory, individualism, scepticism, empiricism and secularity. Eyerman begins to define the intellectuals, therefore, as any group which challenges the existing order in the name of progress; in Mannheimian terms, they are utopians.

There are two versions of this notion of the intellectual as a progressive. The Marxist version is that intellectuals are a segment of the bourgeoisie which breaks away from its class roots to give an articulate expression to the class interests of the proletariat. The specific function of the intellectual is to universalize the particularistic character of working-class trade unionism; the intellectual transforms the local struggle of workers into a historic feature of the global process of revolution. However, as Eyerman points out, there is an ambiguity in Marxism. While in Marxist theory the intellectual must somehow depart from his/her bourgeois origins in order to provide a radical articulation of proletarian interests, there is also an anti-intellectualism in Marxism-Leninism which distrusts the intellectuals precisely because they are *déclassé*. The second approach to the intellectual as an agent of change came from a liberal tradition which sought to protect or to create a public arena in which radical ideas could be discussed and exchanged. The role of the intellectual is seen to be educative. The classic liberals in this tradition were, in England, J. S. Mill, Herbert Spencer and to some extent Mannheim himself. This is the intellectual as educator. Marxist and liberal accounts eventually converged around the importance of democracy against authoritarianism as the political context in which a free exchange of ideas can take place.

The main problem with this aspect of Eyerman's account is that he fails to identify a third response to modernization, namely the so-called conservative and Romantic response to modernization (in England for example from Edmund Burke through Shelley and Wordsworth to poets like T. S. Eliot and J. R. R. Tolkien). I assume he wants to exclude these on the grounds that they are not progressive, but I think this is a mistake. The Romantics were critical of existing conventions and customs; what they wanted to restore was a romanticised utopia of a lost world. The Romantics sought a rural arcadia and a modern version of the Land of Cockaygne. Their response to modernization was nostalgic and national-istic, but it was no less critical and radical. Again it is dangerous to generalise about 'Romanticism' as such. In England, the Lake poets were oppositional in working outside the court; their framework was the 'country', that is, a rural idyll and the nation (Butler 1988).

This great European tradition of the intellectuals was, according to Eyerman, eventually challenged by the entry of the state into the twenti-eth-century welfare system. With the emergence of a welfare consensus in the capitalist democracies, intellectuals were domesticated. They were no longer an external force outside the political system; they became professional academics as a consequence of the educational revolution of the 1950s; they became managers of an academic empire; or they were co-opted into the great army of social workers, welfare analysts and educational bureaucrats. In this regard, Eyerman adopts part of Jacoby's argument in *The Last Intellectuals*, although his own perception of the demise of the intellectuals is based on his analysis of the Swedish welfare system (Eyerman 1985).

Eyerman, however, wants to suggest an alternative future scenario. He argues that, while between the 1940s and 1950s intellectuals were incorporated into the system of agents of rational planning, the growth of alternative new social movements in the 1970s and 1980s (the women's movement, peace movements and the Greens) has created a new social role for the 'movement intellectual'.

However, the nature of this intellectual movement is rather different. The new social movements are, if anything, anti-progressive in the sense that they have questioned the value of unimpeded industrialization by developing alternative enterprises, and they have questioned the desir-ability of unification, universalism and globalism by defending localism. In fact, their response to modernity is, in the literal sense, reactionary, because new social movements are anti-progress. The 'movement intellectuals', according to Eyerman, operate outside the university complex and they are not members of a new middle-class intelligentsia.

This argument is clearly important. It provides an alternative to Jacoby's view that the intellectual died with the creation of the new university boom of the post-war period. It also takes account of the new interests of movement intellectuals: gender divisions, peace, alternative economies and ecology. His argument is underdeveloped, however, in at least three related areas. First, he fails to notice that the reaction against progressive industrialization, mass democracy and universalism was also the agenda of Romantic conservatives. Tolkien's mythologies were also condemnations of a world with street lighting, automobiles and industrial development just as Ludwig Klages of the Heidelberg George Circle (about whom Mannheim was very critical) wanted to return to more natural rhythms of pre-industrial societies in his notion of cosmic love. Heidegger's critical views (1977) on technology and Arnold Gehlen's critique (1980) of the processes of deinstitutionalization in the age of technology can also be regarded as radical conservative criticism of industrial capitalism. In the Weimar period and in the Third Reich, there was a general persistent intellectual relationship between the critique of technology and a conservative cultural reaction, which Herf (1984) calls 'reactionary modernism' as a reworking of the romantic tradition. The question is: How are the movement intellectuals of the 1990s different from the romantic critics of rational capitalism in the nineteenth century?

In passing, we can note that much of his debate was anticipated in the controversy surrounding Weber's 'Science as a vocation' (Gerth and Mills 1991), namely if rationality is self-defeating because it robs the world of the moral legitimation which makes rational inquiry purposeful, what options are still open? Weber of course tried to rule out mysticism and Romanticism as intellectual orientations which he thought were represented in his own day by the prophets around Stefan George. The ethic of responsibility, which calls intellectuals to face up to their times without the false supports of psychotherapy, religion, bohemianism or hedonism, was meant to provide a realistic, if minimalist, answer to the nihilistic implications of instrumental rationalism.

Second, Eyerman fails to consider the possible parallels between a romantic critique of industrialization and a postmodern critique of modernization. If postmodernism challenges modernism by bringing into question the possibility of a unified rationality, then there may be some intriguing possibilities in linking Romanticism and postmodernism. For some writers (Lash 1990), there are strong connections between the classical humanism of the Renaissance and postmodern critiques of the anti-humanism of modernity. While postmodernism is often identified with anti-political cynicism, it may be possible to identify a political or moral

program hidden inside postmodernism. This possibility further complicates the definition of 'progressive' as a basis for identifying oppositional
intellectuals.

Third, there is a weakness in Eyerman's position, because he is, in fact,
attempting to analyse the experience of the Swedish intelligentsia but he
wants to suggest that the incorporation of the intelligentsia in the middle
of the twentieth century was a common, global experience. There is at
least one important difference between the Swedish and other cases.
Eyerman wants to argue that in the nineteenth century intellectuals were
a diverse social group of marginalized, *déclassé* radicals, workers, poets
and private intellectuals, but the great expansion of the welfare state in
the twentieth century produced the state intellectual, regardless of
whether he or she worked in a university, the civil service administration
or wherever. One obvious problem with this generalization is that the
history of the welfare state is extremely different as between, for example,
Sweden, Britain and the United States. In the middle-class social democracies (Scandinavia) and the corporatist systems (Germany), state involvement is high, personal taxes are high and welfare is not confined to
stigmatized social groups. In the liberal welfare states of Great Britain
and the United States, the welfare system is residual, personal taxation
is low and welfare benefits are for target groups, such as the elderly and
the sick. In the liberal welfare states, intellectuals can and do have a
critical role to play, because they emerge as the advocates of the principle
of egalitarian redistribution and the idea of citizenship as necessary and
universal. In short, what we might call the 'Welfare Intellectual' is not
necessarily a co-opted agent of the state. The more important point is
that the role and place of universities in these diverse welfare systems
are also very different, and so the context of intellectual work must be
different. The theoretical point I am trying to make is that Eyerman
treats a specific case history – intellectuals in the context of the growth
of Swedish social democracy – as if it could, without qualification, be
generalized.

Although we can have some view on the global nature of the *fin de
siècle* and on the general functions of the intellectuals, we also need some
understanding of local circumstances and in particular on the indigenous
circumstances determining the role of intellectuals within national cultures. Although sociology, for example, has often aspired to be a science
of 'Man' (Hennis 1988), it typically reflects national problems and values
(Turner 1990a). In order to develop the notion of a 'specific intellectual',
we require a more elaborate understanding of the local conditions which
produce intellectuals.

Drawing extensively on the arguments of Perry Anderson (1964), it is
clear that without an English revolutionary transformation the English
intelligentsia never evolved to assume a critical and decisive social posi-

tion within English cultural life. The English intelligentsia, for these historical and structural reasons, has been unable to fulfil any national function in relation to, for example, the defence of the national language, the Church or the national culture. The English intellectuals have never successfully secured a structural location with a social class or other social stratum, for which they could act as guardian and defender. They have not formed an integrated or truly coherent social group. Although it is clear that Oxford and Cambridge have had a pivotal role in the reproduction of the dominant class, the universities in general have not provided a reliable or valid platform for the support of a national intelligentsia. English intellectuals in this respect have been distinctive by comparison with Irish and Scottish intellectuals, who have been an influential group in the development of a national culture.

If it is the case that England is characterized by an absent intelligentsia (Turner 1990b), it is not at all surprising that there is, in the educated English middle class, a deep embarrassment about the very notion of the intellectual, let alone an intelligentsia. Max Beloff (1985: 402) has noted that 'few Englishmen would have wished or would now wish to be called intellectuals'. English culture has been dominated by empiricism and pragmatism and, as a result, abstract or general theory does not flourish in English institutions. Utilitarianism has penetrated the universities, reinforcing and encouraging the native hostility to abstract thought, especially when undertaken by 'foreigners'. Hostility to abstraction and outsiders has been nicely illustrated in a recent special issue on British sociology in the *British Journal of Sociology* (Halsey 1989).

The enthusiasm for the study of intellectuals which is characteristic of North America, France and the Netherlands is largely absent in Britain. Indeed it is hard to imagine that volumes like Alvin Gouldner's *The Future of Intellectuals and the Rise of the New Class* (1979) or Arthur Kroker's *Technology and the Canadian Mind* (1984) could be written in England. Equally, Konrad and Szelenyi's *Intellectuals on the Road to Class Power* (1979), with its notion of the teleological role of the intellectual, could only make sense in a society in which the intellectual stands in some opposition to the party bureaucracy within a politically regulated system. Mannheim's aspirations about the intellectual as planner in a democratically reorganized post-war Europe probably had a similar cultural origin. The relationship between state and intellectual in England has had a very different character. The absence of a public role for the intellectual is related to the fact that historically the connection between the state and intellectuals in England has been distant and weak. The liberal tradition of the nightwatchman state, the late intervention of the state into higher education, the continuity of the celebration of amateurism, the ethic of the gentleman as scholar and the marginal role of the universities in the training of professionals have not created a public space for the intellectual as a significant figure in the making of public opinion.

A radical intelligentsia is typically the product of the cultural crisis which results from major structural transformations of a national society. These structural transformations are likely to be the consequence of massive class conflict, military takeover, economic collapse or a major natural disaster resulting in chronic epidemics and famine. These catastrophic events, when they pose a major threat to the continuity of a national culture, call forth and constitute a national intelligentsia. Under such crisis conditions, an intellectual stratum may become a self-conscious, committed and coherent intelligentsia. The classical illustrations of this thesis are the Russian and Hungarian intelligentsia. However, if we add to this account of crisis the consequences of large-scale migration and alienation, then further examples might include the Frankfurt School but also the Palestinian intelligentsia. Few English intellectuals could ever occupy the role which has been enjoyed in public by Edward Said.

Within this framework, it is the relative gradualism of English political history, the failure of any conquest after 1066 and the relative success of the state in imposing a national culture which explains the absence of a radical, organized intelligentsia. Here again this account of British history depends heavily on the work of Perry Anderson (1974), Barrington Moore (1968) and Michael Mann (1986). After the political conflicts of the seventeenth century, England made the transition from a traditional agrarian feudal society to capitalism without a successful revolutionary conflict between social classes. The 1688 settlement created some of the preconditions for a parliamentary system, which evolved by gradual steps through the eighteenth and nineteenth centuries. Because the English Civil War had curtailed the development of absolutism, the English state did not acquire a massive repressive apparatus; in the development of the state, the navy rather than a standing army had been the crucial issue. In short, the English upper classes had been demilitarized relatively early and English capitalist society assumed a number of specific features, namely a *laissez-faire* economy, class compromise, a common law tradition, individualism and a liberal political system.

The empiricism of English social thought and the rejection of idealism and grand theory meant that a general theory of (English) society did not develop, because English intellectuals were not called upon to theorise an alternative social system, or to provide a defence of liberal bourgeois democracy against a proletarian revolution or a fascist takeover. Intellectual life was dominated by the utilitarianism of Bentham and Mill, the empiricism of David Hume, the political philosophy of Locke and, later, by the middle-class idealism of T. H. Green. Although the Halévy thesis cannot be swallowed in its entirety, it is the case that Methodist principles probably did more to shape the everyday world of the nineteenth-century working class than either socialism or liberalism. Neither Hegelian nor Marxist grand theory acquired a significant following among the intellectuals.

Intellectual life in England was, and to some degree remains, divided into two separate and distinctive sectors. There is the tradition of the Oxbridge gentleman-academic, who is a person of 'independent means' and for whom the university functioned as a special club within which one could undertake scholarly research and professional engagements. Within this traditional setting, the gentleman-scholar was typically a writer of essays and articles rather than of systematic treatises, because the essay is more compatible with and symbolic of leisure and the cult of the amateur. The general essay avoids any hint of scientific specialization. The gentleman is independent, seeking no patronage from the state. Occasionally the gentleman-scholar might combine these activities with an ecclesiastical living. This habitus produced the concept of a 'fine mind', that is, an intellectual for whom brilliance comes naturally without effort, and whose talents might find expression simultaneously in almost any field from patristic theology to nuclear physics.

By contrast, there was the dissenting scientist of the provinces, whose academic interests were often adjacent to employment in business or industry. They are often associated with provincial scientific societies. These independent academies had often been created by dissenting religious groups (Baptists, Methodists and Quakers). There was an important cultural division between these provincial academies and the traditional elites in the Anglican Church and the ancient universities. To some extent, the origins of English sociology were in the dissenting, provincial milieu of the Midlands and northern England. Herbert Spencer, nonconformist, railway engineer and amateur scientist, was a typical example.

I have employed the idea of an 'absent' intelligentsia to characterise the English intellectual experience. Now the word 'absent' has a number of functions. It refers to the migrant English academics who have in waves left England to work in the United States and what used to be the Commonwealth. It indicates the absence of a cultural centre of the English social system. It refers to the absence of an English core to the global academic field, despite the dominance of English as an international language. It notes the absence of a genuine English model of the intelligentsia which is partly a function of English empiricism and its traditional hostility to universalistic, abstract thought. It points to the cultural ambivalence which surrounds describing oneself in English life as 'an intellectual'. It signifies the absence in England of any debate about intellectuals. Whereas in America there has been a great outpouring of self-critical analysis – *The Last Intellectuals* (Jacoby 1987); *The Winding Passage* (Bell 1980); *The Liberal Mind in a Conservative Age* (Pells 1985); *The New*

York Intellectuals (Wald 1986); *The Closing of the American Mind* (Bloom 1987) and *Prodigal Sons* (Bloom 1986) – there has been little or no discussion of 'the intellectuals' in British life which could compare.

The explanation for this absence has to be sought in a number of macro, long-term features of English social structure and history. The underlying assumption has been that a collection of anomic and anonymous intellectuals are forged into a coherent intelligentsia as a consequence of some massive cultural, social, moral or military threat. Let me highlight the important aspects of this claim. Much of the intellectual excitement of so-called white-settler societies (especially Australia, New Zealand and Canada), especially in the post-war period, has been generated by the cultural confrontation which has been produced by the question: 'What is the national character?' as a consequence of the impact of multi-culturalism on a traditional WASP host system. England by contrast had Englishness imposed on it by a powerful state from at least the sixteenth century. The state exercised a powerful orchestration and articulation of a moral view of English identity. Of course this cultural reach did not successfully include the Celtic fringe, but it is only in the last two decades that this cultural hegemony in England has begun to collapse. Tom Nairn's book *The Break-Up of Britain* (1977) signalled that the traditional consensus was under siege (especially from the Celtic fringe, and more recently from Islam). The affair surrounding Salman Rushdie's *Satanic Verses* has forced English intellectuals, possibly for the first time, to consider seriously what the British 'national identity' actually refers to (Asad 1993).

There is clearly a major issue relating to social class in England in relation to intellectuals. Historically, the great majority of English intellectuals (whether socialist, liberal or conservative) were recruited from the landed upper classes, they were trained within the London-Oxbridge axis, and they were often oppositional to bourgeois-industrial-provincial culture. The expansion of universities in the 1960s created a new stratum of university-trained social critics who were drawn from the middle and lower middle classes and who were educated (often in the social sciences) at provincial universities. Historically, intellectual adoption of Marxism, especially in a discipline like sociology which was largely confined to and contained within a group of provincial universities such as Leicester, Leeds and Hull, signified one's ideological separation from the traditional academic establishment. This social group of 'upstarts' was genuinely detached and *déclassé*, but it had little political or social influence in the system. Those radical academics who are recruited into the university establishment, such as Terry Eagleton, are self-defined outsiders, but they also retain an ambiguous relationship to working-class politics. They could neither connect with the trade-union leadership of the working class in the traditional Labour Party nor expand in any significant numbers into the radical circles of the old university elite. They were also absent. Radical English intellectuals have had an ambiguous relationship, therefore, to their working-class constituency, because their very success in academic terms necessarily cuts them off from their roots. The humorous aspects of these paradoxical social relationships have often been captured successfully in novels such as *The History Man*. In fact, much of the genuine social criticism which has existed in Britain in the post-war period was dominated by British humour. 'The Goon Show' created a new form of humour which, as a radio program, depended on linguistic absurdity. Although 'The Goon Show' provided a radical critique of the class structure it also celebrated English parochialism in its racist stereotyping. More recently, 'Monty Python's Flying Circus' is a form of humour which was originally a public-schoolboy protest against the cultural stupidity of the English class system. The absent English intelligentsia should be contrasted with the radical place of poets, artists and academics as a marginalised intelligentsia in Scotland, Ireland and Wales. The dominance of the cultural revival of Celtic identity – often led by the arts faculties of the Scottish and Welsh universities – can be taken as further support for my argument. Nevertheless, the English case remains something of an enigma. To take one example, between approximately 1945 and 1965, Great Britain witnessed the loss of one of the largest empires in human history, partly under military pressure and partly as a consequence of pragmatic politics and economic realism. Almost no trace of that loss can be found overtly in the intellectual culture of Britain.

The notion that the English intelligentsia has been absent is not to suggest that England has no intellects – far from it. As a counterweight to my own ironic view of intellectual life in England, I want briefly to discuss Perry Anderson's 'A culture in contraflow' (1990), which is primarily concerned with the nature of British intellectual life as it is expressed in the social sciences. I have argued that an intelligentsia arises in response to some major catastrophe or national crisis; for Anderson, the English catastrophe is to some extent Thatcherism. The very success of Thatcherism as a form of authoritarian populism has put left-wing, radical intellectuals to the test. The result, for Anderson, despite the failure and irrelevance of organized socialism, has been a remarkable cultural effervescence. He argues that out of that trial emerged 'the liveliest republic of letters in European socialism' (Anderson 1990: 44). As evidence of this cultural renaissance, he lists *Iron Britannia, Zero Option, Towards 2000, The Road to Wigan Pier Revisited, For a Socialist Pluralism, The Enchanted Glass, The Hard Road to Renewal, Politics for a Rational Left* and *Theatres of Memory*. He also draws our attention to a flurry of new journals which came into existence in the 1970s and 1980s which were typically not dependent on traditional cultural centres and covered the entire range of disciplines. The list includes *Marxism Today, Screen* (1969),

Radical Philosophy (1972), *Economy and Society* (1972), *Critique* (1973), *Oxford Literary Review* (1974), *Critique of Anthropology* (1974), *History Workshop* (1976), *Social History* (1976), *Capital and Class* (1977), *Cambridge Journal of Economics* (1977), *Feminist Review* (1979) and *Theory, Culture and Society* (1982). He also provides a detailed study of four academic figures whom he regards as major contributors to a significant re-evaluation of historical materialism, namely Michael Mann, Anthony Giddens, Ernest Gellner and W. G. Runciman (Hall 1989). In Anderson's view, these intellectual developments constitute a rebirth of British social thought and something approaching a late English intelligentsia.

There are obviously problems with Anderson's enthusiastic celebration of the British republic of letters. As he recognizes (Anderson 1990: 50), most of the best British academics work wholly or partly abroad – MacIntyre, McCabe, Lukes, Heritage, Mann and Anderson. Gellner is part of the white migration and Runciman is an example of the classic industrialist-scholar. For Anderson, also, the essential feature of British sociology is the development of 'large-scale theories of history' which in one way or another have engaged with the critique of Marxist historical materialism, but this judgement ignores some of the achievements and limitations of what many refer to as 'British cultural studies' (G. Turner 1990).

The study of culture in Britain has had a number of distinctive features, but perhaps the central issue has been a concern

> not so much with the relationship between socially shaped interests and knowledge (the German focus) or between the social structure and modes of thought (the dominant French perspective) but with the *natural intimacy* of culture and social relationships and structures – culture as the *way of life* of a people.
>
> (Robertson 1988b: 13).

To be more precise, cultural studies in Britain has been the study of the way of life of social class. The classic studies which laid the foundations for subsequent cultural studies were Richard Hoggart's *The Uses of Literacy* (1957) and Raymond Williams's *Culture and Society 1780–1950* (1958). While Hoggart's study of the impact of the media and commercialization on working-class culture in northern England was a nostalgic recreation of the idea of cultural wholeness, Williams's approach attempted, partly within the literary tradition of F. R. Leavis, to identify patterns of culture and structures of feeling which could be studied as cultural wholes. Another highly influential study from this period was of course E. P. Thompson's *The Making of the English Working Class* (1963), which had an important impact on the development of cultural studies, especially in terms of debates about agency/structure and the base/superstructure metaphor in Marx. These three studies established the paradigm of British cultural studies in its first wave: the notion of the serious academic as politically committed; middle-range theorizing with an antipathy to abstract thought; the merging of historical and anthropological techniques and assumptions about the pattern of cultural life; the privileging of the working class as the principal historical agent, and thus some notion of the working class as a community or *Gemeinschaft*; a nostalgic view of pre-industrial society as more authentic than urban industrial society; and, finally, a covert but resolute commitment to the study of English culture.

Recent historical commentaries on the development of cultural studies have viewed the emergence of British cultural studies as highly discontinuous. Following Terry Eagleton's early criticism in his *Criticism and Ideology* (1978) of the legacy of Williams, subsequent writers have noticed a decisive turn toward more abstract theory under the impact of Althusserian structuralism, a stronger preoccupation with the problems of ideological analysis, especially the Gramscian notion of 'hegemony', a greater openness to other theoretical traditions such as discourse analysis, and a subtle but important shift from the singular notion of culture to the plural view of cultures. These developments were in particular associated with the Birmingham Centre for Contemporary Cultural Studies, which had been established in 1964 under the directorship of Hoggart who was succeeded by Stuart Hall (in 1969), Richard Johnson (1979) and recently by Jorge Larrain. The work of the CCCS has obviously changed over time; the early emphasis on the mass media gave way to the analysis of subcultures; and subsequently new interests emerged around the analysis of texts, subjectivities and ideology.

There are three crucial aspects of British cultural studies which appear to be continuous underlying assumptions of research on culture. First, they have been obsessed with questions of class and ideology, and both have been approached within the paradigm which is heavily influenced by Althusser, Poulantzas and Gramsci. The main theoretical thrust of these approaches has been to break out of the legacy of the base/superstructure notion and the idea of a dominant ideology thesis (Abercrombie *et al.* 1980). Although there have been important and valuable developments in this area, the general problematic of neo-Marxism remains. Research in Britain has focused predominantly on the idea of popular culture as part of the ideological system which, in the last instance, can only be understood by reference to dominant and dominated classes. Thus, 'hegemony' may be a more complex notion than 'dominant ideology' but they still come out of the same stable. For example, David Morley's very important audience studies (1980), which did much to improve our ideas of reception theory, have not gone beyond the original paradigm of ideology. The main addition to the original Althusserian paradigm has been to reject the idea of the passive audience which is interpellated by ideology in favour of the idea of resistance (Hall and Jefferson

1976). Morley's version of reception theory shows that the way audiences receive messages is more active and more complex than orthodox Althusserian versions of ideology allow. The interest in Michel de Certeau's *The Practice of Everyday Life* (1984) is centred on the idea that in everyday life people appropriate space, technologies and utilities which they adapt to their own needs. Thus, while there has been much theoretical elaboration and empirical illustration, the dominant intellectual paradigm has focused on the production of culture and its ideological effects; 'In many accounts of the role of culture, there is a reluctance to face up to the fact that people derive pleasure from their cultural pursuits and that this pleasure requires explanation' (Abercrombie 1990: 199). This theoretical 'reluctance' is connected to the fact that the sociology of consumption in general is a neglected area of sociology. The absence of such a theory makes it very difficult for sociologists (not to mention economists) adequately to understand the *meaning* of consumption for social actors. Perhaps the only important contributions to this problem in recent years have been Colin Campbell's *The Romantic Ethic and the Spirit of Modern Consumerism* (1987), Nicholas Xenos's *Scarcity and Modernity* (1989) and Mary Douglas and Baron Isherwood's *The World of Goods* (1980).

The second feature is the continuing dependence on continental European social theory as the principal source of analytical inspiration. Of course, the strength of the Frankfurt School is still obvious in the notion of 'the culture industry' (Bernstein 1991), although Walter Benjamin's critique of those assumptions in his 'The work of art in the age of mechanical reproduction' in *Illuminations* (1973) has probably been the most influential single article in cultural studies. In recent years the influence of Althusser, Poulantzas and Gramsci has been partly replaced by that of Pierre Bourdieu, especially through his work on cultural capital (Bourdieu and Passeron 1990) and distinction (Bourdieu 1984). Here again Bourdieu has been acceptable within a British tradition because in some respects, his idea of 'cultural capital' supplements existing class-theoretical approaches to culture. Thus continental influences have partly overshadowed the legacy of Williams and Hoggart. Indeed although Williams is normally referred to in fairly reverential terms it is not clear how the Williams legacy will survive, because there is no distinctively Williams school. The dominance of the class/ideology paradigm has meant that important contributions from alternative paradigms have been somewhat marginalized. For example, Bernice Martin's *A Sociology of Contemporary Cultural Change* (1981) did not receive the attention which it so clearly deserved. From a different perspective, the bleak anti-Parsonian and anti-Bell sentiment of post-war British social theory meant that many important American contributions were precluded. Few British sociologists were willing to admit that Daniel Bell's *The Cultural Contradictions of Capitalism* (1976) remains one of the most important and innovative analyses of the relationship between economics, politics and culture of our period (Turner 1990c), or that in his work on values, norms and culture Talcott Parsons had placed cultural sociology at the top of his own research agenda. British theoreticism was both parasitic (on predominantly continental engagements with the ghost of Marx) and totally sectarian.

Third, English social theory acted as an intellectual conduit, whereby these limited selections from Marxist and post-Marxist authors in Paris and Frankfurt could be re-exported along with the migration of English academics themselves, to Auckland, Brisbane, Hong Kong, Adelaide, Toronto, Pittsburgh and California. The scale of this migration in the 1970s and 1980s has yet to be fully appreciated, but it has meant that the British version of cultural studies was successfully exported to a global audience, while the cultural homeland of this global phenomenon was slowly but surely stifled by the decay of British higher education under Thatcherism. It is global diaspora without a 'homeland' and without any self-consciousness of itself as a displaced social movement. Hence the impact of the British translation of European social theory is influential but highly dispersed and fragmented.

In this critical discussion of English intellectual life, I have tried to show that, within the context of the sociology of Mannheim, there is no national intelligentsia, that English intellectual life has been in many ways parasitic on continental European thought, that the legacy of Marxism and the sociology of knowledge have been dominant paradigms for understanding knowledge, ideology and culture and, finally, that this paradigm has been selective and sectarian. For example, while Bourdieu's notion of 'cultural capital' has been embraced by English sociologists (especially in the field of educational sociology), his more interesting notions about practice, habitus and field have received relatively little attention. British cultural studies have been primarily engaged with debates which grew out of a Marxist legacy – that of Althusser, Gramsci, Poulantzas – and with attacks on that legacy – Foucault, Barthes, Baudrillard. In this respect, the English intellectual scene has operated as a conduit between Europe and the global English-speaking community, but this role of intellectual mediation has been combined with a pronounced involvement with and focus on national English questions: primarily the historical transformation of working-class culture and the rise of mass culture. Despite changing theoretical paradigms and vocabulary, it has been centrally concerned with the transformation of a *gemeinschaftlich* working-class culture by commodification and commercialization. Soaps, TV series and films such as 'Coronation Street', 'Eastenders', 'Z-Cars', *Educating Rita* and 'Boys from the Black Stuff' have provided cultural sociologists with a rich documentation of these processes. In this respect, English intellectuals have seen themselves, at least implicitly and covertly, as

Mannheimian intellectuals whose function is to expose the ideological facade of inauthentic culture in pursuit of a utopian alternative of organic class culture. While the radical intelligentsia in Russia, the Middle East and France have been constituted by national struggles especially against external colonialization and military destruction, English intellectuals have been more typically mobilized around the defence of class. It is probably for this reason that English sociologists have typically embraced a *gemeinschaftlich* conception of the working class (Holton and Turner 1989: 160–96) as a combative community, and hence the notion of culture as a way of life which can be understood through the tools of literary analysis. Hoggart's celebrated chapter on the division of 'them' and 'us' is a classic illustration of this claim.

It could be objected that, while many of these claims were true, they are now hopelessly out of date. The impact of feminism, film theory, discourse analysis, postmodernism and deconstructive techniques has been either to demolish the traditional Marxist and neo-Marxist paradigms or at least to marginalize them. The defence of my argument would point to the fact that a number of recent general evaluations of 'culture' and 'cultural studies' (Brantlinger 1990; G. Turner 1990) have seen the specifically British contribution in terms of the couples incorporation/resistance and falsification/authenticity. To assume that Marxist paradigms are dead and buried is to underestimate the long-term impact of Thompson, Hoggart, Williams and the CCCS on British approaches to the field of culture. It is also to underestimate the central impact of literary theory, especially Eagleton (1978) and Macherey (1978) on both the social sciences and humanities. In this respect, Robert Young (1990: 21) strikes exactly the right note when he observed that 'For much of this century Marxist literary criticism monopolised the realm of literary theory, for the simple reason that only Marxists consistently believed in its value and strategic necessity'. However, precisely because these influences have been so powerful, the study of culture has not yet been successfully released from a set of narrow concerns about ideology and knowledge.

Part V

Modernity

Modernity

Chapter 12

From regulation to risk

The concept of risk is fundamental to any notion of modernity. The process of modernization involves a multiplication of risk for both individuals and social groups. One should not be surprised to discover that the theory of risk is central to all attempts to describe modern society. The concepts of risk, hazard and uncertainty have been fundamental to a number of social sciences. However, it is probably within economic theory that the analysis of risk has been particularly prominent as an analytical issue. Economics as a science deals with questions of scarcity and choice, and has focused particularly on problems of uncertainty in economic decision-making and with the inadequacies of knowledge with respect to the choice of economic aims and goals. The study of risk and insurance has been as a consequence a critical feature of the development of economic science. One can plausibly argue that the concept of risk first became prominent in the seventeenth century with the development of long-term trade based upon speculative investments. The growing interest in the problem of risk in relation to capital investments eventually spilled out into other areas of the scientific study of society and culture and analytical enquiry, including theology where philosophers like Pascal came to see faith itself as a personal gamble in a context of salvational risk. The theology of risk can be seen as a definite break with the idea of a divine order based upon regularity and certainty, in which God as a Divine Planner determined the course of history and the life of individuals. Within Protestant circles, because God's purpose could not be fully known, faith became an acute gamble against all the odds.

Within the social sciences in the nineteenth and twentieth centuries, there has been an important elaboration of these elementary notions of risk and uncertainty especially with the development of statistical techniques for the calculation of probabilities. Within economic history and economic theory, it is not surprising to find a central role allocated to the figure of the entrepreneur in the development of social change and economic accumulation. Obviously Karl Marx regarded capitalism as an economy within which the destructive force of trade and investment was a major feature of the process of social change, whereby the traditional securities of feudalism were blown apart by cheap commodities and the expansion of the market-place. Marxist economics, however, did not in the long run place much significance on the idea of entrepreneurial risk. Max Weber's economic sociology distinguished between the old adventure capitalism of the Elizabethan period and the eventual development of rational capitalism in which risk was minimized by long-term planning, the growth of an administrative infrastructure, an effective banking system and rational law. It was writers like Joseph Schumpeter (1939) who developed an economic theory of the capitalist entrepreneur within which the destructive capacities of entrepreneurial activity were seen to be crucial for economic accumulation and change. Furthermore, it was Schumpeter who thought that the indigenous process of economic rationalization and socialization within the capitalist economy would bring about the death of entrepreneurial speculation and risk-taking, with a resulting secular decline of economic activity. In the post-war period with the growth of Keynesian economic policies the theory of entrepreneurial activity went somewhat into decline, being replaced by a new emphasis on rational planning, the involvement of the state in economic change, and development of the welfare state as a cushion against the uncertainties and insecurities of the market-place. In response to the problems of market uncertainty and personal risk as a consequence of illness and unemployment, the welfare states of the post-war period developed an alternative conception of social security, by which the individual in periods of personal and social crisis could be protected from the full rigour of the risky nature of market-place activities. We have seen of course in the 1980s a return to the idea of free markets, monetaristic policies to encourage economic growth, and a significant erosion of welfare supports. It is within this context of the decline of social Keynesianism and a return to free market theories and *laissez-faire* principles that we should see the importance of Ulrich Beck's *Risk Society* (1992). Beck's theory is primarily concerned with the impact of globalization and deregulation within the broader process of the modernization of society. In sociology, it is clear that globalization as a theory of social change has brought about a resurrection of interest in the nature of risk, which is in turn connected with the process of postmodernization.

Various sociological models of the changing nature of capitalist society have been proposed in the wake of the decline of Keynesian economics and the corporatist state. Claus Offe, Scott Lash and John Urry have attempted to outline various aspects of the disorganization of capitalism. The idea of the end of organized capitalism has attempted to conceptualize some of the consequences of the freeing of financial markets, the inability of nation-states to solve their economic problems in isolation, and the general globalization of labour markets and capital transfers.

However, Beck's concept of risk society breaks with many of the assumptions of the periodisation of capitalism in conventional sociology. Beck has largely abandoned any idea of the historical transition from feudalism to competitive capitalism to monopoly capitalism in favour of a more elementary model which makes a basic contrast between traditional or premodern societies and modern societies. Within the concept of modernization, Beck draws a distinction between the incomplete modernization project of industrial society and the radicalized modernity of the present world to which he gives the title 'reflexive modernity'. For Beck, the uncertainties and hazards of the modernization project are not to be characterized by the idea of postmodernity, because he believes that the fragmentation and contradictions of modern society are a fundamental feature of the very process of modernization itself. In this respect, Anthony Giddens in *The Consequences of Modernity* (1990) also follows Beck's argument in suggesting that, rather than talking about postmodernity we should develop the idea of high modernity.

Within this framework, we can understand Beck's analysis of risk society as an attempt to provide a genuinely sociological approach to existing (economic) ideas about risk and uncertainty. Before proceeding to an analysis of Beck's conceptualization of risk, we might, however, note a rather important difference between economics and sociology as sciences of action. Talcott Parsons throughout much of his sociological career, particularly in the influential argument in *The Structure of Social Action* (1937), attempted to develop the notion that the social sciences were underpinned or held together by a general theory of action, and that this theory of action was voluntaristic, in the sense that it drew attention to the importance of the selection of means and ends for the satisfaction of wants. While the different sciences occupy different places within the Parsonian action scheme of goal-attainment, adaptation, integration and latency (politics, economics, sociology and psychology), they are analytically members of a general framework in Parsons's action-system theory (Holton and Turner 1989). In this respect, there is in principle no significant difference between economic and sociological theories of action, because they are both attempts to understand the problems of choice, the selection of means for desirable ends, and the problem of rational behaviour in situations of scarcity. Both economics and sociology attempt to develop theories about behaviour in these circumstances of risk, and both disciplines have at various levels been concerned with questions about choice, uncertainty and hazard. It was for this reason that Max Weber in attempting to establish a general set of concepts for the analysis of sociology in his *Economy and Society* (1968) developed various ideal types of social action, but within this scheme of different types of action he was particularly concerned with the idea of probabilities of action. In Weberian theories of social action, the notion of probable

types of action gives expression to the uncertainty of behaviour in conditions of scarcity, where knowledge and material means are inadequate.
In general terms, however, sociology has attempted to argue that social
behaviour is structured, and that randomness is not a common feature of
social interaction. There is a detailed and well-known discussion in
Weber's *Wissenschaftslehre* (Shils and Finch 1949) in which he argues,
following Kant, that we should not confuse randomness of action with
personal freedom. Weber's notion of personality as a coherent life-project
ruled out any idea that freedom was somehow an indeterminate and
undetermined state of affairs. For sociologists in the Parsonian tradition,
values and norms are critical for structuring the uncertainty of social
interaction. Social actions are in principle predictable.

Drawing upon anthropological research, sociologists have typically
argued that social actors cannot tolerate uncertainty and randomness, and
that they resort to various means whereby social circumstances can be
made predictable and certain. For example, in early theories of magic
and religion, following the work of Bronislaw Malinowski, sociologists
have argued that magical beliefs function to give a structure to otherwise
uncertain and unpredictable circumstances. Malinowski's observations on
the role of magic in giving a meaningful structure to the uncertainties of
outer-lagoon fishing by contrast with the relative absence of ritual and
magic in inner-lagoon fishing was the classical anthropological illustration
of this notion that magic functions to give a sense of predictability to
contexts of insecurity. In contemporary sociology, one could argue that
Niklas Luhmann's systems theory is also fundamentally concerned with
the management of risk. For Luhmann, systems function to reduce complexity, because they are efficient carriers of information. In reducing
'environmental' complexity, systems reduce risk.

While economics and sociology share this common interest in the problem of risk and predictability, there has been a major difference between
sociologists and economists in their general view of the character of
human societies. My claim here is that both sociology and anthropology
have taken an implicit view of human beings as creatures who cannot
tolerate unlimited risk, uncertainty and complexity. Human beings
respond culturally to risk with the overt aim of reducing riskful action
contexts. By contrast, economists have tended to view risk in a more
positive light; risk tends to be regarded as creative risk. The doctrine of
the 'hidden hand' suggested that the unintended consequences of actions
in an environment of scarcity and uncertainty were positive and beneficial.
At the level of societies, as distinct from arguments about human nature,
sociologists have tended to believe that with modernization societies will
become more regulated and organized; in other words, risk will decline
with the evolution of societies towards more regulated social systems. For
example, sociologists of capitalism have argued that the development of

capitalist society will in fact lead to more regulation, more organization and more constraint, because of the tendency for large-scale societies to become subject to such processes as bureaucratization. Weber's image or metaphor of advanced capitalist society was not the naked market-place of endlessly competing individuals engaged in an egoistic struggle over means and ends, but rather an iron cage in which the behaviour of individuals would become subordinated to the needs of a bureaucracy based upon the principles of instrumental rationalism. For Weber, modernization was rationalization, that is, the application of scientific knowledge to every area of everyday life, the erosion of magical and irrational beliefs and practices, the development of a money economy whereby contributions and wants could be measured with precision, the secularization of religious values, and the disenchantment of reality in favour of rational principles of efficiency and calculation. In a similar fashion, Emile Durkheim criticised the economic principles of the Manchester School, and was a bitter opponent of the egoistic utilitarianism of sociologists like Herbert Spencer. Durkheim thought that there was an inherent instability in modern societies which he described with the term anomie or normlessness. There was a great instability of norms and values in periods of economic crisis leading to pathological behaviour such as egoistic suicide. There are of course many problems with the concept of anomie (Lockwood 1992), but the use of the term in Durkheim's sociology is a rather useful indicator of his concern for the growing uncertainty and unpredictability of a society subject to major and unpredictable economic booms and slumps. This legacy from Durkheim and Weber eventually found its way into the so-called sociology of the problem of order, and it was again Parsons (1937) who developed a general theory of social order in which he criticized the legacy of economic theories of rational behaviour arguing that they could not solve the Hobbesian problem of order without inconsistently appropriating notions about collective sentiments, shared interests or common values.

It has often been thought that the sociology of social order has produced a somewhat conservative response to the analysis of social institutions and social relations. It has been suggested by critics of Parsons that an interest in social order has precluded a concern for social change based upon the conflict of interests and the struggle between social classes. However, while Marx often saw capitalist society as a chaotic system of inherently contradictory relations, the critical theory of the twentieth century has drawn more from the legacy of Weber's analysis of bureaucratic capitalism than it has from either Schumpeter's view of the entrepreneur or Marx's view of the inherent contradictions of the capitalist mode of production. Horkheimer and Adorno (1972) in their analysis of the *Dialectic of the Enlightenment* saw capitalist renunciation and regulation very much within the perspective of a Weberian analysis of the iron cage of bureaucracy. Capitalism negated the natural needs and instincts of human beings, channelling them towards a regulated society which was hostile to the development of human personality. The rise of Taylorism and Fordism convinced critical theorists from Gramsci onwards that capitalism imposed a detailed, regulated and scientific system of controls and organization. In recent years, Habermas's critical analysis of the contradictory relationship between the life-world and the social system has given a contemporary expression to this rather conventional notion that human interests and needs cannot be adequately satisfied in a society dominated by bureaucratic instrumental relations, and that the spread of science and bureaucratic social organisation destroys the life-world of individuals. Social system and everyday life are seen to be contradictory.

Of course, Habermas, as a contemporary exponent of a tradition of critical theory which goes back to Marx's analysis of capitalism, has in *Legitimation Crisis* (1976) drawn attention to the inherent contradictions within capitalist society and to the unpredictable nature of capitalist institutions. However, the dominant image of modern society in critical theory and in Habermas's sociology is that of the regulated system, which orders and organizes reality in ways which are often incompatible with the human needs of individuals. Furthermore, within German sociology, while there have been major disagreements with the legacy of Marx and Habermas, much of the analysis of modern society has focused on the idea of its systematicity and regulation. Indeed, as I have indicated, the basic idea behind Luhmann's analysis of social systems is precisely that systems function to reduce complexity and uncertainty, and that systematization is a necessary requirement for functional communication which reduces 'noise'. In his recent analysis of the social effects of 'McDonaldization', George Ritzer (1993) has continued the tradition of Weber's theory of rationalization by treating the application of Fordism to the fast food industry as an illustration of the growing impact of instrumental rationality on everyday life. The point of McDonaldization is to remove unpredictable circumstances from both the production and consumption of food. By eliminating 'surprises' from the consumption of food, McDonaldization also removes risk.

I have drawn attention to various traditions within sociology which paradoxically suggest that modernization produces more regulation, more organization and more predictability in social life. While the underlying economic and class relations of capitalism may be chaotic and contradictory, various writers from a wide variety of political backgrounds have noted that bureaucracy, scientific administration, the development of a rational money system, McDonaldization, the organization of commercial and criminal law, and the functional organization of the state have all contributed to the stabilization and regulation of social relations in a capitalist economy. This stability of capitalist social order may be periodically punctured by booms and slumps in the economy, by military catastrophe, or occasionally by natural disasters, but the dominant image has been that of the iron cage in Weberian sociology, the theme of discipline and panopticism in the work of Foucault, the concept of 'the administered society' in Adorno, and so forth; that is, an image suggesting that social relations become more rather than less regulated and organized. My argument is that the implication of these perspectives is that risk declines rather than increases with the development of capitalism.

These arguments about regulation and risk have been central to much of economic sociology and in particular to those branches of sociology which have been significantly influenced by the work of Marx, Weber and Schumpeter. However, there are other types of sociology which also see modern society as more rather than less regulated and stabilized which do not draw their inspiration from these economistic arguments. As I have briefly noted, there is an important strand in sociological theory which suggests that human beings, either individually or collectively, cannot tolerate a high level of uncertainty and unpredictability in social relations. Much of the research of anthropology has been concerned with the problem of how primitive societies, or at least societies with rather low levels of technical resources, cope with the inevitable unpredictability and uncertainty of social life, especially in an environment where natural resources may be limited or uncertain. In general, anthropologists such as Mary Douglas have developed the argument that all human societies construct elaborate cosmologies which attempt to make social relations meaningful and predictable against the background of inevitable uncertainty and anxiety. It is for this reason that Douglas has suggested that a fundamental dichotomy within these cosmologies is that between purity and danger. Sociological approaches to individual anxiety and uncertainty have also been influenced by the work of Arnold Gehlen (1988) and Sigmund Freud, and these social theorists have been concerned with questions of plausibility and legitimacy on the one hand, and with the regulation of inter-personal contact by the processes of culture and civilization on the other.

We can briefly examine two versions of this type of argument in the work of Peter Berger (1969) and Norbert Elias (1978). Following the philosophical anthropology of Gehlen, Berger has argued that human beings are biologically unfinished and that they require culture to structure the life-world which they inhabit. Within nature, the animal world is organized by instincts, but human beings live in an instinctually open reality, where culture and institutions function to regulate human needs, desires and interests. It follows that social reality is socially constructed, and that societies resist any threat to this sacred canopy; culture is always surrounded by the threat of anarchy, and anomie. All social organizations require plausibility structures which defend individuals and groups from the possibility of anomie, and which constantly reproduce the cultural assumptions which normatively underpin such social relations. Risk and uncertainty in social life represent, as it were, a sociological version of the religious problem of theodicy, because they constantly challenge and threaten the nomos of social reality. Within this paradigm, social institutions exist to minimize and preclude risk. However, modern societies are peculiarly unstable and the plausibility structures of modern societies are tenuous and precarious. Modern life is precarious because of its complexity, and because the differentiation of social spheres and institutions is accompanied by a pluralization of life-worlds which in turn results in a greater complexity of values and norms. We may regard secularization in this context as an erosion of the stability and facticity of meaning structures, which are thereby rendered constantly implausible. As a result modern individuals frequently become detached from these traditional institutions and structures, and are significantly exposed to the challenge of scientific rationalism, the pluralism of values, and the secularization of society. As I have argued in earlier chapters, fundamentalism in both Christianity and Islam is a response to these changes to everyday life. Pluralism means that individuals experience societies rather like supermarkets within which they are offered a multiplicity of lifestyles and values. The globalization of culture tends to reinforce this experience of the diversity and differences of cultural life. Pluralism cannot be avoided. This view of society has been shared by a number of sociologists, who draw the conclusion that societies cannot exist on the basis of this complex pluralism. Much of the conservative thinking about pluralism has been influenced by Helmut Schelsky's concept of 'permanent reflectiveness' in which he asked whether constant questioning of social institutions was compatible with stable social life. Sociologists, who doubt that the complete secularization of society is possible, have argued that modernization must be a limited project and that there has to be some maintenance of a system of common values and institutions whereby the risky, uncertain and unplausible character of modern life could be contained.

Finally, we can turn to Norbert Elias's general theory of the civilizational process (1978), which I want to treat as an argument which suggests that modern life becomes more rather than less regulated as a consequence of the spread of civilized norms and values regulating individual aggressive behaviour. There has been much debate about the intellectual background and origins of Elias's general theory of civilization. In the context of this discussion, however, it is important to recognise Elias's dependence on a Freudian psychoanalytic theory of instincts; we can see Elias's work as a sociological version of Freud's arguments in *Civilisation and its Discontents*. While Freud's analysis of the contradictions between civilization and instinct was largely ahistorical, the strength of Elias's theory is the attempt to locate the debate about civilizational processes within a clear view of the relationship between feudalism and bourgeois society, and between civilization and the growth of a modern state. Briefly, Elias argued that in premodern societies based upon a warrior ethic, inter-personal behaviour was typically unregulated, and disputes and arguments were characteristically solved by resort to violent means. The man of arms was the ideal of feudal society, and as a result strong emotions and passions were celebrated and cherished. With the development of court society, however, these violent relations between men had to be modified in the interests of a new social order and a new code of courtly behaviour emerged celebrating the ideals of the civilized knight, who exercised restraint and compassion towards the weak, the elderly, women and children. These court values were elaborate and complex; particular attention was given to questions of etiquette, inter-personal behaviour and comportment. Civilization produced inter-personal civility. Elias draws attention to the interesting development of table manners and table utensils, so that with the evolution of medieval society men came to eat at table without knives, swords or spears. Instead, particular moral emphasis was given to good manners, including the proper management of bodily secretions. These behaviour patterns gave rise to a whole culture of courtesy within which social order came to depend upon self-restraint and regulation rather than on force and violence. With the development of the modern state, the demilitarization of the aristocracy and the decline of medieval institutions, new patterns of behaviour emerged which were associated with such groups as the bourgeoisie and civil servants within the state apparatus. There followed a greater emphasis on individualism and education, and eventually the idea of the gentleman cultivated by education replaced the image of the courtier and the knight. Aristocratic values were gradually replaced in Germany, France and England by the bourgeois values of privacy, education and bourgeois civility.

Now we can see Elias's theory of society as a theory of moral regulation which has the consequence of reducing uncertainty in social life, because we can predict the behaviour of persons, especially strangers, on the assumption that their instinctual behaviour has been socialized and regulated by certain cultural values and norms. According to this theory, inter-personal violence should diminish with the growth of civilization and, as a consequence, the unpredictable nature of encounters with strangers should also diminish. These norms of control between strangers are obviously important for societies which are being transformed by a globalization. In this sense, we can say that a civilized society is a regulated society in which the risky relations between strangers are contained and controlled.

There are a number of important problems within Elias's theory, which relate directly to this question of risk. A number of writers have drawn attention to a fundamental historical problem in Elias's theory, namely that it was written on the eve of the fascist takeover of Germany, which was in turn the context of the Holocaust. Fascism as an ideology drew heavily upon militaristic values, emphasized the instinctual life, drew much of its imagery from sexual violence and celebrated the values of blood and soil. We can, however, regard the Holocaust not as an aberration in the modernization process but precisely as an expression of rational organization, regulation and instrumental rationalism. Bauman, in his famous study of the Holocaust (Bauman 1989), attempts to show that the destruction of the Jews was compatible with the very core values of modernization and civilisation. Another objection to Elias's theory would be to question whether the theory of the civilizational process has any comparative value. For example, it is unclear whether Elias's arguments would apply satisfactorily to the history of Japanese feudalism or, taking a contemporary society, the widespread availability of firearms in American culture might be viewed as an argument that modernization does not necessarily bring about the demilitarization of the population, or the monopolistic transfer of the means of violence to the state. In short, Elias's theory of moral regulation represents a particularly German view of the relationship between culture and civilization, which cannot be easily extended to societies like Britain and North America.

These historical and comparative criticisms of Elias may not be the most appropriate in the context of my argument about civilization and risk. A more interesting commentary on Elias's theory of civilization has been presented by Cas Wouters (1986) who has argued, commenting on the youth movements of the 1960s and the oppositional cultural movements of the 1970s, that on the basis of a formalization of values by the norms of civilization, we have seen in various societies a strong informalization of social norms and values. Informalization suggests that there is no necessary evolutionary development towards more formal norms of inter-personal relations and regulation, but there can be distinctive shifts in the pattern of civilizational processes. Wouters has made an important contribution to Elias's theory of society; we can assume that an informalization of social relations will in fact increase the uncertainty and risk which is involved in social relations which have to be constantly negotiated and renegotiated.

We can now proceed, having considered various aspects of the relationship between risk and regulation in social science, to a more explicit and detailed account of Beck's influential analysis of the risky character of contemporary society. In an advanced industrial society, risk is increasingly a function of our very dependence on social institutions, such as the state, professional medicine and the labour market. Risk grows out of the essential social precariousness of such institutionalized patterns of existence. In the context of high modernity within an advanced capitalist system, risk follows from the production of wealth itself. Whereas risks in traditional and early modern society were primarily personal, now they are global and they threaten the entire system of human societies. For Beck, therefore, traditional risks were obvious, palpable and observable, whereas today's risks often escape easy detection; they are not necessarily palpable. Beck does not argue that risk is merely the product of contemporary circumstances, because the very concept of risk is obviously indigenous to social science as such. However, the transformations of modern society are so profound that risks in modern society can no longer be adequately calculated according to existing paradigms. Ecological crises, which are treated by Beck as direct effects of modernization, are inevitably global. For example, the threats to life which are a consequence of atomic accidents are simply not regarded as insurable risks. There is no easy method for calculating the insurance risks of interplanetary travel.

While Beck does not provide a clear definition of risk, we can detect certain broad assumptions behind his account. Environmental risks often do irreversible harm, but they generally remain invisible and as a result they are under the scrutiny of legal and scientific professions which become central to the modern political process. The nature of modern risk also illustrates the problem of the nation-state in the context of these environmental and scientific risks, because risks no longer respect national boundaries; risk society is a globalized society, because many of the hazards and problems of contemporary society derive from a general environmental and scientific crisis. The debate about the nature of risk and its political importance becomes central to the whole international context of governmental negotiations.

For Beck, the modern character of risk is radically different from those hazards and difficulties which characterized traditional and early modern societies. As we have seen, risks are no longer observable, local and personal. They are unobservable, global and impersonal. In addition, risks have become, as it were, democratized because they have an impact on all human existence, and they are no longer simply hierarchical. Beck argues that 'poverty is hierarchic; smog is democratic' (Beck 1992: 36). In this respect, Beck insists upon what he calls the boomerang effect, that is the diffusion of risks beyond the origins to all social classes regardless of their power and wealth. It is clear that the working classes are still the most exposed to contemporary environmental risk, but risk becomes generalized and crosses the class structure.

These observations on the modern nature of risk lead Beck to make some important comments on the character of solidarity in contemporary societies. For example, he argues that, while solidarity in premodern societies was based upon need, the solidarity of the contemporary world is based upon anxiety. That is, societies were organized to protect themselves against lack and most welfare systems were articulated around some notion of need and necessity. However, contemporary societies are often societies of abundance, but they are bound together by a common appreciation of the nature of globalized risk and uncertainty. As a result, the political goals and ambitions of modern governments tend not to express positive views about growth and wealth, but negative views about the containment of existing dangers and problems.

In arguing that environmental pollution and disaster have produced a new type of risk, Beck may not be saying anything particularly original but merely articulating the political concerns and viewpoints of various aspects of the green movement. However, Beck's thesis may be more interesting when we realize that he is basically arguing that the risks of modern society are the unintended but inevitable consequences of the very process of modernization, and in particular they are the product of the scientific management of society and nature. The result has been a major politicization of science, because science and scientific bureaucracies attempt to deny or obscure the character of environmental and scientific risks by attempting to develop the apparently neutral concept of 'acceptable levels' of risk. It is the application of instrumental rationalism in the form of science to the production of wealth and the management of nature which is itself the core of the risk society, because the unintended consequences of this rationality are in fact to destabilize human societies, or at least to open them up to overwhelming hazard.

Beck illustrates these arguments through a number of examples, but his commentary on medical science, medical professionalization and patient risk is central to his general thesis (Beck 1992: 205–14). Medical practice is protected by the development of the clinic. This institution provides an organizational roof where research, medical training and practice can be securely interconnected. It is within this context that medicine operates in what Beck calls an arena of 'sub-politics', that is, medicine can bypass the formal political structures of parties and parliaments to develop its own interests and power base. In short, medicine in the clinic and the experimental laboratory operates beyond the regulation of the law and the state. Given the speed of medical development and technological innovation, the general public is typically presented with the results of problems of medical innovation long after they are relatively well established in experimental medicine. Beck calls this 'a policy of *faits accomplis*' (Beck 1992: 210). Some negative illustrations of this policy would include thalidomide babies, 'mad cow disease' and inadvertent forms of Creutzfeld Jakob Disease.

Beck's critical attitude towards scientific rationalism may be traced back to earlier attacks on instrumental rationalism in Weber and the critical theorists. However, Beck's argument, while overtly about the nature of risk, may be more accurately perceived as a theory of reflexive modernization. In order to appreciate more fully the nature of Beck's thesis, we can concentrate briefly on his idea of reflexivity. Now clearly the notion of reflexivity includes that of self-reflexive rational criticism and self-reflexive critical inspection. Reflexivity in this sense implies a constant critical discussion or analysis of the circumstances of modernity at both the personal and institutional level. Here again Beck's argument may follow an earlier Weberian model of modernization as rationaliz-ation, that is, the application of critical scientific knowledge to the every-day world and everyday social reality. Risk society is associated with a new form of individualism in which the self becomes a project. However, it is probably a mistake to place the burden of this notional reflexivity at this subjective level. Beck's concept of risk is based upon the idea that modernization brings about a multiplication of the problems and contra-dictions which beset modern institutions and, as a result, social institutions become reflexive in the sense that the weight and complexity of the problems which they face forces them into processes of collective self-evaluation and relegitimization. Modernization as problematization pro-duces an increase in the contradictions within institutions, threatening their continuity and stability. These processes of problematization and contradiction are conceptualized by Beck as a process of de-traditionaliz-ation. Here again, one can assume that Weber's views on the erosion of tradition and charisma as sources of value must be influential in Beck's account of de-traditionalization as modern reflexivity. Because Beck sees industrial society as an incomplete project of radical modernity, he places a special emphasis on the individualizing process of late modernization. He notes that 'the process of individualisation is conceptualised theoreti-cally as the product of reflexivity, in which the process of modernisation as protected by the welfare state de-traditionalizes the ways of living built into industrial society' (Beck 1992: 153).

Beck's principal illustrations of these patterns of reflexive modernity are taken from the complexities of family life, the problems of scientific legitimacy, the instabilities of the flexible labour market and the negative consequences of the medicalization of life. For Beck, it is the family which perhaps most clearly illustrates these contradictions and tensions, because sexual relations as ascriptive relations are particularly problematic within an advanced modern system which is overtly based upon achievement and equality. The ascriptive nature of gender is rather like a modern estate or feudal relationship inside modernization itself. In fact, market society should have been a society without the family at all and ultimately without children. The creative and destructive pattern of market relations, based upon assumptions of achievement and universality, should have broken down the ascriptive character of familial and gender relations. The family has been drawn into the project of reflexive modernization, because it is a social institution which is riddled with contradictions and difficulties, and in particular a contradiction between the growing demands for high-quality childcare and motherhood as against the demands of economic participation which is experienced by both partners. The demands for intimacy and interaction with children are not easily reconciled with part-time or full-time employment. These tensions within the family are only too easily illustrated by high levels of divorce and domestic violence. In some respects, we can regard Anthony Giddens's arguments in *The Transformation of Intimacy* (1992) as an elaboration of this idea that there is a fundamental set of contradictions between the demands for intimacy, or the pure relationship as Giddens calls it, and the broader demands for egalitarian participation within the public sphere.

I have now presented Beck's argument about risk within the context of the broader consideration of the relationship between regulation and risk. This analysis can now be drawn to a conclusion with a consideration of some possible criticisms of Beck's position. Beck could be criticized on the grounds that he has failed to take into account earlier analyses of risk and uncertainty, and therefore tends to present his own argument as if it were a completely new perspective on society. The absence of any discussion of the anthropology of risk in the work of Mary Douglas is peculiar. For example, Beck's analysis of uncertainty and flexibility in the labour market, and his general concern for the impact of communication and technology on existing society could in some ways be seen as a modern version of Daniel Bell's analysis of post-industrial society. More generally speaking, Beck's concept of risk society is probably best seen as a sociological version of economic arguments about post-Fordism and deregulation. Although Beck wants to locate the notion of risk within the idea of scientific rationalism, the general sense of risk and hazard in advanced industrial societies is a specific consequence of the decline of social Keynesianism, and thus a consequence of the application of economic rationalism in advanced capitalism. Risk, for the great majority of citizens, particularly those who are in some respects socially dependent, is a function of the transformation of welfare capitalism, the political attack on the very notion of social security and the globalization of deregulation. Thatcherism, in so far as it was an attack on the so-called 'nanny state', was thus an ideological confrontation with earlier notions of the importance of security, and the debate about risk should therefore at least be located within these quite specific political struggles over the nature of the welfare state.

Perhaps a more serious criticism of Beck's arguments would be to suggest that risk has not changed so profoundly and significantly over the last three centuries. For example, were the epidemics of syphilis and bubonic plague in earlier periods any different from the modern environmental illnesses to which Beck draws our attention? That is, do Beck's criteria of risk, such as their impersonal and unobservable nature, really stand up to historical scrutiny? The devastating plagues of earlier centuries were certainly global, democratic and general. Peasants and aristocrats died equally horrible deaths. In addition, with the spread of capitalist colonialism, it is clearly the case that in previous centuries many aboriginal peoples such as those of North America and Australia were engulfed by environmental, medical and political catastrophes which wiped out entire populations. If we take a broader view of the notion of risk as entailing at least a strong cultural element whereby risk is seen to be a necessary part of the human condition, then we could argue that the profound uncertainties about life, which occasionally overwhelmed earlier civilizations, were not unlike the anxieties of our own *fin-de-siècle* civilizations. The seventeenth-century crisis, which was often accompanied by witchcraft movements, spiritual uncertainty and social instability gave rise to a Baroque mentality which can be seen to be the cultural and personal elaboration of these notions of risk and hazard. Perhaps as I have suggested earlier the analysis of risk should be seen within a more general sociological discussion of the theodicy problem. Within the tradition of writers like Gehlen, Berger and Luckmann the specific nature of modern risk has to be seen as merely an illustration of the more general notion of contingency in human and social life. The implications of Berger's view of social construction is that there are likely to be quite distinctive responses to the multiplication of risk, which is in various ways to reassert the importance of a sacred canopy. Risk will produce 'religion', by which I mean any generalized view of social reality which emphasizes the meaningfulness of social existence against the threat of chaos and disorder. Beck appears to neglect the question: Are there any predictable limitations to the multiplication of risk? I have already suggested through an examination of Berger and Elias that one might as a sociologist expect certain societal responses to the democratization of risk, the multiplication of contradictions, and the elaboration of hazard.

There does not appear to be an easy or obvious answer to the question: Has life become inherently more risky? From an historical perspective, one can imagine that a sociologist who had been educated in the tradition of Elias might want to argue that, on the contrary, everyday life becomes more predictable, more secure and more comprehensible as a consequence of a long-term process of civilization which has contained and regulated violence and inter-personal abuse. One potential solution to this sociological difficulty would be to suggest that we should examine risk at different levels. Crudely speaking, if we draw a distinction between the micro and the macro level, it could be argued that everyday life has become more secure for reasons which are contained within Elias's view

of civilizational norms. In addition, one might add that legislative attempts
to regulate everyday life, combined with a powerful bureaucracy and
state administration have indeed created the conditions whereby risk,
uncertainty and violence might be minimized at the everyday level. However, there do appear to be good reasons for accepting Beck's view of
the macro risks of a modern globalized society where environmental
hazard, industrial pollution, food contamination, and the uncertainties of
the deregulated economy have produced incalculable levels of risk for
modern individuals. Within the advanced societies, as a consequence of
the modernization process, there is an obvious contradiction between the
subjective experience of everyday normality and the global or macro
condition of hazard.

Chapter 13

The self and reflexive modernity

In this collection of essays I have been concerned to identify important connections between three social phenomena, namely, orientalism, postmodernism and globalization. In this chapter I am primarily interested in the debate about postmodern social theory, with special reference to the issue of the reflexive self and the body. However, the linking theme in these essays has in fact been the emergence and development of globalism, which is producing a new cultural context within which intellectuals are forced to operate and, at the same time, the process of cultural globalization is transforming the nature of intellectual work. Globalization has resulted in a new level of multiculturalism which has challenged much of the traditional dominant cultures of nation-states. The constant reproduction of the old high culture of the elite is now problematic and has been questioned by marginal groups within the nation-state and by educated groups rising to cultural dominance as a consequence of decolonization. In addition, globalization has rendered much of the discussion of East and West in orientalism redundant. From the seventeenth century onwards, orientalism had constituted a profound sense of otherness with respect to alien cultures. This sense of otherness was in fact the foundation of the anthropological project in traditional society (Hodgen 1964). This colonial experience of otherness was a significant problem for the idea of a great chain of being within which God had determined the status of both animal and human species. With globalization and the emergence of multicultural politics as a prominent dimension of all political systems, the sense of the strangeness of the outside world is difficult to sustain since the other has been, as it were, imported into all societies as a consequence of human mobility, migration and tourism. Otherness has been domesticated. Of course, with the collapse of communism and the erosion of the traditional cold-war politics of the post-war period, Islam may well function as a substitute for the dangers represented by a communist menace. However, while communism was associated with the outside and the threat of Soviet military aggression, Islam is increasingly, as it were, part of the 'inside' of the Western world. Islam functions as a profound cultural challenge to the Western political system, but this challenge is from within. I have noted in previous chapters the strange impact of the Rushdie affair in Britain which has served to generate a debate about the nature of British identity, because the British cultural elite has been forced into a recognition of the emergence of a multi-cultural civil society in the United Kingdom. The same issues are also significant, for example in Germany and the Netherlands. Because Dutch society has constitutionally recognized the existence of separate communities in the United Provinces, which have been traditionally referred to as pillars, it is difficult for the Dutch system to resist the process whereby Islam will itself become a new pillar in Dutch society, alongside the Catholic, Protestant and humanistic pillars. In the post-war situation, Germany had, comparatively speaking, a relatively homogenous ethnic base to the state, but the increase in Turkish migrant workers and other migrant communities in the 1980s has posed a problem for social order in the new united Germany. It is difficult to see how, in this context, Islam could be easily assimilated, given the fundamentalization of Islam which requires separate legal and social conditions for its members.

I have also taken the view in this collection of essays that globalization is one of the social causes of the postmodernization of culture. Globalization brings about increasing diversification and complexity of cultures by interposing a variety of traditions within a given community. Cultural globalization, therefore, forces upon modern societies, and upon intellectuals in particular, a new reflexivity about the authenticity of cultures, their social status and the nature of cultural hierarchy. Although human societies have always been faced with the issue of alien cultures and foreign intervention, globalization is producing a completely new level of multiculturalism and cultural diversity. This cultural diversity cannot be simply ignored and my argument, therefore, is that globalization requires a new cultural reflexivity, which in turn gives a special role to the intellectual as passing a judgement on the nature of national cultures. The old anthropological problematic of alien cultures becomes a persistent theme of modern intellectual enquiry as such, because nation-states are forced to enquire into the character of their national cultural identities. Globalization raises the possibility that all cultural systems are local cultures, because it is difficult to sustain the idea, for example, that British culture is a global culture. Reflexivity and cultural propinquity in a global context also produces a new focus on the self in postmodernity, because the relation between individual and national identity becomes highly unstable and uncertain.

Postmodernity is typically analysed as an effect of new technical means of communication and new patterns of information storage. In popular culture, the impact of radio, television, film and video on attitudes and practice has been enormous. The experiential impact of virtual reality is to suggest in a relatively direct way that the simulation of reality is technically feasible. Cultural postmodernism is also seen by sociologists to be a broad social response to rational modernism, particularly in architecture and domestic design. My intention is not to reject these theories of the social causes of the process of postmodernization; the point of my argument is to draw attention to the special role of globalization in the social production of postmodernity. Within this scenario, cultural tourism is a particularly potent force in the postmodern diversification of cultural experience. Global tourism increases intercultural exchange and forces cultural elites to come to terms with the heritage industry. Tourist fantasy permits the self to assume diverse social roles in exotic settings; tourism invents and demands empathy to play out short-term fantasy roles. Tourism tends to make cultures into museums, as cultural phenomena which can be viewed as quaint, peculiar and local. Tourism paradoxically is a quest for authentic local cultures, but the tourist industry, by creating an illusion of authenticity, in fact reinforces the experience of social and cultural simulation. The very existence of tourism rules out the possibility of authentic cultural experience. More importantly, ethnic or national cultures become local or folk cultures which are available to the tourist gaze.

As an illustration of this argument we could take Jean Baudrillard's account of *America* (1988). We can treat Baudrillard's study as in fact an intellectual tourist commentary on American postmodern culture. In particular, the style of Baudrillard's work creates the illusion of a car journey across the American landscape. A postmodern style of reading involves channel-hopping, random grazing and depthless scanning rather like a tourist pursuing culture through an *ad hoc* sample process (Rojek and Turner 1993). The implication of postmodernism, therefore, is that in the postmodern world we are all tourists or, to use a term which is full of sociological significance, strangers in our own society. Thus the global diversity of cultures creates an alien environment in which all cultures appear strange. The counterpart of course for postmodern cultural alienation is nostalgia, that is, the nostalgic quest for real communities, real experience and real culture. Postmodernization produces a profound sense of the artificial and constructed nature of both social arrangements and cultural forms. All cultural artefacts appear, therefore, to be mere artefacts.

It is important to recognize that the process of postmodernization is also in many respects a process of secularization, because it is difficult for religions to protect themselves from the critique of postmodern culture which regards all religious accounts of the world as merely 'grand narratives'. Secularization is an essential ingredient to the idea of the reflexive self and most traditional theories of the self, individualism and individuality have assumed a profound process of social disenchantment of belief.

Pluralistic belief, random commitment and religious experimentation would be compatible with a postmodern lifestyle, that is, with the idea of secularization as cultural pluralism. Postmodernism makes commitment to a single grand narrative unlikely. However, I do not want to suggest that the secularization of the faith takes place at this merely cognitive or intellectual level. It is not the case that people stop believing in God merely as a consequence of rational criticism, rather they stop believing in God when religious belief is eroded by transformations of everyday life which make belief either irrelevant or impossible. The postmoderniz-ation of culture in creating an experience of artificiality also brings religion into question at this everyday level. The multiplication of religious faiths in a multicultural society has in this everyday world a profoundly relativizing effect. This relativism is not of the old atheistic type about which Ernest Gellner has written in his *Postmodernism, Reason and Religion* (1992). The relativism of postmodern cultures is more to do with the daily experience of consumerism in a context of global diversity and difference; in short, we have to see experiential secularity as the product of globalization. While Gellner has attempted to treat postmodernism as simply philosophical relativism, my argument has attempted to examine the impact of consumerism and postmodern cultural diversity on everyday experience and practice. In turn, fundamentalism should be regarded as a religious response to globalization, multiculturalism and postmodern pluralism. Western consumerism erodes the foundation of traditional life-styles and therefore corrodes traditional religious practices not at the level of consciousness but at the level of what Pierre Bourdieu has called the habitus.

If postmodernism is a challenge to religion, it is also a challenge to the traditional role of intellectuals. As we have seen, one of the significant social functions of the intellectual has been the guardianship of high culture and the protection of high culture from popular debasement. Postmodernism mixes high and low culture in a new system of kitsch culture and through the mode of parody and irony, and in so doing it undermines and questions traditional hierarchical patterns of high and low culture. At the same time, the consequences of globalization are to mix up local and global culture in a new melting pot of multiculturalism. Since high culture cannot be local culture, this effect of globalization has important consequences for the very possibility of the intellectual as a social role. Of course, postmodernism at the same time opens up new possibilities for the intellectual as an interpreter of the postmodern condition.

In this discussion I have self-consciously treated postmodernism and postmodernity as real states of affairs. I have restricted the notion of postmodernism to theories about postmodernization, that is, I have treated postmodernism as an intellectual movement in social thought and as a cultural criticism of modernism. By postmodernity, therefore, I refer to the social condition of modern societies which are going through a process of postmodernization. Postmodernity involves cultural differentiation and complexity, the loss of the authority of high culture, the growth of urban multiculturalism as a consequence of processes of globalization, and the prevalence of certain stylistic devices in culture, such as simulation, parody and irony. Postmodernization produces the experience of the artificial and constructed nature of culture and cultural experiences. In taking this view of postmodernism I am also self-consciously distinguishing this position from arguments presented by Anthony Giddens and Ulrich Beck. As we have seen, Beck and Giddens prefer to define modern societies in terms of either risk society or high modernity or reflexive modernity. They have specifically rejected the notion that postmodernization is a valid account of the transformation of modern culture. Their account of high modernity and risk society depends heavily on a particular view which they develop of the modern self, namely of the self as a project. The reflexive self is a core feature of the general progress of detraditionalization in high modernity.

I want to suggest therefore that contemporary sociology is faced with two major questions; the first is whether society has gone through a profound change such that its very character has been transformed. The second addresses the problem of social theory in relation to these radical social changes by suggesting that an entirely new theoretical framework is required to understand these radical changes. Beck and Giddens are trying to propose that we are living in an entirely radicalized and transformed social reality. Because high modernity is a new condition, we also need to develop new theories for analysing these societies. If we combine these two questions (Is it a new type of society and do we need new theories to describe this reality?), then we can produce a property space with four boxes as in Table 3:

Table 3 A property space relating new types of society and new theories

New society

		+	−
New theories	+	Postmodernization risk society	Feminism
	−	Post-industrialism	Marxism

This new reality is described in terms of the theory of reflexive modernization which is presented as an alternative to the idea of postmodernization. We can identify highly traditional forms of explanation which want to deny that we exist in a new society and therefore deny that we need new theories. For example, those theorists who are trying to defend a traditional Marxist/Leninist theory want to claim that there has been no fundamental change to capitalism. Mainstream feminists are presumably trying to argue that we are not living in a new type of society; indeed the old patriarchal structures are still in place and there is no significant change in the sexual division of labour and inequality, but we need new types of theories to analyse these circumstances because social science is itself shaped by patriarchy. Daniel Bell's theory of post-industrialism might illustrate a third position which argues that there has been a radical change in the nature of social organization and culture, but there is no need to abandon classical sociological theory. I am not in this chapter so much interested in these three theoretical strategies because I want to focus on risk society and postmodernity. What Beck and Giddens are explicitly or implicitly trying to do is to reject postmodernism as a plaus-ible option in the social sciences, specifically to counteract theories of the postmodernization of society. While Giddens does not discuss the work of Jean Baudrillard, we could see the development of contemporary sociology as a struggle between those theories that want to retain a foundationalist view of contemporary social reality by describing it as risk society or late modernity or high modernity, and those theories which want to reject the traditional idea of 'the social'. We could see these theories of high modernity in competition with the work of writers like Baudrillard, Lyotard and Bauman, who have argued that there are no appropriate or viable sociological theories that we can inherit from tra-ditional social science, including Marxism, which are able to grasp the global complexity of postmodern societies. Thus, behind the debate about detraditionalization and the radicalization of the self is a social struggle between different theoretical groupings in sociology, namely those who believe that modernity is best understood as risk society or as reflexive modernity and those who believe that the process of postmodernization is the dominant feature of change and that the condition of *posthistoire* most adequately characterizes our epoch. The basic question is: Can classical sociology still be regarded as relevant to the understanding of late twentieth-century society?

This critical view of the current health of classical social theory follows from Giddens's earlier arguments in *The Consequences of Modernity* (1990) to the effect that sociology in its existing form is not adequate as an analysis of modern conditions, primarily because sociology has been based upon a false equation of the nation-state with society and cannot therefore cope analytically with the pattern of globalization which has emerged in modern societies. Classical social theory is too unidimensional to serve as a relevant and informative perspective on our times.

I believe that Giddens's position can be challenged by considering, for example, Max Weber's account of personality in the context of the debate about the *Bildungsbürgertum* or a cultured middle class. This criticism of Giddens might initially sound rather trivial. However, it achieves two important objectives. It shows that some aspects of classical sociology are indeed highly relevant to understanding modern society, but, in the course of examining Weber, I can show that Giddens's notion, that reflexive selfhood is a specifically late feature of high modernity, is untenable from a historical point of view. Weber's notion of personality has in fact much in common with Giddens's debate about the detraditionalization of the self and the rise of self-reflexivity. Weber thought that the personality was a project; indeed personality was that rational project of the self which distinguished human beings from the non-human. Thus in Weber's sociological perspective having a personality was not a natural fact about human beings but something which was produced by culture and education. Weber went on to elaborate the notion of individuality and personality via the concept of singularity. The idea of the rational project of personality in this German tradition emphasized the idea of individuality and individual singularity. Weber undertook this discussion of personality as a life project in the context of a traditional German debate about the relationship between culture and civilization. Personality in this framework was the development of culture against civilization, that is, against the materialism which was thought to be typical of the Anglo-Saxon industrial nations, especially English materialism. Personality is a calling or vocation whereby a singular individual imposes on himself or herself the ascetic disciplines or rationality to produce the self as an effect of training. This view of personality was closely related therefore to Weber's sociology of vocations and to his analysis of world religions in terms of their specific soteriologies. This feature of Weber's sociology has been analysed brilliantly by Harvey Goldman in his *Politics, Death and the Devil: Self and Power in Max Weber and Thomas Mann* (1992). Weber's study of the Protestant ethic concludes with the tragic picture that the calling has been undermined by the self-destruction of Protestant values in secular capitalism. Weber's argument has much in common with Simmel's view of 'the tragedy of culture' in which the most successful values tend to be self-defeating and in which content is submerged by the crystallization of form. In fact, Goldman analyses Thomas Mann's major novels (especially *Buddenbrooks* and *Death in Venice*) as explorations of Weberian themes about the self which attempt to come to terms with the erosion of bourgeois culture, namely the high culture of the *Bildungsbürg-ertum*. In particular the *Buddenbrooks* novel is an exploration of the decline of bourgeois culture and the secularization and decay of the ascetic vocation within the Protestant ethic. The theme of decay and destruction, or more generally of nihilism, was in any case a major theme of late nineteenth-century German intellectual culture. *Fin-de-siècle* decay and decadence was very much in the air. These topics of familial decay and personal decline were fundamental to Mann's novels, especially in the analysis of demonic forces and intellectuality in *Dr Faustus* and in *The Magic Mountain* where personal illness serves as a metaphor of national decline. These novels provided a literary expression of the sociological themes of disenchantment, tragedy and personal heroism in Weber's sociological theories.

Weber's main anxiety was that personality would be undermined by the growth of scientific rationalization and the bureaucratic dominance of the everyday world by the state. Weber's sociological views on the cultivation of the self against the constraints of a rational secular system thus anticipated at least some aspects of the current debate about the reflexive self under conditions of modernization. More importantly, Weber's analysis of personality and in particular his views on the impact of Protestant spirituality on the growth of the modern self influenced a variety of twentieth-century social theorists who have contributed to a distinctive sociology of the modern self. Of particular significance in this group of writers influenced by Weber was Benjamin Nelson whose *On the Roads to Modernity: Conscience, Science and Civilizations* (1981) is a major historical analysis of the evolution of the idea of conscience in Western cultures specifically within the framework of Weber's historical sociology. Nelson's task was no less than a history of the self and civilization. He was particularly important in providing a detailed analysis of the impact of urban culture, Protestantism and rationalism on the origins of conscience. The point of this commentary is basically to indicate the fact that Giddens's analysis of the reflexive self is not necessarily an original contribution to sociology since there are a number of well-established traditions in classical sociology (Weber, Simmel, Nelson, Dumont and Elias) by which the self can be approached and understood as a reflexive project in modernity. The consequence of this argument is to suggest that there is no automatic justification for abandoning or rejecting traditional or classical sociology as a paradigm since there are well-established traditions by which the idea of reflexive modernity, especially the reflexive self, can be understood. Giddens's exclusionary strategy cannot be wholly supported in this crucial area of the sociology of the self.

This sociological debate about the self is also fundamentally connected with the recent emergence of a sociology of the body, to which Giddens has marginally turned his attention in two recent works *The Transformation of Intimacy* (1992) and *Modernity and Self-Identity* (1991). The major issue is that in contemporary society the body has become a site of regulative beliefs and practices which help to constitute the body as a project. Medical technology has made the idea of creating our own bodies through transsexual surgery, cosmetic surgery, dentistry, and so forth a real option, at least for the middle classes. Several writers on the body have recently argued that 'in conditions of high modernity, there is a tendency for the body to become increasingly central to the modern person's sense of self-identity' (Shilling 1993: 1). However, to put this issue of the body/self as a project in a wider historical framework, perhaps in Western cultures the body has always been problematized by the cultural legacies of Christianity, Judaism and Islam. The critique of the flesh, the denigration of sex and the denial of the body, which is the legacy of a radical Pauline theology, actually meant that in Western civilization, the body was a problematic dimension of Western cultures (Asad 1993). One important feature of Christianity which was a radical departure from earlier traditional forms of religion, is that because Christ was a God without children, he was a non-generative God. In Christianity, ascension replaces reproduction. In Christianity therefore one has the paradox of a religion in which the body is a central topic (the resurrection of the dead, the idea of Christ's incarnation, and Christ as a tormented and bleeding God), but which also denies the body. The idea of the embodiment of divine energy is essential to Christian orthodoxy, but the legacy of Pauline theology cut the body off from the self, transforming the body, at best, into a vessel or vehicle for cognitive and spiritual activity. It is for that reason that sovereign power in Christianity was divided into the king's two bodies – a spiritualized body and a decaying, degenerative and secular body. In the Judaeo-Christian legacy, there are various versions of this dualism, and they have different manifestations in various theories of Mariology, gnosticism and resurrection, but what I want to argue is that within Western cultures, reflexivity about the body has been an inescapable cultural fact, precisely because in the Christian religion there has been an attempt to erase the body from social practice. In my work on the sociology of the body (Turner 1992), I have tried to focus on the idea of diet as a way of talking about the body as regulated and to think about the body as the target of 'institutions of normative coercion' such as medicine and law. The word 'diet' is sociologically interesting because 'diet' means regime or government. In the idea of dieting, we are already talking about a government of the body or a regulation of our flesh. One of the main transitions from traditional to modern society may involve a major cultural inversion. In the traditional Christian legacy, one dieted the body in order to subordinate the flesh, that is, in order to regulate and produce the soul. The idea was that the government of the body was the production of the soul and only by this regulation of bodies could the soul emerge as some pure entity. In modern societies it is the other way round; we regulate the body in order to produce pleasure, and we diet the body in order to enhance the surface of the body as a system of sexual symbolism. In modern societies, consumer culture has made the project of the body a general activity throughout the population. The idea of the body beautiful has transformed this traditional dieting practice in the opposite direction, and the regulation of the body has resulted in a fetishization of sexuality. We regulate the body in order to produce sexuality, not to deny it. The Protestant ethic is thus turned inside out and the body becomes a project alongside the reflexive self and is inextricably bound up with the self as a project. To take one specific issue, in a culture in which the surface of the body is seen to be that which carries the signs of inner moral condition, ageing is a process which has to be denied. Diet is a regime of the self which aims to sustain the illusion of youth. I would like to put this idea in a slightly different way, namely, that ageing intensifies the reflexivity which is forced upon us in a world in which we are all forced to choose a lifestyle embodying tastes. The ageing process is bound up with the reflexivity of modernity. The debate about the aestheticization of everyday life means that the body becomes a project and it becomes a project for a variety of reasons, such as the centrality of the gymnasium to modern culture, the idea of sport and personal fitness. The debate about the nature of sexuality in both gay and feminist literature has also problematized the body. Thus, if we are going to talk about a project of the self and the detraditionalization of the self, we are inevitably going to have to talk about a detraditionalization of the embodied self. However, it is also the case that, because of the nature of the Christian culture which we have inherited, the body has always been in some respects a project, because it required discipline, surveillance and regulation. It could not be taken for granted.

Another feature of this argument against the theoretical strategy proposed by Giddens and Beck is to question the periodization of detraditionalization in their analysis of the reflexive self. In the recent writing of Zygmunt Bauman, for example, in *Intimations of Postmodernity* (1992), we have a very elegant, persuasive and morally impressive defence of the idea that we are living in a totally different type of world, but I am not convinced that there was necessarily such a hiatus in the historical development of Western society. In particular, I have been impressed by the notion that the baroque crisis of the seventeenth century was based upon the idea of society as artifice and of the very precariously constructed nature of the society (Turner 1990). The notion of society as an artifice emerged out of the crisis of the clash of ideological cultures and as a consequence of the process of economic globalization going on in world trade in that period and of the crisis of the relationship between the court and society. Shakespeare's tragic plays which were a feature of baroque culture, were based on the assumption that the world was merely a stage and that the social actors thereupon were merely players within an artificial reality. In fact we can regard the sixteenth and seventeenth centuries as a period when writers from More to Shakespeare were specifically concerned with the idea of 'self-fashioning'. Indeed, in the sixteenth century 'there appears to be an increased self-consciousness about the fashioning of human identity as a manipulable, artful process'

(Greenblatt 1980: 2). Perhaps a more significant challenge to Giddens's position would be to ask the question: Were the religious confessional practices of the sixteenth and seventeenth centuries cultural institutions in which the self began to emerge as a project? The development of the idea of the confessional in Western religiosity can be regarded as a technique of the self that produced the idea of the self as a project. Confessional manuals provided the disciplines whereby a new concept of the interior self could flourish. This claim is not to suggest necessarily that there was a contest between Protestant and Catholic cultures. In the Protestant diary and in the collective confessional practices of the pietist and Methodist sects, one also finds the idea of the self as a project. As I have already indicated the work of Benjamin Nelson is important in this context since he was able to identify an evolutionary development of consciousness through the confessional practices of both the Catholic and Protestant traditions.

In fact, the historical evidence about the nature of individuality and the self represents a significant challenge to Giddens's view of the modern development of the reflexive self. For example, there is an extensive literature which draws upon historical research to suggest that the discovery of the individual as a subject and of individual self-awareness goes back to at least the twelfth century (Bynum 1980). The emphasis on the confessional in twelfth-century religious literature indicates a new self-awareness emerging through the religious reforms of the monastic orders. Caroline Bynum suggests that twelfth-century religious writing showed a specific interest in the inner landscape of the psyche and a concern for the development of models of moral consciousness and ethical behaviour. For Bynum, therefore, this discovery of the self was not a discovery of the isolated individual, because religious writers were particularly concerned with the development of models for moral behaviour which was to take place within a communal setting. Thus, historical research on the growth of the self provides a strong criticism of the periodization of self-development implicit in Giddens's view of modernity.

These studies are unfortunately rather parochial in their view of the nature of individuality and the individual by concentrating rather exclusively on Western history. This focus on Western individualism has, of course, been a persistent feature of orientalism, but recent historical and artistic research throws into doubt any claim that the idea of individuality (Abercrombie, Hill and Turner 1984) is a peculiar feature of Western society. In Islam, of course, the representation of the individual was precluded by theological problems about representation, which partly explains why calligraphy was such an important aspect of cultural development in Islam. However, if we take the case of China it is clear that portraiture had been traditionally used to express the social functions of individuals as rulers or heroes, but in the seventeenth century there was a valorization of portraiture as a widespread social practice aimed at constructing diverse cultural identities, supplanting the more restricted, broadly commemorative functions of earlier periods. This phenomenon suggests a rising self-consciousness or spirit of individualism in the culture at large.

(Vinograd 1992: 68)

This stimulation of self-reflexivity in the production of the portrait reflected broader changes in the structure of late Ming society: urbanization, changing social class relationships, changes in professional distinctions and rising social ambiguity in role relations. Recent research in Japanese culture also indicates that a reflexive self-awareness has been an important aspect of self-identity even in traditional society. Although post-war interaction with the West has given a new urgency to reflexivity, there were elements of the traditional culture which fostered a critical, reflexive notion of the self in relation to the outside and the other (Rosenberger 1992).

Finally I come to the topic of secularization. The analysis of the reflexive self and risk society presupposes a theory of the secularization of society, but neither Beck nor Giddens pay any specific attention to the role of secularization in creating the conditions for modern reflexivity. The idea of detraditionalization, which is a central feature of both their approaches, clearly depends upon a theory about the process of secularization and the detraditionalization of the sacred. Here again their views on detraditionalization are very much in line with the classical sociological tradition of writers like Marx, Weber, Troeltsch, Durkheim and Simmel. These social theorists believed that capitalism was undermining the authority and dominance of the church and exposing sacred reality to the corrosive impact of industrialist capitalist relations. Durkheim in particular was conscious of the profound changes in the nature of sacred reality. He assumed that the traditional religious bases of society would necessarily collapse as a consequence of social differentiation and the emergence of new forms of reciprocity in urban society. As a consequence, Durkheim specifically addressed the question of moral individualism as an alternative to the view of the hedonistic and egotistical individual which was characteristic of utilitarian social thought. Weber's concept of disenchantment expressed his tragic view of the end of religious certainty, the emergence of pluralistic belief systems and the erosion of religious meaning by science. Disenchantment was a condition of the crisis of personality in late nineteenth-century social thought. This view of the transformative character of capitalism was shared by all social theorists regardless of their specific ideological persuasions. It was after all Karl Marx who had recognized that with capitalism 'all that is solid melts into air' (Berman 1982).

This classical view of the process of secularization has been challenged by contemporary sociologists of religion who have shown that this uni-dimensional view of secularization is inadequate and superficial. For example, if we follow the approach of the theologian Paul Tillich that religion addresses those things which ultimately concern us, then we might view the alleged secularization of society in a rather different manner. Indeed, for a number of contemporary writers the individual self is pre-cisely the ultimate concern of modernity and it is important, therefore, to reject any simplistic view of the decline of religion as being merely the erosion of orthodox official faith. We might expand this view to suggest that the project of the embodied self is the ultimate concern of late twentieth-century society and that again following some of the implications of Durkheim's sociology of religion, the self has become the sacred arena of contemporary social thought and practice. Postmod-ernism suggests of course that there cannot be one but many ultimate concerns. Certainly the traditional world of a sacred/profane split cannot be regarded as an adequate perspective on modern and postmodern religiosity. Robert Bellah (1964) perceptively noted that in modern times life is not a 'one possibility thing' but an infinite possibility. Individuals are forced to seek out their own meanings and form their own lives. In this respect, Giddens's notion of the self as project re-asserts Bellah's view of the reversibility of the self.

In conclusion, I have attempted to reject much of Giddens's recent analysis of modernization by bringing into question one specific aspect of that process, namely the emergence of self-reflexivity in high modernity. I have sought to question Giddens's view of self on a number of grounds, namely that it fails to look seriously at the question of embodiment, it exaggerates the originality of the theory, it produces an inappropriate view of historical periodisation, it lacks a comparative perspective and finally it assumes a somewhat unidimensional view of secularization. Are we to conclude, therefore, that there has been no significant change in Western society from the twelfth century? This is not the conclusion I wish to draw from this analysis. The discovery of the self in the twelfth century and the subsequent evolution of confessional practices indicate a process of change within the upper classes of traditional society. The confessional, the diary, the mirror and spiritual practices were techniques specifically directed at the elite. By contrast the project of the embodied self in the late twentieth century is a mass movement which is bringing a new conception of self to the whole of society. In my view, Giddens is correct in suggesting that the new pattern of intimacy which he described in *The Transformation of Intimacy* (1992) presupposes a democratization of social relations in contemporary society. The project of the self and the project of the body which are generating new patterns of intimacy are social changes which affect all social groups in the modern world;

they are not an elite practice of the upper strata of society. This democratization of sensibility might within the paradigm adopted in this book also
be regarded as a postmodernization of the self in the sense that the new
structure of intimacy involves an interpenetration of high and low culture;
self-construction in contemporary times also involves a large measure
of self-parody and irony. In the seventeenth century as we have seen,
there was an elite for whom the self appeared to be socially constructed.
In the modern world this artificial nature of the self (the idea of the self
as reversible) has penetrated all sectors of modern society. The globalization of cultural diversity and the institutionalization of multiculturalism
have both contributed to the development of the notion that the self is
constructed. Everything is reversible; everything is constructed; everything
is ironized.

Chapter 14

Conclusion

In recent years there has been a significant change in the interpretation of Max Weber's contribution to sociology. Although Weber was originally and narrowly associated with the Protestant ethic thesis, that is, a specific debate about the impact of Protestant asceticism on economic development, contemporary scholarship on Weberian sociology has associated him with the general process of modernization. Choosing almost at random from modern interpretations of Weber one could mention the work of Lawrence S. Scaff *Fleeing the Iron Cage* (1989), Ralph Schroeder *Max Weber and the Sociology of Culture* (1992) and Wilhelm Hennis *Max Weber Essays in Reconstruction* (1988) as major contributions to this cultural interpretation of the process of modernization. These interpretations of the Weber thesis as an analysis of modernization have a number of points in common. First, they identify the philosophy of Friedrich Nietzsche as the major contribution to the development of Weber's sociology. Second, they identify the notion of culture as a primary concern of his sociology as a whole. Third, they situate Weber's anxieties about bureaucratization and disenchantment within the broader context of late nineteenth-century nihilism and finally, therefore, they focus on the antinomies of Weber's attitude towards cultural modernity as a highly irrational form of life from the point of view of everyday concerns. Weberian sociology was concerned with the differentiation of the various spheres of life within which culture and religion had a primary place.

These interpretations of the modernization thesis in Weber have strangely located him within the debate about postmodernization (Turner 1992). Weber's uncertainties and anxieties about the modernization process and his location within the nihilistic debate suggest that there was a theme of postmodernization hidden, so to speak, within his general sociology. This anxiety about the contradictions of capitalism focussed on well-known dichotomies such as the relationship between charismatic revolutions and rational culture, the impact of instrumental reason on religious values, the fatalistic impact of asceticism on religious systems and finally the possibility of cultivating personality in the context of a highly rationalistic system. Of course, Weber's views on international politics, warfare and economic struggles, which was derived from Nietzsche, also painted a picture of the modern world as a violent, destructive and nihilistic place. On a biographical basis Weber's personal life and in particular his views on eroticism and sexuality also anticipated a number of significant themes in twentieth-century debates about sexuality in relation to modernity and postmodernity. Here again, the hidden impact of debates about eroticism in Weber's sociology have only recently fully emerged.

There are two points to this commentary. First, it suggests an interesting continuity between classical sociology and contemporary discussions of postmodernism. I have suggested that the peculiar debates in classical sociology in the late nineteenth century about *fin-de-siècle* values in many respects reproduced in advance the peculiar debates in the late twentieth century between theories of modernity and postmodernity. In this collection of essays I have sought to draw upon this classical tradition to interpret various features of modern society and therefore I have attempted to provide an alternative to the perspective of Anthony Giddens and Ulrich Beck on the alleged failures of classical sociology and its inability to understand the modern processes of globalization, reflexivity and institutional change. There is no need to cling ritualistically to classical sociology, but many of the insights of writers like Weber are still specifically relevant to many contemporary issues and debates. This view of Weber also provides a very neat and parsimonious method of defining the relationship between modernism and postmodernism by special reference to the Protestant ethic thesis. Weber's sociology offers a particularly powerful definition of the process of modernization which involved the routinization of everyday life, the disenchantment of religious values, the differentiation of spheres of life, the growth of bureaucratic systems of management, the growing dominance of urban, technical and scientific values over everyday life, and finally the economic dominance of Western urban capitalism. In this particular study I have defined postmodernism as an alternative set of theories of social change and approached postmodernity as a state of affairs standing in opposition to Weber's view of modernization or as a state of affairs coming after rationalist modernization. Postmodernity therefore involves a de-differentiation of spheres, a decline in the confidence expressed towards instrumental rationality, a new focus on the emotions and the human body, a greater concern for the intimate, the secret and the everyday, an erosion of certainty in the value of economic capitalism and a growing awareness of the importance of environmental and green issues. Postmodernity emphasizes the local, the oppositional, the contextual, and the locally specific. While the Protestant ethic suggests a life of intense seriousness (in fact religion can be defined as the serious life), postmodernism draws attention to the importance of play, parody, irony and simulation. Of course, as I have noted, Weber's sociology contains an element of this postmodern critique, because following the influence of Nietzsche on his social philosophy, there was a strong element of scepticism in Weber's world view with respect to the ultimate outcome of the rationalization process.

Second, the value of this approach to the modernity/postmodernity debate is that it draws attention to the peculiar role of religion and religious cultures in shaping the world in which we live. Weber's specific attitude towards 'Eastern religions', therefore, sheds a great deal of light on the contemporary problems of culture, religion and social change. Of course 'other cultures' have always represented a problem for the inner core of a dominant cultural tradition. Does the outside confirm the authenticity of the inside reality or is it a fundamental challenge to the legitimacy and dominance of a core set of values and beliefs? In Weber's sociology, the attempt to establish the authenticity of the (German) Lutheran ascetic tradition was an important feature of his general world view which sought, largely covertly, to protect and celebrate a German cultural perspective on world religions. Weber's criticisms of the eroticism of Islam are relatively well known, but we should remind ourselves that Weber also to some extent dismissed the 'religions of India' as really a collection of views and attitudes generated by local gurus. Sanskrit studies have in many respects suffered the same attitude of orientalism as Islamic cultural studies. 'Other religions' like 'other cultures' lacked the seriousness of purpose and calling which dominated both Weber's sociology and his personal views on ethics, prophecy and charisma.

Here again we see the importance of the notion of the calling and vocations in the German educated middle classes. In his study of *Politics Death and the Devil*, Harvey Goldman (1992) draws attention to the historical and ethical significance of Dürer's 'knight, death and the devil' as a symbol of a particularly melancholic but disciplined orientation to cultural reality. In *The Birth of Tragedy*, Nietzsche also noted the importance of the symbol of the armed knight in iron, who looking into the distance in pursuit of his terrible obligations and undeterred by the gruesome companionship of the devil and death, sets out alone on horseback with his dog. Harvey Goldman noted that Thomas Mann in his *Reflections of an Unpolitical Man* also identified this Dürer engraving as representative of his own Nordic ethical Protestant and essentially German world. Finally Hermann Braus also paid a tribute to his friend Weber as someone who was the modern incarnation of Dürer's isolated knight caught between death and the devil but nevertheless pursuing this iron calling or duty. Given Weber's commitment to this type of ethical principle, it is hardly surprising that he should have openly regarded Freudian psychoanalysis as merely an hygienic excuse for sexual dalliance. Similarly Weber rejected any return to the arms of the church as a solution to modern ethical relativity. His idea was that an ethic of responsibility, dedicated either to politics or to science, was the only type of vocation which could still give a person some sense of honourable commitment in society.

This moralistic and ascetic view of culture in Weberian sociology, and more broadly within the German educated classes of the nineteenth century, has been profoundly challenged by at least three modern developments which are considered in this collection of essays. Although Weber had argued that Islam was incapable of providing values and inspiration necessary for the development of rational capitalism, Islamic culture has been remarkably successful in the twentieth century both as the host of economic development in the oil-rich societies of the Middle East and the developing societies of Asia and South-east Asia, and as a third-world leader in political reform, revolution and change. Of course the economic success of Islamic communities around the world has often been dismissed by Western commentators as merely a growth which is parasitic upon global capitalism, particularly in terms of the West's dependency on oil. However, it is difficult to support this argument given the industrial success of a variety of Islamic societies and cultures as illustrated by the development of Indonesia, Malaysia and Pakistan. The political turbulence of Islamic communities has also been a target of criticism by many Western commentators. Once again we might note a certain irony in Weber's political stance. Weber believed that charismatic political breakthroughs were part of the political structure of premodern societies which he saw in terms of a dichotomy between tradition and charismatic authority. In particular, the tension between the priest and the prophet symbolized for Weber the whole legacy of traditional politics. However, in the twentieth century Islam has produced a number of profoundly important charismatic leaders, of whom the Ayatollah Khomeini is perhaps one of the most outstanding examples. We should not be surprised therefore that Michel Foucault saw the Iranian Revolution as a profoundly spiritual event in the wasteland of modern politics. These changes in Islam are no longer part of the outside or external context of Western politics, but part of the essential constitution of global politics. In a variety of multicultural societies such as Australia, Canada and the United States, Islamic issues become increasingly a major dimension of domestic politics. Societies like Holland and Australia, which have in some respects welcomed cultural diversity, cannot easily ignore the implication of Islamic politics for local educational systems, the working of the law and even for concepts of national identity.

In this volume I have argued that this multicultural diversity has to be seen from a sociological point of view as part of the more intriguing development of postmodernism in contemporary culture. When sociologists think about postmodernism, they typically think about the film industry, advertising and fashion. However, cultural diversity, Islamization

and multicultural politics could also be seen as part of the postmodernization of politics; to some extent they challenge the idea of a 'grand narrative' of a single national homogenous identity. The nation-state typically
arose on the back of the idea of ethnic coherence; this is why we use the
word 'nation' in describing the modern state as a 'nation-state'. It is based
upon the assumption that a unified polity has to have a unified ethnic
base and indeed the nineteenth-century nation-states had a strong policy
of unification and integration which required the subordination of local
dialect, regional culture and domestic diversity. In this respect the United
Kingdom is no exception to the rule, since the Celtic fringe was regarded
as an embarrassment to the coherence of the state. Ethnic diversification
and multicultural politics challenge the idea of the political grand
narrative of national democracy, national coherence and national
unification.

The postmodern debate in the social sciences has bifurcated around
politics and culture. In North America, postmodernism is most typically
associated with changes in the nature of film, communication, consumerism and culture generally. It has not been seen as a dangerous or threatening development; instead postmodernization has been seen necessarily as
a 'fun development' in popular culture which is nevertheless a challenge
to the traditional role of intellectuals. Baudrillard's *America* (1988) is a
good illustration of an ironic commentary on de Tocqueville's analysis of
popular democracy. By contrast, in Germany, postmodernization has been
seen as a challenge to the rational order of society and in particular
Habermas's critique of (French) postmodern and post-structural social
theory has been one of the leading aspects of recent contests. Habermas
has sought to protect and to sustain the idea of a public community
within which rational discourse can occur. Habermas clearly has perceived
the postmodern challenge to language and reason as a political threat
to the idea of rational communication and public discourse. It is for these
reasons that the debate about citizenship has come back to the political
agenda of the late twentieth century. Although citizenship within the
English tradition of social theory was almost exclusively associated with
the legacy of writers like T. H. Marshall who contributed significantly
to the debate about social policy and the welfare state, in recent years
the debate about citizenship has expanded to consider specific problems
and issues relating for example to the status of women and children in
society, the problem of growing ethnic diversity, and the ecological questions of sustainable economic growth. I do not believe therefore that the
postmodernization of politics rules out serious political debate. Rather it
draws attention to the inevitability of ethnic and cultural pluralism, the
problem of difference, the negative consequences of universalistic paradigms of membership and, in general, to the legacy of the grand narratives
of the nineteenth century which had in practice an exclusionary social

function. Weber's narrow view of the importance of the power state and his critical objection to the ethnic diversity of the eastern provinces of Germany is out of touch with the needs of modern political tolerance and the global role of human rights in the protection of minority groups.

I have suggested first that Weber's vision of history has been challenged by the strength and continuity of so-called Asian religions, particularly by Islam, and second that Weber's rather unidimensional view of sexuality, politics and culture has been challenged by the postmodernization of cultural practices in the late twentieth century. Finally, Weber's view of power politics has also been questioned by the globalization of culture, economics and political relations. In his *The Consequences of Modernity*, Anthony Giddens (1990) has criticized traditional sociology for its focus on the nation-state which has been equated simply with the idea of society. Giddens's own view of time–space distanciation has been developed as an alternative to the notion of the nation-state. One might also add that when sociologists did enter the field of comparative political analysis, it was often in terms of international relations theory. Weber cannot be accused of having ignored this aspect of social life, since much of his political sociology was precisely focused on the problem of foreign relations. It is well known that Weber saw the dominance of North America and Britain in the international field of economic exchanges as a significant challenge to the political and cultural life of Germany. Indeed his inaugural lecture at Freiburg in 1895 clearly saw the public role of economics and social science in the service of the power state. Weber's language in the analysis of international relations was shaped by the quasi-Darwinistic views of Nietzsche (Stauth and Turner 1988). Contemporary theories of globalization, however, have attempted to transcend this limited nineteenth-century view of nation-states locked in a struggle over scarce resources. Contemporary globalization theory is far more concerned with the cultural perception of 'the world', with the development of international cultural networks, with the impact of tourism, social and geographical mobility, with self-identity and cultural identity. I have attempted to show the relationship between globalization and postmodernization, suggesting that the globalization of cultures creates a greater reflexivity about personal and cultural identity. The mixing and fusing of cultures raises questions about authenticity, originality, tradition and continuity in cultural practices. This reflexivity leads to a greater awareness about the nature of simulation, artificial reproduction, heritage industries and ironic presentation of cultural identity. To take an Australian illustration, the comic figure of Dame Edna Everage is in fact a hyper-caricature of certain features of post-war white suburbia in the development of Australian society, but through popular culture and the globalization of kitsch 'she' has emerged as a globally comic figure and also as a self-parody of Australian national identity. Dame Edna Everage has of course no 'real' role within the multicultural context of Australia, being essentially a white Anglo Saxon representation of Australian suburban culture. However, given the impact of global mass culture, 'she' is a figure who is larger than life.

These cultural processes in popular culture and global culture have brought about a greater sense of reflexivity about self-identity and social role. Here again Anthony Giddens in *The Transformation of Intimacy* (1992) has captured an important development of contemporary debate, particularly at the popular level. Of course, I have in this study been critical of Giddens's periodization of high modernity, postmodernization and the rise of the reflexive self, since I have argued that there are important antecedent developments in medieval culture around the notion of the confessing self. Giddens's implied argument that his perception of the reflexive self is a distinctive break with traditional sociology cannot be sustained. It can be argued that many of these analyses of the self were anticipated by writers like Troeltsch, Nelson, Weber, Dumont and Simmel. In fact, Simmel's writing on aesthetics, sexuality, tourism, the modern self in relation to the metropolis and the idea of the stranger have captured much of the mood of postmodern cultural studies: the idea of the aestheticization of everyday life, the growth of reflexivity about aesthetics and the notion that aesthetics has replaced morality were ideas which were worked out in Simmel's cultural sociology and which have become central to much of the postmodern debate about culture. Simmel's views on the city and the estrangement of personality were ideas which have been taken up by writers like Walter Benjamin and Christine Buci-Glucksmann in much postmodern writing on the self, society and culture. In this volume I have suggested that this identification of Simmel and Weber with postmodern debate is a product of the fact that both were profoundly influenced by Nietzsche's critique of the pretensions of national culture and the neurotic character of rational life. Giddens is correct, however, in suggesting that the growth of intimacy, the emergence of self-help manuals in the emotional life, and the challenge of feminist culture are features of a democratization of inter-personal relations which was not featured in classical sociology and which was not part of the structural arrangements of medieval systems of confessional culture. This democratization of intimacy can also be connected with contemporary debates about citizenship and the problematic nature of the relationship between the public and the private sphere.

The globalization debate has made the concept of 'society' problematic and hence has represented a rather direct challenge to the intellectual legitimacy and coherence of sociology itself. Once more, Baudrillard's challenge that the 'social' has disappeared or imploded is a very specific critical challenge to the legacy of classical sociology (Rojek and Turner 1993). Giddens in his *The Consequences of Modernity* (1990) has addressed this problem of the nature of the social and society, arguing that much of classical sociology cannot cope with this problematization of the social. There is of course much to support and to justify such a critical response to classical social theory. However, this charge cannot be levelled at Simmel who saw the social, not as a reified phenomenon, but as sociation and social process. Similarly, Norbert Elias in his studies of the civilizing process argued that processual sociology would also avoid any reification of its major concepts. Hence, Elias talked about civilizing processes rather than about civilizations. It is also unclear whether this criticism could be successfully levelled at Weber's formal sociology in the introductory sections to *Economy and Society*. Weber also sought to avoid any reified or concrete concepts of society, state and economy in his formulation of the theory of social action. In fact Weber went so far as to say that his whole sociology sought to reject and to destroy any reified or collectivistic concepts in sociological theory. Thus institutions like the economy and the state were defined by Weber in terms of social action. In fact, classical sociology was concerned to provide an analysis of this complexity of different forms of sociations (*Vergesellschaftungen*). However, classical sociology also saw these sociations as having a spatial dimension which eventually provided a distinctive form of society. In short, there was a great deal of ambiguity in traditional social theory about the nature of the social and this ambiguity has so to speak been exposed by the globalization of cultural and social relationships.

Within this context the orientalist tradition, comparative religious studies and civilizational analysis are interesting, since the major religions of the world have tended to perceive themselves as 'world religions'. Now the tradition of religious studies in terms of the analysis of world religions obviously constructed the notion of 'the world' within an orientalist dimension, but nevertheless civilizational analysis emerging out of religious studies has never had a reified view of the nation-state. Both Christianity and Islam had a primitive notion of the world which shaped their concept of the Household of Faith and the church. Although the idea of the national church developed alongside the nation-state, there have always been strong globalizing tendencies within Islamic and Christian cultures. Contemporary fundamentalism therefore has questioned any attempt to localize the religious faith of Christianity, Islam, Judaism and so forth. While fundamentalization has been a check upon the spread of global consumerism, it is the case that fundamentalization actually increases the globalization of the religious debate about identity and commitment. Any simplistic notion of secularization as merely religious decline could never capture the importance and significance of these contemporary changes in the global positioning of the world religions.

An important theme in this volume has been the changing nature of the intellectual and the role of an intelligentsia within social systems where the classical distinction between high and low culture has been eroded by postmodernization and by globalization. The traditional intellectual was a defender of national culture, which in practice meant a guardian of high cultural distinction and elitism. The work of Pierre Bourdieu in his analysis of the scientific field has been highly influential in contemporary views of the intellectual. Bourdieu's work has been a specific contribution to the sociology of knowledge and the sociology of the intellectuals which presents an alternative to the legacy of Karl Mannheim. Bourdieu's critique of the idea of the 'free-floating intellectual' has caused some offence to intellectuals who want to see themselves as not determined by social forces (Bourdieu 1993). I have shown in this collection of essays that there is a good deal of nostalgia amongst critical social scientists who would like to return to a conventional role as guardians of high culture and discipline. Critical theorists like Adorno and Marcuse saw the development of mass culture and the culture industry as a threat to the authenticity of cultural distinction. The consequence of their rejection of mass culture was paradoxical in that there was a convergence between conservative and critical responses to the mechanisation of artistic production, growth of a culture industry and the global impact of mass popular culture. Postmodernism can be seen as an extension of this mixing of high and low culture. Indeed, postmodernism is a celebration of these changes. The ascetic calling of the traditional academic and the free-floating intellectual has relatively little social relevance in the context of popular and postmodern culture. The classical notion of the responsibility of the intellectuals and the idea of an adversary culture are now arcane. There is in fact 'no respect' for the traditional intellectual (Ross 1989). The idea of the 'last of the intellectuals', the sense of intellectual decline, and indeed a feeling of intellectual betrayal are now popular themes in the sociology of the intellectuals, and the perception of the closing of the mind is a widespread cultural response to these changes, particularly in North America and Europe.

The traditional home of the intellectual was of course the academy, but in the second half of the twentieth century there has been a massification of higher education as a consequence of the establishment of new universities in the 1960s. The rebellions of the 1960s and 1970s amongst undergraduate students were in part a product of the mixing of a conservative and mass educational system. The democratization of the post-war university system produced a profound shock to a more traditional and elitist culture. In Europe the revolutions of 1968 were closely associated with sociology and Marxism, resulting in new intellectual movements such as the situationists who came eventually to have a major impact on the development of postmodern theory in the work of writers like Lyotard, Castoriadis, Debord and Baudrillard. While the whole tradition of English literature and the canon of classical studies was being challenged by subaltern studies in the third world, so mainstream academic disciplines were being challenged by minority groups, by feminism, by black studies, by gay studies and finally by postmodernism. At a trivial level this led to questions about the status of Shakespearean studies in relation to popular cultural studies (Is Mickey Mouse better than Hamlet?), but at a more interesting level it produced a variety of debates about reorganizing and transforming traditional forms of rational research, conventional forms of argumentation and representation, and traditional modes of study. Here again we can see a conflict between the traditional ascetic world of the Weberian scholar pursuing an isolated life of intensive study and specialization, and the postmodern world of the late twentieth century involving diversity, discontinuity and difference in academic styles and intellectual pursuits. Dürer's engraving of the knight, death and the devil is hardly appropriate as an image of intellectual life in the late twentieth century, although there is a strong melancholic dimension to intellectual life which, I have argued, is associated with a nostalgia for tradition, discipline and vocation.

Is there a limit to the process of postmodernization? Certainly the classical sociological tradition saw certain limits to the process of modernization. Durkheim was concerned that utilitarian individualism, the decline of community and the absence of a system of professional ethics would lead to a profound situation of anomie, which was manifest in high levels of egoistic suicide. As we have seen, Weber saw the limits to rationalization in the problem of meaningfulness in social relations, because instrumental rationalism could never replace the values which had been eroded by the very process of social change and modernization. Even Marx looked forward to a period of solidarity and collectivist values which would provide an alternative to the conflicts and divisions of industrial capitalism. Within the debate about reflexivity, postmodernism and contemporary nihilism, there may also be a parallel debate about the limits of postmodernity. Some direction for this debate could be gathered from Helmut Schelsky's article on 'Can continual questioning be institutionalised?' (1969), an article which had a profound impact on the sociology of religion which was developed by Peter Berger and Thomas Luckmann. For Schelsky, the modern consciousness of perpetual self-reflexivity had in fact destroyed much of the traditional community of Christianity within which there was a close interconnection between religious life and the total public and private existence of human beings. Reflexivity had created a sense of the end of religion and the end of history. Schelsky wondered whether such a process could be sustained indefinitely without the erosion of social relations as such. One finds a similar mood in Robert Bellah's brilliant essay on 'Religious evolution' (1964) in which he stressed the importance of the individual in modern society as the ultimate source of all moral solutions, in a context where

traditional forms of ritual and practice had been replaced by individualistic symbolism and ritual. One would predict that, while postmodernism
is a challenge to the grand narratives of both Islam and Christianity, the
postmodern period will not be without its own religious dimension.

In retrospect it may turn out that religion, and not the self or the body,
provides the link between classical modernism at the end of the nineteenth century and postmodernism at the end of the twentieth century.
It was, after all, writers like Weber, Simmel and Troeltsch who probed
the modern consciousness in terms of a debate about asceticism, polytheistic values, the disenchantment of the Garden and the problem of
other religions. While Weber rejected any flight to the church, he was
only too well aware that private belief, mysticism and individualized
religiosity would be the lifestyle appropriate for a modern soteriology of
contemporary times. Weber noted that the disenchantment of the world
was the 'fate of our times' but also noted that precisely under these
circumstances the individual would seek out the most sublime values
within the transcendental realm of mystical experience. Therefore it is
not an accident that in our time the most significant works of art tend to
be both intimate and personal rather than monumental. In personal
relations, religion would express itself pianissimo. In a similar fashion
much post-structural and postmodern thinking has been influenced by the
work of Martin Heidegger who was of course highly critical of modern
technology, modern capitalism and the modern state which threatened to
destroy many of the traditional forms of spiritual life. The notion of the
sublime has emerged as a fundamental issue in postmodern philosophy
around the work of writers like Emmanuel Levinas, Maurice Blanchot and
George Bataille. In postmodern philosophy the question of the sublime is
related to the possibility of unconditional love under the untrammelled
nature of beauty. The debate about the sublime had its origins in aesthetic
philosophy particularly with the work of Kant on aesthetic judgement,
and on the analysis of aesthetics presented by Edmund Burke in his
*Philosophical Enquiry into the Origin of Ideas of the Sublime and Beauti-
ful* which was published in 1757. In these works, the sublime is concerned
with the shock of beauty, with effervescence of religion and emotional
intensity. The growth of a mass market in art, however, suggests that
sublime experience is a religious experience which cannot be reproduced
in the modern world, because the aura which surrounds traditional art
has been destroyed by modern technology. Here again the role of the
intellectual, the avant-garde and the university cannot be separated from
these changes in the nature of the art market and the concept of the
beautiful and the sublime. Nostalgia is therefore an important theme
within the question of the limits of postmodernization; the quest for the
local, the contextual and the everyday represents a quest for a point of
security and stability within a world characterized by an incomprehensible

plethora of viewpoints, lifestyles, modes of discourse and opinions. In short, we are confronted by the postmodernization of polytheism.

References

Abaza, M. (1987) *The Changing Image of Women in Rural Egypt: Cairo Papers in Social Science*, vol. 10, monograph 2, Cairo: The American University of Cairo Press.

Abercrombie, N. (1990) 'Popular culture and ideological effects', pp. 199–218 in N. Abercrombie, S. Hill and B. S. Turner (eds) *Dominant Ideologies*, London: Unwin Hyman.

—— Hill, S. and Turner, B. S. (1980) *The Dominant Ideology Thesis*, London: George Allen & Unwin.

———— (1984) *Sovereign Individuals of Capitalism*, London: Allen & Unwin.

Adorno, T. W. (1984) *Aesthetic Theory*, London: Routledge & Kegan Paul.

Adorno, T. W. and Horkheimer, M. (1944) *Dialectic of the Enlightenment*, New York: Social Studies Association.

Ahmed, A. (1992) *Postmodernism and Islam*, London: Routledge.

Albrow, M. and King, E. (eds) (1990) *Globalisation, Knowledge and Society*, Newbury Park, CA: Sage.

Alexander, J. C. (1987) *Twenty Lectures, Sociological Theory Since World War II*, New York: Columbia University Press.

—— (ed.) (1988) *Durkheimian Sociology: Cultural Studies*, Cambridge: Cambridge University Press.

Althusser, L. (1969) *For Marx*, London: Allen Lane.

—— (1971) *Lenin and Philosophy and Other Essays*, London: NLB.

—— (1972) *Politics and History: Montesquieu, Hegel and Marx*, London: NLB.

—— and Balibar, E. (1970) *Reading Capital*, London: New Left Books.

Amin, S., Arrighi, G., Frank, A. G. and Wallerstein, I. (1982) *Dynamics of Global Crisis*, New York: Monthly Review Press.

Anderson, P. (1964) 'The origins of the present crisis', *New Left Review* 23: 26–53.

—— (1974) *Lineages of the Absolutist State*, London: New Left Books.

—— (1977) 'The antinomies of Antonio Gramsci', *New Left Review* 100: 5–78.

—— (1990) 'A culture in contraflow', *New Left Review* 180: 41–57.

Archer, M. S. (1988) *Culture and Agency: The Place of Culture in Social Theory*, Cambridge: Cambridge Review Press.

Asad, T. (1993) *Genealogies of Religion: Discipline and Reasons of Power in Christianity and Islam*, Baltimore: John Hopkins University Press.

Avineri, S. (1968) *The Social and Political Thought of Karl Marx*, Cambridge: Cambridge University Press.

—— (ed.) (1968) *Karl Marx on Colonialism and Modernization*, New York: Doubleday Anchor.

Bailey, A. M. and Llobera, J. K. (eds) (1981) *The Asiatic Mode of Production*, London: Routledge & Kegan Paul.

Banani, A. (1975) 'Islam and the West', *International Journal of Middle East Studies* 6(2): 140–7.

Baudrillard, J. (1987) 'The year 2000 has already happened', pp. 35–44 in A. Kroker and M. Kroker (eds) *Body Invaders*, London: Macmillan.

—— (1988) *America*, London: Verso.

—— (1990) *Cool Memories*, London: Verso.

Bauman, Z. (1987) *Legislators and Interpreters: On Modernity, Post-modernity and Intellectuals*, Cambridge: Polity Press.

—— (1989) *Modernity and the Holocaust*, Cambridge: Polity Press.

—— (1992) *Intimations of Postmodernity*, London: Routledge.

Beck, L. W. (1988) *Kant, Selections*, New York: Macmillan.

Beck, U. (1986) *Risikogesellschaft: Auf dem Weg in eine andere Moderne*, Frankfurt: Suhrkamp.

—— (1992) *Risk Society*, London: Sage.

Bell, D. (1976) *The Cultural Contradictions of Capitalism*, London: Heinemann.

—— (1980) *The Winding Passage: Essays and Sociological Journeys 1960–1980*, New York: Basic Books.

Bellah, R. (1964) 'Religious evolution', *American Sociological Review* 24: 358–74.

Beloff, M. (1985) 'Intellectuals', pp. 401–3 in A. Kuper and J. Kuper (eds) *The Social Science Encyclopedia*, London: Routledge & Kegan Paul.

Benda, H. J. (1958) 'Christiaan Snouck Hurgronje and the foundations of Dutch Islamic policy in Indonesia', *Journal of Modern History* 30: 228–37.

Bendix, R. (1977) 'The province and the metropolis: the case of eighteenth-century Germany', pp. 199–249 in J. Ben-David and T. N. Clark (eds) *Culture and its Creators: Essays in Honor of Edward Shils*, Chicago and London: University of Chicago Press.

Benjamin, W. (1973) *Illuminations*, London: Collins/Fontana.

Berger, P. L. (1969) *The Social Reality of Religion*, London: Faber & Faber.

—— and Hsiao, H. M. (1988) *In Search of an East Asian Model of Development*, New Brunswick: Transaction.

—— and Luckmann, T. (1967) *The Social Construction of Reality*, London: Allen Lane.

Berman, M. (1982) *All That is Solid Melts into Air*, New York: Simon & Schuster.

Bernstein, J. M. (1991) 'Introduction' to Theodor W. Adorno *The Culture Industry: Selected Essays on Mass Culture*, London: Routledge.

Berque, J. (1972) *Egypt, Imperialism and Revolution*, London: Faber & Faber.

Bhabha, H. (1983) 'Difference, discrimination and the discourse of colonialism', pp. 190–205 in F. Baker *et al.* *The Politics of Theory*, Colchester: University of Essex.

Bhatnagar, R. (1986) 'Uses and limits of Foucault: a study of the theme of origins in Said, "Orientalism" ', *Social Scientist* 158: 3–22.

Black, Cyril (ed.) (1976) *Comparative Modernization*, New York: Free Press.

Bloch, E. (1986) *The Principle of Hope*, Oxford: Basil Blackwell.

Bloom, A. (1986) *Prodigal Sons: The New York Intellectuals and Their World*, New York and Oxford: Oxford University Press.

—— (1987) *The Closing of the American Mind*, New York: Simon & Schuster.

Bolz, N. and Reijen, van, W. (1991) *Walter Benjamin*, Frankfurt: Campus Verlag.

Bonne, A. (1960) *State and Economics in the Middle East*, London: Routledge & Kegan Paul.

Bourdieu, P. (1984) *Distinction: A Social Critique of the Judgement of Taste*, London: Routledge & Kegan Paul.
—— (1988) *Homo Academicus*, Cambridge: Polity Press.
—— (1993) *Sociology in Question*, London: Sage.
—— and Passeron, J.-C. (1990) *Reproduction in Education, Society and Culture*, London: Sage.
Boyne, R. (1990) *Foucault and Derrida: The Other Side of Reason*, London: Unwin Hyman.
Brandt Commission, The (1983) *Common Crisis: North-South Co-operation for World Recovery*, Cambridge, MA: MIT Press.
Brantlinger, P. (1990) *Crusoe's Footprints: Cultural Studies in Britain and America*, New York: Routledge.
Brubaker, R. (1984) *The Limits of Rationality: An Essay on the Social and Moral Thought of Max Weber*, London: Allen & Unwin.
Buci-Glucksmann, C. (1984) *La Raison Baroque, de Baudelaire a Benjamin*, Paris: Editions Galilee.
Butler, N. (1988) 'Romanticism in England', pp. 37–67 in R. Porter and M. Teich (eds) *Romanticism in National Context*, Cambridge: Cambridge University Press.
Bynum, C. W. (1980) 'Did the twelfth century discover the individual?', *Journal of Ecclesiastical History* 31(1): 1–17.
Campbell, C. (1987) *The Romantic Ethic and the Spirit of Modern Consumerism*, Oxford: Basil Blackwell.
Capaldi, N. (1975) *David Hume: the Newtonian Philosopher*, Boston.
Certeau, M. de (1984) *The Practice of Everyday Life*, Berkeley: University of California Press.
Chenu, M.-D. (1969) *L'Eveil de la conscience dans la civilisation medievale*, Montreal: Institute of Medieval Studies.
Chirot, D. (1986) *Change in the Modern Era*, San Diego: Harcourt Brace Jovanovich.
Coleman, J. A. (1990) *Foundations of Social Theory*, Cambridge, MA: Belknap/Harvard University Press.
Coulson, M. A. and Riddell, D. S. (1970) *Approaching Sociology: A Critical Introduction*, London: Routledge & Kegan Paul.
Dahrendorf, R. (1968) *Essays in the Theory of Society*, London: Routledge & Kegan Paul.
Daniel, N. (1960) *Islam and the West: the Making of an Image*, Edinburgh: Edinburgh University Press.
Davis, H. B. (1965) 'Nations, colonies and social classes: the position of Marx and Engels', *Science and Society* 29: 26–43.
Deleuze, G. (1983) *Nietzsche and Philosophy*, London: The Athlone Press.
Dennis, N., Henriques, F. and Slaughter, C. (1956) *Coal is Our Life*, London: Eyre & Spottiswoode.
Denzin, N. K. (1991) 'Paris, Texas and Baudrillard on America', *Theory, Culture and Society* 8(2): 121–33.
Dews, P. (1986) 'Adorno, post-structuralism and the critique of identity', *New Left Review* 157: 28–44.
Douglas, M. (1970) *Purity and Danger: An Analysis of Concepts of Pollution and Taboo*, Harmondsworth: Penguin.
Douglas, M. and Isherwood, B. (1980) *The World of Goods*, Harmondsworth: Penguin.
Dumont, L. (1983) *Essais Sur l'Individualisme*, Paris: Seoul.

—— (1986) 'Collective identities and universalistic ideology, the actual interplay', *Theory, Culture and Society* 3: 25–34.

Durkheim, E. (1951) *Suicide: A Study in Sociology*, Glencoe: Free Press.

—— (1957) *Professional Ethics and Civic Morals*, London: Routledge & Kegan Paul.

Durkheim, E. (1961) *The Elementary Forms of Religious Life*, New York: Collier Books.

—— (1978) 'Two laws of penal evolution', pp. 153–80 in M. Trangott (ed.) *Emile Durkheim on Institutional Analysis*, Chicago: University of Chicago Press.

Eagleton, T. (1978) *Criticism and Ideology*, London: Verso.

Eisenstadt, S. N. (ed.) (1986) *The Origins and Diversity of Axial Age Civilizations*, New York: State University of New York Press.

—— and Curelaru, M. (1976) *The Form of Sociology: Paradigms and Crises*, New York: Wiley.

El Guindi, F. (1982) 'The killing of Sadat and after: a current assessment of Egypt's Islamic movement', *Middle East Insight* 2: 17–29.

Elias, N. (1978) *The Civilising Process: Vol. 1 The History of Manners*, Oxford: Basil Blackwell.

Enayat, H. (1982) *Modern Islamic Political Thought*, London: Macmillan.

Esposito, J. L. (1984) *Islam and Politics*, New York: Oxford University Press.

Eyerman (1985) 'Rationalising intellectuals', *Theory and Society* 40: 77–87.

—— (1990) 'Intellectuals and progress: the origins, decline and revival of a critical group', pp. 91–105 in J. C. Alexander and P. Sztompka (eds) *Rethinking Progress: Movements, Forces and Ideas at the End of the Twentieth Century*, Boston: Unwin Hyman.

Farias, V. (1989) *Heidegger and Nazism*, Philadelphia: Temple University Press.

Featherstone, M. (1987a) 'Lifestyle and consumer culture', *Theory, Culture and Society* 4(1): 55–70.

—— (1987b) 'Consumer culture, symbolic power and universalism', pp. 17–46 in G. Stauth and S. Zubaida (eds) *Mass Culture, Popular Culture and Social Life in the Middle East*, Frankfurt: Campus Verlag.

—— (1991) *Consumer Culture and Postmodernism*, London: Sage.

Ferry, L. and Renaut, A. (1990) *Heidegger and Modernity*, Chicago and London: University of Chicago Press.

Finkelkraut, A. (1987) *La Défaite de la pensée*, Paris: Gallimard.

Finley, M. (1980) *Ancient Slavery and Modern Ideology*, London: Chatto & Windus.

Fleming, D. and Bailyn, B. (1969) (eds) *The Intellectual Migration: Europe and America 1930–1960*, Cambridge, Mass: Belknap Press.

Foucault, M. (1972) *The Archeology of Knowledge*, New York: Pantheon Books.

—— (1973) *The Birth of the Clinic*, trans. A. M. Sheridan Smith, New York: Pantheon Books.

—— (1977) *Discipline and Punish, The Birth of the Prison*, London: Tavistock.

—— (1988) *Politics, Philosophy, Culture: Interviews and Other Writings 1977–1984*, London: Routledge.

Fox, R. A. (1976) *The Tangled Chain: The Structure of Disorder in the Anatomy of Melancholy*, Berkeley and Los Angeles: University of California Press.

Frank, A. G. (1972) *Sociology of Underdevelopment and the Underdevelopment of Sociology*, London: Monthly Review Press.

Friedman, T. L. (1987) 'How secular Israel? Orthodox right poses challenge', *International Herald Tribune* 1 July.

Frisby, D. (1983) *The Alienated Mind: The Sociology of Knowledge in Germany 1918–1933*, London: Heinemann Educational Books.

Gaskin, J. C. A. (1976) 'Hume's critique of religion', *Journal for the History of Philosophy* 14: 301–11.

Geertz, C. (1966) 'Religion as a cultural system', pp. 1–46 in M. Banton (ed.) *Anthropological Approaches to the Study of Religion*, London: Tavistock.

—— (1968) *Islam Observed: Religious Development in Morocco and Indonesia*, New Haven: Yale University Press.

Gehlen, A. (1980) *Man in the Age of Technology*, New York: Columbia University Press.

—— (1988) *Man: His Nature and Place in the World*, New York: Columbia University Press.

Gellner, E. (1962) 'Concepts and society', *Transactions of the Fifth World Congress of Sociology Louvain* 1: 153–83.

—— (1969) *Saints of the Atlas*, London: Weidenfeld & Nicholson.

—— (1979) 'The social roots of egalitarianism', *Dialectics and Humanism* 4: 27–43.

—— (1980) 'In defence of orientalism', *Sociology* 14: 295–300.

—— (1981) *Muslim Society*, Cambridge: Cambridge University Press.

—— (1992) *Postmodernism, Reason and Religion*, London: Routledge.

Gerth, H. H. and Mills, C. W. (eds) (1946) *From Max Weber: Essay in Sociology*, New York: Oxford University Press.

—— (eds) (1991) *From Max Weber: Essays in Sociology*, London: Routledge.

Giddens, A. (1990) *The Consequences of Modernity*, Cambridge: Polity Press.

—— (1991) *Modernity and Self-Identity: Self and Society in the Late Modern Age*, Cambridge: Polity Press.

—— (1992) *The Transformation of Intimacy: Sexuality, Love and Eroticism in Modern Societies*, Cambridge: Polity Press.

Gilsenan, M. (1973) *Saint and Sufi in Modern Egypt*, Oxford: Clarendon Press.

Giner, S. (1976) *Mass Society*, London: Martin Robertson.

Glick, T. F. (1970) *Irrigation and Society in Medieval Valencia*, Cambridge: Harvard University Press.

Goldman, H. (1992) *Politics, Death and the Devil: Self and Power in Max Weber and Thomas Mann*, Berkeley: University of California Press.

Goldmann, L. (1973) *The Philosophy of the Enlightenment*, London: Routledge & Kegan Paul.

Gouldner, A. W. (1958) 'Introduction to Emile Durkheim' in *Socialism*, New York: Collier Books.

—— (1970) *The Coming Crisis of Western Sociology*, New York: Basic Books.

—— (1979) *The Future of Intellectuals and the Rise of the New Class*, New York and London: Oxford University Press.

Gramsci, A. (1971) *Selections from the Prison Notebooks*, trans. and ed. Quintin Hoare and Geoffrey Nowell Smith, New York: International Publishers.

Greenblatt, S. (1980) *Renaissance Self-fashioning: From More to Shakespeare*, Chicago and London: University of Chicago Press.

Grunebaum, G. E. von (1937) *Die Wirklichkeit der fruharabischen Dichtung. Eine literaturwissenschaftliche Unterschung*, Vienna: Selbsverlag des Orientalischen Institutes der Universitat.

—— (1944) 'The concept of plagiarism in Arabic theory', *Journal of Near Eastern Studies* 3: 234–53.

—— (1946) *Medieval Islam: A Study in Cultural Orientation*, Chicago: University of Chicago Press.

—— (1955a) *Islam: Essays in the Nature and Growth of a Cultural Tradition*, London: Routledge & Kegan Paul.

—— (1955b) *Unity and Variety in Muslim Civilization*, Chicago: University of Chicago Press.

—— (1958) *Muhammadan Festivals*, London: Abelaird-Schuman.

—— (1962) 'Byzantine iconoclasm and the influence of Islamic environment', *History of Religions* (2) 1: 1–10.

—— (1970) *Classical Islam, A History 600–1258*, trans. Katherine Watson, Chicago: Aldine.

—— and Caillois, R. (eds) (1966) *The Dream and Human Societies*, Berkeley and Los Angeles: University of California Press.

Guha, R. (1981) *Subaltern Studies: Writings on South Asian History and Society*, Delhi: Oxford University Press.

Habermas, J. (1976) *Legitimation Crisis*, London: Heinemann.

—— (ed.) (1979) *Geistigen Situation der Zeit*, 2 vols, Frankfurt: Suhrkamp.

—— (1987) *The Philosophical Discourse of Modernity*, Cambridge: Polity Press.

Hall, J. A. (1989) 'They do things differently here, or, the contribution of British historical sociology', *British Journal of Sociology* 40(4): 544–64.

Hall, S. and Jefferson, T. (eds) (1987) *Resistance Through Rituals, Youth Sub-Cultures in Post-War Britain*, London: Hutchinson.

Halsey, A. H. (1989) 'A turning of the tide? The prospects for sociology in Britain', *British Journal of Sociology* 40(3): 353–73.

Harman, L. D. (1988) *The Modern Stranger: On Language and Membership*, Berlin: Mouton de Gruyter.

Hartung, F. (1957) *Enlightened Despotism*, London: Routledge & Kegan Paul.

Hayward, J. E. S. (1959) 'Solidarity: the social history of an idea in nineteenth-century France', *International Review of Social History* 4: 261–84.

Hegel, G. W. F. (1956) *The Philosophy of History*, New York: Dover Publications.

Heidegger, M. (1977) *The Question Concerning Technology and Other Essays*, New York: Harper & Row.

Hennis, W. (1988) *Max Weber: Essays in Reconstruction*, London: Allen & Unwin.

Herf, J. (1984) *Reactionary Modernism, Technology, Culture and Politics in Weimar and the Third Reich*, Cambridge: Cambridge University Press.

Hindess, B. and Hirst, P. Q. (1975) *Pre-Capitalist Modes of Production*, London: Routledge & Kegan Paul.

Hodgson, M. T. (1964) *Early Anthropology in the Sixteenth and Seventeenth Centuries*, Philadelphia: University of Pennsylvania Press.

Hodgson, M. G. S. (1955a) *The Order of Assassins: The Struggle of the Nizari Ismailis against the Islamic World*, The Hague.

—— (1955b) 'How did the early Shi'a become sectarian?', *Journal of the American Oriental Society* 75: 1–13.

—— (1960) 'A comparison of Islam and Christianity as a framework for religious life', *Diogenes* 32: 49–60.

—— (1974) *The Venture of Islam*, 3 vols, Chicago: University of Chicago Press.

Hoggart, R. (1957) *The Uses of Literacy*, London: Chatto & Windus.

Holton, R. J. and Turner, B. S. (1986) *Talcott Parsons on Economy and Society*, London: Routledge & Kegan Paul.

—— (1989) *Max Weber on Economy and Society*, London: Routledge.

Horkheimer, M. and Adorno, T. (1972) *Dialectic of Enlightenment*, New York: Herder & Herder.

Hourani, A. (1962) *Arabic Thought in the Liberal Age*, Oxford: Oxford University Press.

Hughes, H. S. (1959) *Consciousness and Society: The Reorientation of European Social Thought 1890–1930*, London: MacGibbon & Kee.

Hulliung, M. (1981) 'Montesquieu's interpreters: a polemical essay', *Studies in Eighteenth Century Culture* 10: 327–46.

Hume, D. (1963) *On Religion*, London: Routledge.

Jacoby, R. (1987) *The Last Intellectuals: American Culture in the Age of Academe*, New York: Noonday Press.

Jameson, F. (1984) 'Post-modernism or the cultural logic of late capitalism', *New Left Review* 146: 53–93.

—— (1985) 'Postmodernism and consumer society', in H. Foster (ed.) *Postmodern Culture*, London and Sydney: Pluto Press.

Janz, C. P. (1981) *Friedrich Nietzsche*, 3 vols, Munchen: DTV.

Jay, M. (1988) *Fin-de-siècle Socialism*, London and New York: Routledge.

Kadarkay, A. (1991) *Georg Lukács: Life, Thought and Politics*, Oxford: Basil Blackwell.

Kalberg, S. (1987) 'The origin and expansion of Kulturpessimismus: the relationship between public and private spheres in early twentieth century Germany', *Sociological Theory* 5: 150–65.

Käsler, D. (1988) *Max Weber: An Introduction to his Life and Work*, Cambridge: Polity Press.

Kaufman, W. (1950) *Nietzsche: Philosopher, Psychologist, Antichrist*, Princeton, New Jersey: Princeton University Press.

Kavolis, V. (1982) 'Social movements and civilizational processes', *Comparative Civilizations Review* 8(Spring): 31–58.

Keddie, N. and Beck, L. (eds) (1978) *Women in the Muslim World*, Cambridge, MA: Harvard University Press.

Kellner, D. (1983) 'Critical theory, commodities and the consumer society', *Theory, Culture and Society* 1(3): 66–84.

—— (1988) 'Postmodernism as social theory: some challenges and problems', *Theory, Culture and Society* 5: 239–270.

Kiernan, V. G. (1972) *The Lords of Human Kind: European Attitudes to the Outside World in the Imperial Age*, Harmondsworth: Penguin Books.

King, A. D. (ed.) (1991) *Culture, Globalization and the World-System*, Binghamton, NY: University of New York Press.

Klibansky, R., Panofsky, E. and Saxl, F. (1964) *Saturn and Melancholy: Studies in the History of Natural Philosophy, Religion and Art*, New York: Basic Books.

Knox (1940) 'Hegel and Prussianism', *Philosophy* (January): 51–63.

Koebner, R. (1951) 'Despot and despotism, vicissitudes of a political term', *Journal of the Warburg and Courtauld Institutes* 14: 275–302.

Kolakowski, L. (1968) *Positivist Philosophy, from Hume to the Vienna Circle*, New York: Doubleday.

—— (1974) 'Marxist philosophy and national reality', *Round Table* 253: 43–55.

Konrad, G. and Szelenyi, I. (1979) *Intellectuals on the Road to Class Power*, New York: Harcourt Brace Jovanovich.

Kroeber, A. L. (1952) *The Nature of Culture*, Chicago: University of Chicago Press.

Kroker, A. (1984) *Technology and the Canadian Mind: Innis/McLuhan/Grant*, Montreal: New World Perspectives.

——, Kroker, M. and Cook, D. (1989) *Panic Encyclopedia*, London: Macmillan.

Kronman, A. (1983) *Max Weber*, London: Arnold.

Laroui, A. (1973) 'For a methodology of Islamic studies: Islam seen by G. von Grunebaum', *Diogenes* 81(4): 12–39.

—— (1976) *The Crisis of Arab Intellectuals*, Berkeley: University of California Press.

Lash, S. (1990) 'Postmodernism as humanism? Urban space and social theory', pp. 62–74 in B. S. Turner (ed.) *Theories of Modernity and Postmodernity*, London: Sage.

—— and Urry, J. (1987) *The End of Organised Capitalism*, Cambridge: Polity Press.

Lechner, F. J. (1985a) 'Fundamentalism and socio-cultural revitalization in America: a sociological interpretation', *Sociological Analysis* 46: 243–60.

—— (1985b) 'Modernity and its discontents', pp. 157–78 in J. C. Alexander (ed.) *Neofunctionalism*, Beverly Hills: Sage.

Lerner, D. (1958) *The Passing of Traditional Society*, Glencoe, Illinois: The Free Press.

Lewis, B. (1972) 'Islamic concepts of revolution', pp. 35–40 in P. J. Vatikiotis (ed.) *Revolution in the Middle East and other Case Studies*, London: George Allen & Unwin.

Liebersohn, H. (1988) *Fate and Utopia in German Sociology 1870–1923*, Cambridge, Mass.: The MIT Press.

Lockwood, D. (1992) *Solidarity and Schism*, Oxford: University of Oxford Press.

Lowe, L. (1991) *Critical Terrains: French and British Orientalisms*, Ithaca and London: Cornell University Press.

Lubeck, P. M. (1987) 'Structural determinants of urban Islamic protest in northern Nigeria', pp. 19–108 in W. R. Roff (ed.) *Islam and the Political Economy and Meaning: Comparative Studies of Muslim Discourse*, Berkeley and Los Angeles: University of California Press.

Luce, D. R., Smelser, N. J. and Gerstein, D. R. (1989) *Leading Edges in Social and Behavioural Science*, New York: Russell Sage.

Luckmann, T. (1967) *The Invisible Religion: The Transformation of Symbols in Industrial Society*, New York: Macmillan.

Lukes, S. (1973) *Emile Durkheim, His Life and Work*, London: Allen Lane.

Luhmann, N. (1984) 'The self-description of society: crisis, fashion and sociological theory', *International Journal of Comparative Sociology* 25: 59–72.

Lyotard, J.-F. (1984) *The Postmodern Condition*, Minneapolis: University of Minnesota Press.

McClelland, D. (1961) *The Achieving Society*, New York: van Nostrand.

Macherey, P. (1978) *A Theory of Literary Production*, London: Routledge & Kegan Paul.

MacIntyre, A. (1971) *Against the Self-Images of the Age: Essays on Ideology and Philosophy*, London: Duckworth.

—— (1981) *After Virtue: A Study in Moral Theory*, London: Duckworth.

Mani, L. and Frankenberg, R. (1985) 'The challenge of Orientalism', *Economy and Society* 14(2): 174–192.

Mann, M. (1986) *The Social Sources of Power: Volume 1, A History of Power from the Beginning to A.D. 1760*, Cambridge: Cambridge University Press.

Mann, T. (1985) *Pro and Contra Wagner*, London: Faber and Faber.

Mannheim, K. (1956a) *Essays on the Sociology of Culture*, London: Routledge & Kegan Paul.

—— (1956b) *Conservatism: A Contribution to the Sociology of Knowledge*, London: Routledge.

—— (1986) *Conservatism: a Contribution to the Sociology of Knowledge*, London: Routledge.

—— (1991) *Ideology and Utopia*, London: Routledge.

Marcuse, H. (1964) *One Dimensional Man*, London: Sphere Books.
—— (1968) *Negations*, London: Allen Lane.
Martin, B. (1981) *A Sociology of Contemporary Cultural Change*, Oxford: Basil Blackwell.
Marx, K. (1970) *Capital*, London: Lawrence and Wishart.
—— and Engels, F. (1953) *The Russian Menace in Europe*, London: George Allen & Unwin.
—— (1965) *The German Ideology*, London: Lawrence & Wishart.
—— (1972) 'The future results of the British rule in India' (1853) in pp. 81–7 K. Marx and F. Engels *On Colonialism*, New York: Doubleday.
Mauss, M. (1968–9) *Oeuvres*, Paris: Presses Universitaires de France.
Meja, V. and Stehr, N. (1990) *Knowledge and Politics: The Sociology of Knowledge Dispute*, London: Routledge.
Mill, J. (1972) *The History of British India*, London and New Delhi: Associated Publishing House.
Mill, J. S. (1859) *Dissertations and Discussions*, 2 vols, London: John W. Parker and Son.
Mitchell, M. M. (1931) 'Emile Durkheim and the philosophy of nationalism', *Political Science Quarterly* 46: 87–106.
Mitchell, R. (1969) *The Society of Muslim Brothers*, New York: Oxford University Press.
Montesquieu, C. (1923) *Persian Letters*, London: G. Routledge & Sons.
—— (1949) *The Spirit of the Laws*, New York: Hafner Pub. Co.
—— (1965) *Considerations on the Causes of the Greatness of the Romans and Their Decline*, New York: Free Press.
Moore, B., Jr. (1968) *The Social Origins of Dictatorship and Democracy*, Harmondsworth: Penguin Books.
Moore, W. E. (1966) 'Global sociology: the world as a singular system', *American Journal of Sociology* 71: 475–482.
Morley, D. (1980) *The 'Nationwide' Audience*, London: BFI.
Nagata, J. (1984) *The Re-Flowering of Malaysian Islam: Modern Religious Radicals and Their Roots*, Vancouver: University of British Columbia Press.
Nairn, T. (1977) *The Break-Up of Britain*, London: New Left Books.
Needham, J. (1954) *Science and Civilisation in China*, Cambridge: Cambridge University Press.
Nehemas, A. (1985) *Nietzsche: Life as Literature*, Cambridge, Mass.: Harvard University Press.
Nelson, B. (1981) *On the Roads to Modernity: Conscience, Science, and Civilizations*, Totawa, NJ: Rowman and Littlefield.
Nettle, J. P. (1969) 'Ideas, intellectuals and structures of dissent', pp. 53–124 in P. Rieff (ed.) *On Intellectuals: Theoretical Studies. Case Studies*, New York: Doubleday.
Niel, R. van (1956) 'Christian Hurgronje. In memory of the centennial of his birth', *Journal of Asian Studies* 16: 591–594.
Nietzsche, F. (1910) *The Genealogy of Morals: A Polemic*, Edinburgh: University of Edinburgh Press.
—— (1968) *The Anti-Christ*, Harmondsworth: Penguin Books.
—— (1979) *Ecce Homo*, Harmondsworth: Penguin Books.
Nisbet, R. A. (1967) *The Sociological Tradition*, London: Heinemann Educational Books.
Novak, M. (1982) 'Pluralism in humanistic perspective', pp. 27–56 in William

Peterson, Michael Novak and Philip Gleason (eds) *Concepts in Ethnicity*, Cambridge, MA: Harvard University Press.

Offe, C. (1985) *Disorganised Capitalism: Contemporary Transformations of Work and Politics*, Cambridge: Polity Press.

O'Hanlon, R. and Washbrook, D. (1992) 'After orientalism: culture, criticism and politics in the third world', *Comparative Studies in Society and History*, 34(1): 141–67.

O'Leary, D. L. (1949) *How Greek Science Passed to the Arabs*, London: Routledge & Kegan Paul.

Parsons, T. (1937) *The Structure of Social Action*, New York: McGraw-Hill.

—— (1963) 'Christianity and modern industrial society', pp. 33–70 in E. A. Tiryakian (ed.) *Sociological Theory, Values and Socio-Cultural Change: Essays in Honor of Pitirim Sorokin*, New York: Free Press.

—— (1966) *Societies: Evolutionary and Comparative Perspectives*, Englewood Cliffs, NJ: Prentice Hall.

—— (1968) *The Structure of Social Action*, New York: Free Press.

—— (1971) *The System of Modern Societies*, Englewood Cliffs, NJ: Prentice Hall.

—— (1977) *The Evolution of Societies*, Englewood Cliffs, NJ: Prentice Hall.

Peel, J. D. Y. (1969) 'Understanding alien belief systems', *British Journal of Sociology* 20: 69–84.

Pells, R. (1985) *The Liberal Mind in a Conservative Age: American Intellectuals in the 1940s and 1950s*, New York: Harper & Row.

Pels, D. (1991) 'Treason of the intellectuals: Paul de Man and Hendrik de Man', *Theory, Culture and Society* 8(1): 21–56.

Philips, D. (1986) 'Americans in Holland', pp. 64–9 in D. Bok (ed.) *Harvard and Holland*, N.V. Indivers.

Plant, G. (1973) *Hegel*, London: Unwin University Books.

Popper, K. (1945) *The Open Society and its Enemies*, London: Routledge & Kegan Paul.

Poulantzas, N. (1973) *Political Power and Social Classes*, London: NLB, Sheed and Ward.

Prager, J. (1985) 'Totalitarian and liberal democracy: two types of modern political order', pp. 179–210 in J. C. Alexander (ed.) *Neofunctionalism*, Beverly Hills: Sage.

Rabinbach, A. (1985) 'Between Enlightenment and apocalypse: Benjamin, Block and modern German Jewish messianism', *New German Critique* 34: 78–124.

Rammstedt, O. (1986) *Deutsche Soziologie 1933–1945*, Frankfurt: Suhrkamp.

Rattansi, A. (1982) *Marx and the Division of Labour*, London: Macmillan.

Reijen, W. van (1987) 'Post-scriptum', pp. 9–36 in W. van Reijen and D. Kamper (eds) *Die Unvollendee Vernunft: Moderne versus Postmoderne*, Frankfurt: Suhrkamp.

Reischauer, E. O. *The Japanese Today: Change and Continuity*, Cambridge, MA: Harvard University Press.

Renan, E. (ed.) (1896) 'Islamism and science', in *Poetry of the Celtic Race and Other Studies*, London: W. Scott.

Ritzer, G. (1975) *Sociology: A Multiple Paradigm Science*, Boston: Allyn and Bacon.

—— (1991) *Metatheorizing in Sociology*, Lexington, MA: Lexington/Heath.

—— (1993) *The McDonaldization of Society*, London: Sage.

Robertson, R. (1970) *The Sociological Interpretation of Religion*, Oxford: Basil Blackwell.

—— (1978) *Meaning and Change: Explorations in the Cultural Sociology of Modern Societies*, Oxford: Basil Blackwell.

—— (1982) 'Parsons on the evolutionary significance of American religion', *Sociological Analysis* 54(4): 307–26.

—— (1985a) 'Max Weber and German sociology of religion', pp. 263–305 in N. Smart *et al.* (eds) *Nineteenth Century Religious Thought in the West*, Cambridge: University of Cambridge Press.

—— (1985b) 'The sacred and the world system', pp. 347–58 in P. E. Hammond (ed.) *The Sacred and the Secular Age: Towards Revision in the Scientific Study of Religion*, Berkeley: University of California Press.

—— (1987a) 'From secularisation to globalisation', *Journal of Oriental Studies* 26: 28–32.

—— (1987b) 'Globalisation and societal modernisation: a note on Japan and Japanese religion', *Sociological Analysis* 46(5): 35–42.

—— (1988a) 'Liberation theology, Latin America and Third World under-development', pp. 117–34 in R. L. Rubinstein and J. R. Roth (eds) *The Politics of Latin American Liberation Theology*, Washington D.C.: Washington Institute Press.

—— (1988b) 'The sociological significance of culture', *Theory, Culture and Society* 6(1): 3–24.

—— (1989a) 'Globalization, politics and religion', pp. 10–23 in James Beckford and Thomas Luckmann (eds) *The Changing Face of Religion*, London: Sage.

—— (1989b) 'A new perspective on religion and secularization in the global context', pp. 66–77 in J. K. Hadden and A. Shupe (eds) *Secularization and Fundamentalism*, New York: Paragon House.

—— (1990a) 'Mapping the global condition: globalization as the central concept', *Theory, Culture and Society* 72(2–3): 15–30.

—— (1990b) 'After nostalgia? Willful nostalgia and the phases of globalization', pp. 31–44 in B. S. Turner (ed.) *Theories of Modernity and Postmodernity*, London: Sage.

—— (1991a) 'Social theory, cultural relativity and the problem of globality', pp. 69–90 in Anthony D. King (ed.) *Culture, Globalization and the World-System*, London: Macmillan.

—— (1991b) 'Globality, global culture and images of world order', pp. 395–411 in H. Haferkamp and N. Smelser (eds) *Social Change and Modernity*, Berkeley: University of California Press.

—— (1991c) 'The globalization paradigm. Thinking globally', pp. 207–24 in D. G. Bromley (ed.) *Religion and Social Order*, Greenwich, CT: JAI Press.

—— (1992) *Globalization: Social Theory and Global Culture*, London and Newbury Park, CA: Sage Publications.

—— (n.d. a) 'Civilization' and the civilizing process; Elias, globalization and analytic synthesis.

—— (n.d. b) 'Community, society, globality, and the category of religion', in Eileen Barker *et al.* (eds) *Religion, Secularization, and Sectarianism* (tent. title).

—— and Chirico, J. (1985) 'Humanity, globalization and worldwide religious resurgence: a theoretical exploration', *Sociological Analysis* 46: 219–42.

—— and Garrett, W. R. (eds) (1991) *Religion and Global Order*, New York: Paragon House.

—— and Holzner, B. (eds) (1980) *Identity and Authority: Explorations in the Theory of Society*, Oxford: Basil Blackwell.

—— and Lechner, F. (1985) 'Modernization, globalization and the problem of culture in world-systems theory', *Theory, Culture and Society* 2(3): 103–118.

—— and Nettle, J. P. (eds) (1968) *International Systems and the Modernization of Societies*, London: Faber; New York: Basic.

—— and Turner, B. S. (eds) (1991) *Talcott Parsons: Theorist of Modernity*, Newbury Park: Sage.

Rodinson, M. (1961) *Mahomet*, Paris: Editions de Senil.

—— (1966) *Islam et capitalisme*, Paris: Editions de Senil.

Roff, W. R. (1987) Editor's introduction, in W. R. Roff (ed.) *Islam and the Political Economy of Meaning: Comparative Studies of Muslim Discourse*, Berkeley and Los Angeles: University of California Press.

Rojek, C. and Turner, B. S. (eds) (1993) *Forget Baudrillard?*, London and New York: Routledge.

Rorty, R. (1986) 'Foucault and epistemology', pp. 41–9 in Hoy, B. (ed.) *Foucault, A Critical Reader*, Oxford: Basil Blackwell.

Rose, G. (1978) *The Melancholy Science: An Introduction to the Thought of Theodor W. Adorno*, London: Macmillan.

Rosenberger, N. R. (ed.) (1992) *Japanese Sense of the Self*, Cambridge: University of Cambridge Press.

Rosenthal, F. (1973) 'In memoriam', *International Journal of Middle Eastern Studies* 4(3): 355–8.

Ross, A. (1989) *No Respect: Intellectuals and Popular Culture*, New York and London: Routledge.

Roth, G. amd Schluchter, W. (1979) *Max Weber's Vision of History: Ethics and Methods*, Berkeley: University of California Press.

Said, E. W. (1978a) *Orientalism*, London: Routledge & Kegan Paul.

—— (1978b) *Covering Islam*, New York: Pantheon.

—— (1985) 'Orientalism reconsidered', *Race and Class* 27(2): 1–15.

—— (1993) *Culture and Imperialism*, London: Chatto and Windus.

Scaff, L. A. (1989) *Fleeing the Iron Cage: Culture, Politics and Modernity in the Thought of Max Weber*, Berkeley: University of California Press.

Schelsky, H. (1969) 'Can continual questioning be institutionalized?', pp. 418–23 in N. Birnbaum and G. Lenzer (eds) *Sociology and Religion: A Book of Readings*, New Jersey: Prentice Hall.

Schluchter, W. (ed.) (1987) *Max Webers Sicht des Islams, Interpretation und Kritik*, Frankfurt: Suhrkamp.

Scholem, G. (1981) *Walter Benjamin: The Story of a Friendship*, Philadelphia: The Jewish Publication Society of America.

Schroeder, R. (1992) *Max Weber and the Sociology of Culture*, London: Sage.

Schumpeter, J. A. (1939) *Business Cycles: A Theoretical Historical and Statistical Analysis of the Capitalist Process*, 2 vols, New York and London: McGraw-Hill.

Screech, M. A. (1985) 'Good madness in Christendom', pp. 25–39 in W. F. Bynum, R. Porter and M. Shepherd (eds) *The Anatomy of Madness, People and Idea*, vol. 1, London: Tavistock.

Shari'ati, A. (1979) *On the Sociology of Islam*, Berkeley: Mizan Press.

—— (1980) *Marxism and Other Western Fallacies*, Berkeley: Mizan Press.

Shaw and Shaw, E. K. (1977) *History of the Ottoman Empire and Modern Turkey*, Cambridge: Cambridge University Press.

Shilling, C. (1993) *The Body and Social Theory*, London: Sage.

Shils, E. (1980) *The Calling of Sociology and Other Essays on the Pursuit of Learning*, Chicago and London: University of Chicago Press.

Shils, E. A. and Finch, H. A. (eds) (1949) *The Methodology of the Social Sciences*, New York: Free Press.

Shoshan, B. (1986) 'The politics of notables in medieval Islam', *Asian and African Studies* 20: 179–215.
Shupe, A. (1990) 'The stubborn persistence of religion in the global arena', pp. 17–26 in Emile Sahliyeh (ed.) *Religious Resurgence and Politics in the Contemporary World*, Albany: State of New York University Press.
Silk, M. S. and Stern, J. P. (1981) *Nietzsche on Tragedy*, Cambridge: Cambridge University Press.
Simmel, G. (1971) 'The stranger', pp. 141–9 in D. N. Levine (ed.) *Georg Simmel on Individuality and Social Forms*, Chicago and London: University of Chicago Press.
—— (1978) *The Philosophy of Money*, London: Routledge & Kegan Paul.
—— (1991) 'Money in modern culture', *Theory, Culture and Society* 8(3): 17–31.
Simpson, J. H. (1989) 'Globalization, the active self, and religion: a theory sketch', pp. 29–38 in William H. Swatos Jr. (ed.) *Religious Politics in Global and Comparative Perspective*, Westport, CT: Greenwood Press.
Sloterdijk, P. (1988) *Critique of Cynical Reason*, London: Verso.
Smith, D. E. (ed.) (1974) *Religion and Political Modernization*, New Haven: Yale University Press.
Smith, N. (1970) *Man and Water: A History of Hydro-Technology*, Cambridge: Harvard University Press.
Smith, W. C. (1964) *The Meaning and End of Religion*, New York: Mentor Books.
Sombart, W. (1962) *The Jews and Modern Capitalism*, New York: Collier Books.
Sorokin, P. A. (1966) 'Comments on Moore and Biersted', *American Journal of Sociology* 71: 91–92.
Southern, R. W. (1962) *Western Views of Islam in the Middle Ages*, Cambridge: Harvard University Press.
Stauth, G. and Turner, B. S. (1986) 'Nietzsche in Weber oder die Geburt des Modernen Genius in Professionellen Menschen', *Zeitschrift fur Soziologie* 15: 81–94.
—— (1988) *Nietzsche's Dance: Resentment, Reciprocity and Resistance in Social Life*, Oxford: Basil Blackwell.
Stauth, G. and Zubaida, S. (eds) (1987) *Mass Culture, Popular Culture and Social Life in the Middle East*, Frankfurt: Campus Verlag.
Stelling-Michaud, S. (1960) 'Le mythe du despotisme oriental', *Schweizer Beitrage zur Allgemeinen Geschichte*, 18–19: 328–46.
Swatos, W. H., Jr. (ed.) (1989) *Religious Politics in Global and Comparative Perspective*, Westport, CT: Greenwood Press.
Taylor, K. (1975) *Henri Saint-Simon 1760–1825: Selected Writings on Science, Industry and Organisation*, London: Croom Helm.
Tentler, T. N. (1974) 'The Summa for Confessors as an instrument for social control', pp. 103–26 in C. Trinkhaus and H. H. Oberman (eds) *The Pursuit of Holiness in Late Medieval and Renaissance Religion*, Leiden.
Thompson, E. P. (1963) *The Making of the English Working Class*, New York: Vintage.
Tikku, G. L. (1971) (ed.) *Islam and its Cultural Divergence, Studies in Honor of Gustave E. von Grunebaum*, Urban, Chicago: University of Illinois Press.
Tillich, P. (1951) *The Protestant Era*, London: Nisbett.
Tiryakian, E. A. (ed.) (1984) *The Global Crisis: Sociological Analyses and Responses*, Leiden: E. J. Brill.
Tocqueville, A. de (1946) *Democracy in America*, ed. Philip Bradley, New York: A. A. Knopf.

Tönnies, F. (1957) *Community and Association*, East Lansing, Michigan: Michigan State University Press.

Tribe, K. (1983) 'Prussian agriculture – German politics: Max Weber 1892–7', *Economy and Society* 12: 181–226.

Tu, Wei-Ming (1991) 'Core values in economic culture: the Confucian hypothesis', paper presented at a conference on 'The Confucian Dimension of the Dynamics of Industrial East Asia', the American Academy of Arts and Sciences, Cambridge, MA.

Tucker, J. E. (1985) *Women in Nineteenth Century Egypt*, Cambridge: Cambridge University Press.

Turner, B. S. (1974a) 'The concepts of social stationariness: utilitarianism and Marxism', *Science and Society* 38: 3–18.

—— (1974b) *Weber and Islam: A Critical Study*, London: Routledge & Kegan Paul.

—— (1978a) *Marx and the End of Orientalism*, London: George Allen & Unwin.

—— (1978b) 'Orientalism, Islam and capitalism', *Social Compass* 25: 371–94.

—— (1979) 'The middle classes and entrepreneurship in capitalist development', *Arab Studies Quarterly* I: 113–34.

—— (1981a) *Citizenship and Capitalism*, London: Allen & Unwin.

—— (1981b) *For Weber, Essays on the Sociology of Fate*, London: Routledge & Kegan Paul.

—— (1984a) 'Une interpretation des representations occidentales de L'Islam', *Social Compass* 31(1): 91–104.

—— (1984b) *The Body and Society: Explorations in Social Theory*, Oxford: Basil Blackwell.

—— (1986a) *Equality*, Chichester: Ellis Horwood; London: Tavistock.

—— (1986b) *Citizenship and Capitalism, the Debate over Reformism*, London: Allen & Unwin.

—— (1987a) 'A note on nostalgia', *Theory, Culture and Society* 4(1): 147–56.

—— (1987b) 'State, science and economy in traditional societies: some problems in Weberian sociology of science', *British Journal of Sociology* 38(1): 1–23.

—— (1988a) *Status*, Milton Keynes: Open University Press.

—— (1988b) 'Classical sociology and its legacy', *The Sociological Review* 36: 146–57.

—— (1990a) 'The two faces of sociology: global or national?' *Theory, Culture and Society* 7: 343–58.

—— (1990b) 'The absent English intelligentsia', *Comenius* 38: 138–51.

—— (ed.) (1990c) *Theories of Modernity and Postmodernity*, London: Sage.

—— (1992) *Regulating Bodies: Essays in Medical Sociology*, London: Routledge.

Turner, G. (1990) *British Cultural Studies, An Introduction*, London: Unwin Hyman.

Van Wolferen, K. (1989) *The Enigma of Japanese Power*, New York: Random House.

Vatikiotis, P. J. (ed.) (1975) *Revolution in the Middle East and Other Case Studies*, London and Totowa, New Jersey: Rowman & Littlefield.

Vidich, A. J. (1991) 'Baudrillard's America', *Theory, Culture and Society* 8(2): 135–44.

Vinograd, R. (1992) *Boundaries of the Self: Chinese Portraits 1600–1900*, Cambridge: University of Cambridge Press.

Waardenburg, J. (1963) *L'Islam dans le miroir de l'occident*, The Hague.

Waines, D. (1976) 'Cultural anthropology and Islam, the contribution of G. E. von Grunebaum', *Review of Middle East Studies* 2: 113–23.

Wald, A. (1986) *The New York Intellectuals: The Rise and Fall of the Anti-Stalinist Left*, Chapel Hill: University of North Carolina Press.
Wallerstein, I. (1974) *The Modern World System 1*, New York: Academic Press.
—— (1980) *The Modern World System 2*, New York: Academic Press.
Weber, M. (1930) *The Protestant Ethic and the Spirit of Capitalism*, London: Allen & Unwin.
—— (1958a) *The Religion of India*, Glencoe, Ill.: Free Press.
—— (1958b) *The City*, New York: Free Press.
—— (1966) *The Sociology of Religion*, London: Methuen.
—— (1968) *Economy and Society: An Outline of Interpretative Sociology*, New York: Badminister Press.
—— (1973) 'The power of the state and the dignity of the academic calling in imperial Germany', *Minerva* 4: 571–632.
—— (1980) 'The national state and the economy policy', *Economy and Society* 9: 428–49.
Wernick, A. (1991) *Promotional Culture*, London: Sage.
Wertheim, W. F. (1972) 'Counter-insurgency research at the turn of the century – Snouck Hurgronje and the Acheh War', *Sociologische Gids* 19: 320–328.
Wiley, N. (1985) 'The current interregnum in American sociology', *Social Research* 52: 179–207.
Williams, B. A. O. (1963) 'Hume on religion', pp. 77–88 in D. F. Pears (ed.) *Hume: A Symposium*, London: Routledge & Kegan Paul.
Williams, R. (1958) *Culture and Society, 1780–1950*, New York: Harper & Row.
Willmott, P. and Young, M. (1957) *Family and Kinship in East London*, London: Routledge & Kegan Paul.
Wittfogel, K. (1957) *Oriental Despotism: A Comparative Study of Total Power*, New Haven and London: Yale University Press.
Wolf, E. (1971) *Peasant Wars of the Twentieth Century*, London: Faber and Faber.
Wolin, R. (1990) *The Politics of Being: The Political Thought of Martin Heidegger*, New York: Columbia University Press.
Wouters, C. (1986) 'Formalization and informalization, changing tension, balances in civilisating processes', *Theory, Culture and Society* 3(2): 1–18.
Wuthnow, R. (1987) *Meaning and Moral Order: Explorations in Cultural Analysis*, Berkeley: University of California Press.
Young, R. (1990) *White Mythologies, Writing History and the West*, London: Routledge.
Xenos, N. (1989) *Scarcity and Modernity*, London and New York: Routledge.

Index